Earth's

Messages for Our Times from Nature's Guardians

Laura Newbury

Tatterdemalion Blue

First published by **Tatterdemalion** Blue in 2022

Words © Laura Newbury 2022
Illustrations © Laura Newbury 2022
Nature Sketches © Canva (see Image Credits) 2022
Photographs (see Image Credits) 2022

Laura Newbury has asserted her right to be identified as the author of this work in accordance with the Copyright, Design and Patents Act 1988

All rights reserved. No part of this publication may be reproduced, stored in a retrieval system, or transmitted in any form or by any means, electronic, mechanical, photocopying, recording or otherwise, without the prior permission of the copyright owner

A CIP catalogue record for this book is available from the British Library

Cover design and layout by Kate Peros and Laura Newbury

ISBN 978-1-915123-12-1

Tatterdemalion Blue
74 Maxwell Place
Stirling
FK8 1JU

www.tatterdemalionblue.com

Earth's Voices

Messages for Our Times from Nature's Guardians

Laura Newbury

Dedication

I dedicate this book to the memory of my mother,
Patricia Mary Newbury (1933-2019),
who sang, laughed and cared for all life,
all of her life.

Contents

Frontispiece	I
Preface	III
Prologue: A Call of the Trees	XII

Part One: Preparation For The Journey
1. Hidden in the Hills: Ancient and Modern Pilgrimages — 1
2. Angels, Devas and Fairies of the Mountains — 16
3. Following the Calling — 24
4. The Water Sprites Would Wish to Speak to You! — 34

Part Two: Entering The Landscape
5. Music on the Moor: The Deva Immortelle Speaks — 39
6. Shifts in Consciousness: Time Travel Beyond the Kitchen! — 55
7. We will Be Here as Long as the Rain Will Fall on Earth — 62
8. Message from the Source of Immortelle's Burn: It is Time for Humans to Co-operate in Earth's Healing — 81
9. Sacred Commission — 91
10. Midsummer, Magic and Manifestation — 104
11. Where is Your Heart Connection? — 111
12. Gaia: Her Kingdoms and Hierarchies — 114

Part Three: Be Still And Listen
13. Rosemarkie and the Fairy Glen: A Message from the Sìthichean — 133
14. Messages From the Water Elementals of Clava — 140
15. The River Elementals of the Upper Findhorn — 145
16. The Lady of the Lake: The Elementals of the Lake of Menteith — 153
17. Now It is Time for Healing! — 157
18. Our Raison d'Etre is Love ~ Our d'Etre is Joy — 165
19. We Need You to Stay Strong and Be in Tune with Us — 172
20. Seeing an Elf Child — 185

Part Four: Creating Our Future Together With Nature's Guardians
    21. The Wee Folk and the Fairy Realms   199
    22. The Spirit of the Rock Speaks to You   209
    23. Enchantment of Sounds and Places   217
    24. Meeting New Findhorn Friends   228
    25. Temples to the Planets   230
    26. Fracking Nature and the Sound of OM   241
    27. The Coming of the Children of Light   250
    28. Remembering the Ancestors   256

Part Five: Now You Are Listening!
    29. Dream Vision of the Eagle, the Owl and the Wolf   263
    30. Children as Caretakers of Our Planet   267
    31. The Great Grey Man ~ Am Fear Liath Mòr   280
    32. The Secret of Clava   286
    33. The Tide has Turned!   305

Epilogue   317
References   319
Image Credits   329
Appendices A   333
Appendices B   337
Appendices C   339
Acknowledgements   341
About the Author   343
Notes Pages   345

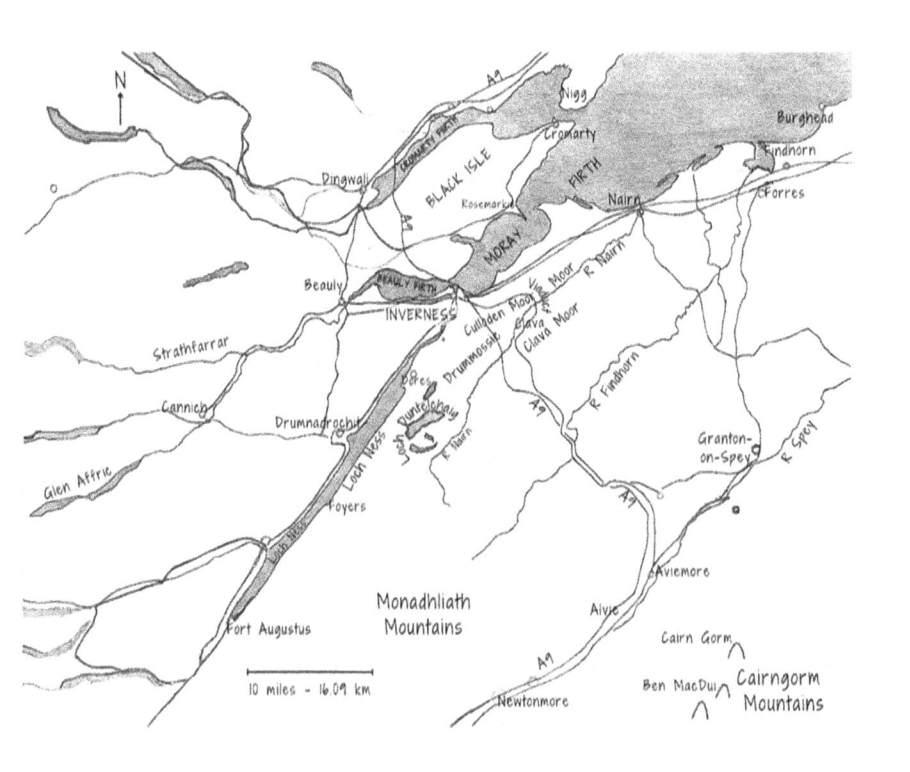

Map of the British Isles with Inset Map of area surrounding the River Nairn, Scottish Highlands - intended as a guide as not all major routes or towns are shown, and distances are approximate.

Frontispiece

Years ago I made a promise. As I walked under the trees, by the water and on the mountainside, I spoke the promise out loud and my words blew away on the wind. I promised the nature spirits that I would bring their messages back from the angelic realms to humankind. One day, I began to hear their words.

This book describes my journey into their realms, and records the messages I have collected over the last ten years. It is for everyone who recognises the need to support the balance and respect between humans and the Earth. I see this as a homecoming to the sacred and essential interdependence between us, as a re-attunement to life in its awe-inspiring aspect in our current times.

Our ancestors listened to their land. We can learn to listen again. As we raise our awareness, we engage the power needed to heal and to create our future.

I hope this book will reach young and old guardians of animals, woodlands, seas, rivers and plants; educators, parents and children; environmentalists, scientists, lawyers of human rights and Nature's rights, and all who have power over decisions on how our landscape is used, developed and cared for.

The dialogue of this book is based on my true experience of the places I know and love in Scotland, particularly the area of Drummossie Moor and Clava in Strathnairn. Though the book is based in Scotland, bringing forward Scottish fairy history, folklore, culture and history, these messages regarding humanity's relationship with Nature are universal messages.

I trust that you, the reader, will see beyond my simple human perception and description of the natural beauty of this land and its spiritual realms and will hear the voice of Earth through the recorded messages.

The messages I received from the devas, Nature's guardians, emphasise that we are intrinsically connected to Nature, and that Nature is not a commodity for us to plunder. We are caretakers of our planet.

Across the globe, citizens are coming together with this vision of caretaking the planet, and what was prophesied by the nature spirits is now shaping our reality today. Momentum is gathering as these human guardians step forward and take action to save our beautiful Earth.

Preface

Angel guidance has taught me that experiencing the silence of the mountains or being close to Nature are two of the best ways of feeling our connection to the Divine.

I grew up with a love of trees, mountains and wilderness, which led me through a portal of beauty into experiences of magic and mystery. From a young age I'd been taken on walks in the Cairngorms in the Central Highlands of Scotland. My favourite mountain was Ben MacDui.

Documented throughout the history of the Cairgorm landscape is the phenomenon of the Great Grey Man (*Am Fear Liath Mòr*, in Gaelic). I'd heard of Norman Collie, a well-known 19th century scientist, world mountaineer and explorer, who pioneered first ascents of Ben Nevis, the highest of Scotland's mountains, as well as the Cuillins of Skye in the west of Scotland. He also wrote famously about his meeting with the Great Grey Man of Ben MacDui.

In 1982, on a week's hillwalking expedition in the Cairngorms with friends from university, we encountered a man who had also experienced seeing the Great Grey Man in the form of a giant figure in the mist. He burst into the Sinclair Memorial Hut, the bothy where we were staying the night. After calming down and regaining his composure, he vividly described the phenomenon of the Great Grey Man in a way that matched Norman Collie's account in my Cairngorm guidebook. It was the last night of our long walk and we were looking forward to our dessert of dried apple rings heated in custard. The memory of this encounter has stayed with me… the terrified man, his story, the meal we were able to offer him cooked on a primus stove.

This wasn't the first time I had encountered a mystery

in the mountains. In 1980 I had walked with my father in Glen Affric, which is considered one of the most beautiful glens in the Highlands and seems to feature on every calendar depicting Scottish scenery. We came down from the summit of *Sgùrr na Lapaich* (Gaelic for Peak of the Bog) in snow showers, sometimes following the tracks of a cross country skier whom we believed to be about half an hour ahead of us, judging by the freshness of the ski tracks. The tracks kept disappearing when visibility was limited, then reappeared on patches of newly fallen snow ahead. The tracks led us to a 'snow bridge', which was the only possible way to cross a fast-flowing river.

My father went first whilst I held the rope belayed round a rock. I then put the rope around my waist and crossed over. Shortly after crossing we noticed that the tracks had stopped. Feeling impelled to check on the safety of the skier, we retraced our steps back uphill to find that the bridge had completely disappeared, with only a rushing torrent visible below the level of the snow that would now be impossible to cross. The skier had clearly made it over the bridge. The tracks were still visible in the snow on both sides of the river where the bridge had been, but stopped abruptly with no sign of a person or footprint anywhere in sight. I often wondered who this skier was who had led us safely down the mountain before doing a disappearing act!

There are no trespassing laws in Scotland. As long as we don't cause damage, enter a person's private garden, or blatantly wander through farm or estate land in the lambing, grouse nesting, shooting or deer culling seasons, we are legally free to roam. I was privileged to be taken on hill walks in some of the wildest and remotest of Scotland's Highland glens and mountains: Cairngorms, Torridon, Glen Affric, the great wilderness of the Fisherfields and Letterewe.

As a teenager, I accompanied my father and sometimes his hillwalking companions on the long cross-country routes from Glen Affric to Kintail and Dundonnell to Poolewe. Some of the walks were long and arduous and probably too strenuous for a teenager. My health was fragile and I often walked with pain, but have nevertheless survived to tell the tale and am indebted to my father for his introduction to these wild places.

My father had been a climber in his youth in the days of hobnail boots, hemp rope and no helmets. Aged only sixteen, he once hitchhiked to Scotland from the Midlands of England with a coil of rope in his suitcase. Later, he gave up hard rock climbing after a fall of three hundred feet from Ben Nevis' Tower Ridge. As they were roped together, he pulled his climbing partner with him into soft snow, where both escaped unscathed.

My parents moved to Scotland in the 1950s and began their married life in a small cottage on Culloden Moor, near Inverness. My mother recollected that she thought she was in heaven when hanging clothes on the washing line, from where she could see the clear vista over the Moray Firth to the Black Isle and Ben Wyvis floating on the horizon to the north, like a mirage. She always sang happily around the house and in the kitchen, but wasn't too keen on hillwalking.

My father, on the other hand, remained a keen hillwalker and footpath conservationist and was passionate about keeping the wilderness accessible and unspoiled for people to enjoy. Our bookshelves at home were lined with volumes of poetry and literature, as well as natural history and mountaineering guidebooks. There were accounts of the lives of indigenous people and autobiographies of Native North Americans. Lame Deer, Chief Sitting Bull, Black Elk and Crazy Horse were familiar names on the books' jacket covers.

I wasn't much of a reader, but the books were a testimony to a way of life where Nature was revered as sacred. This belief in the divinity of the natural world resonated deeply within me and formed a background to my school studies. I was brought up with two siblings: my sister, who became a scientist in the field of cell biology, and my brother, who from childhood has been a gifted musician and composer. Meanwhile, I pursued a career in art and teaching, keeping quiet about my personal spiritual encounters for fear of being thought fey or ethereal, as a high schoolteacher once wrote on my report card.

I remember at about the age of six watching coloured lights in the trees and leaving notes for the fairies. Our next-door neighbour, a large lady, would walk down the lane with me, prodding her walking stick at the flowers, asking me their names. I quickly learned as many as I could so that she would not catch me out. My respect for her was huge because she once unravelled an entire new roll of tinfoil simply to get to the cardboard tube that I needed for my art project. As I watched the pristine and shining silver sheet stretch out, I shyly asked if she believed in fairies. "Of course!" she boomed. I shrank back, stunned that an adult would admit such a thing so emphatically!

I treasured books of wildflowers and trees, beginning with the first *Flower Fairies* books I was given. Later, with money from school art and geography prizes, I bought *The Concise British Flora* and Scottish *Highland Flora*. I went in search of plants that were specific to a particular habitat, such as saxifrages in the rocks on a hillside, or bog plants growing in damp woodland. Some of the mountain flowers in the Scottish Highlands are too specialised or uncommon to be included in the mainstream British Floras, but appear in the Northern Europe and Scandinavian Floras,* which to my joy I discovered many years later.

I wandered in the woods, with the family dog as my companion. She waited close by, guarding, as I sat on the

Footnote: * see References

ground drawing portraits of the trees that I had come to regard as friends. On summer afternoons after work I cycled from Balloch to Daviot through a tunnel under the A9 road a few miles south of Inverness, then up to Loch Duntelchaig, Loch Ashie and over a moor to Errogie. Duntelchaig, the largest of the lochs in that area, is the local water supply for Inverness.

Sometimes my schoolfriend and I would swim in the smaller lochs there. It was an unspoiled landscape then, wild with rocky outcrops and ancient birch forest, where one might hope to see wildcats and eagles. There's a moor above the slopes with dramatic views down to Loch Ness and a ring of mountains all around. The tributaries of the rivers Farigaig and Foyers flow from there, falling steeply over to Loch Ness on the west side. From the east side, tributaries of the Nairn, Dulnain and Findhorn rivers descend from the Monadhliath Mountains to join the Moray Firth at its southern coastline.

I left home to study Fine Art in Edinburgh. On my visits back to Inverness from art college and university, I cycled in search of places beyond our village where I could paint outdoors. A friend from university, who was also from Inverness, told me about the perfect place to work undisturbed, and to which I could easily carry my painting gear. It was a safe, secret place, hidden in the folds of hills on the moors above Culloden Battlefield and the 4000-year-old Bronze Age Clava Cairns.

In the hot summer of 1983 I spent hours there, painting and preparing work for my art college exhibition, whilst my friend sat patiently beside the waterfall, singing in Gaelic. I tried to encapsulate the essence and feeling of being in Nature, amongst the flowers and grasses that were so specific to that environment, painting on large sheets of card laid on the ground and weighted down with small rocks.

I often wondered about the connection between spirituality and Nature, as I wasn't able to separate them. I had a limited knowledge of religions, although being brought up a

Quaker I had read about the testimonies of the early Friends and was vaguely familiar with the Bible. As a teenager, I once tried to read the Bible from beginning to end by torchlight under my bedclothes. I soon gave up on who begat whom, but liked the psalms because they were like poems about landscapes.

Quakers are a minority religious group in Scotland, although well known worldwide for their pacifism and belief in the Light of God that shines in every man, woman and child. In those days, the Quaker Meeting in Inverness met at Scaniport Hall, which had once been a church mission hall. It was situated in a beautiful, peaceful place on the road to Dores at the head of Loch Ness.

There wasn't a separate room for a children's class at that time. I enjoyed looking after the children who had come to Meeting with their parents, and in summer took them for walks in the beech woods and down the banks to the nearby River Ness to look for otters, before heading back to take part in the last fifteen minutes of worship.

I remember the sound of flies that had followed us in from the brightness outside, buzzing round the assembled company and disturbing the silence. The presence of God was within the silence of the group but could also be felt all around in the sunlit trees waving outside and in the calling of birds. The place, its woods, fields and nearby river seemed so special, that I could not decide if I felt the presence of God most strongly outdoors or in the worshipping group of Quakers.

I knew I could feel the spirit of God in Nature, although I never dared to voice this openly. I had adopted the belief that you had to engage in a religion to experience God, but the call of the trees seriously challenged this, at least for me. I could never have guessed at the time that many years later I would be led to hear the words of angels, devas and Nature's guardians. I now know that my experiences of being in Nature were an essential background and preparation for scribing the messages that make up the chapters of this book.

The writing of *An Angels' Guide to Working with the Power of Light* came first. I began taking down the messages in April 2006 and completed the script in 2009. The book was published in 2011.

An Angels' Guide to Working with the Power of Light is a compilation of messages transmitted to me telepathically by angels from divine source through a process that I realised was a form of *channelling*. It had all begun at a time of illness and physical pain. Being concerned for my teenage son, who was also unwell at the time, I had literally written an S.O.S. and experienced what appeared to be two miracles of healing for my son and myself. The book was to become more than a personal guide to healing. My angel guides led me to have it published, so that others could also be helped.

I was only part way through the *Angel* book when I received guidance that I would write another book on Nature's guardians, the devas.

The first information about the devas turned up in messages that I channelled for others from 2007. I kept this material entirely separate from the *Angel* book script. In 2007, 2009 and 2011, I visited the hills under the guidance of my angels for the purpose of *sending Light* for the work of the devas in specific locations. The angels explained that *sending Light* simply meant directing an intention for the purity of air and water, the integrity and sanctity of the Earth and the life it supports. This was to be done by focusing the mind on visualising a beam of Light from the heart, sent out with the intention for healing to reach the required places. The process is almost identical to sending prayer or healing to a person, as described in *An Angels' Guide to Working with the Power of Light*.

I asked why I was being called to write another book. The angels' messages to me were insistent:

> We wish that you write this book because of your lifelong love and connection with us, because of your

desire to help, because of your active involvement in our destiny.

    The compilation of research and messages for this second book took me back into the mountains and the heartland of the area where I was born and spent my formative years.

    Here I found a changed landscape due to an expanding population and increased housing, a changed economy and the need for new green industry, all of which had infiltrated much of the wild and more remote scenery.

    In these sacred landscapes I was still able to find the spirit of the land in the quiet, hidden places, where I could hear the voices of the devas and the angelic guardians of the Earth and record their messages for our times.

Prologue:

A Call of the Trees

I'm walking uphill through sunlit birch trees, shafts of light falling through the leafy canopy to soft grass on the forest floor... a gentle wind catches the scent of leaves and myrtle. The woodland is open, airy and many flowering plants are growing under the trees. The air is pure and mild.

There's a great feeling of expectancy on approach to a place that seems to call from beyond the trees. Hurrying with quickening pace towards the feeling of being called... I stop in a glade in front of two tall birch trees, which grow side by side.

Down from the sunlit canopy, down from the white trunks of the trees glide simultaneously two tall beings, male and female.

Their beauty is beyond anything that is possible to describe and it's difficult to look at their faces because of the overwhelming feeling of awe they evoke within me.

They appear completely naked, apart from some garlands of leaves around their waists and genital areas. Their skin is pale green silvery white, a colour which resembles the very bark of birch trees.

The female *being* has armlets of leaves and a wreath of leaves on her head. Her incredible beauty creates Light, which emanates from her so strongly. Her male companion is taller and his stature totally commanding. His beauty is equal to hers and his presence is immense.

As they are naked, yet so powerful and shining, one would feel ashamed to be in their presence wearing clothes.

Unbelievably they are coming forward, holding out their arms. The words are clear. There is no mistaking them.

Please help us!

I am stunned into silence, filled with deep awe. I look downwards at my feet, not wishing to stare directly, yet perceiving their Light, afraid to look as they come down the tree and walk forward.

Then I wake with a pain through my heart so real that I think it's physical.

This dream, which came to me in the late 1990s, was so powerful that I dressed hurriedly and ran out that morning to see if there was a tree being in trouble near my flat in Stirling. How does one identify a tree with its *being* in trouble? There was a birch tree recently cut down. It had been a beautiful one with long cascades of leaves, and I had always admired it on my way home walking from town. Although I was sad to see it chopped down, I didn't feel that my dream related to that particular tree. Finally, I came to the realisation that the dream was about birch trees further afield, in places of wilderness. Perhaps the town trees had a connection with their relatives in the wild?

The dream had come so powerfully through my subconscious mind that I have never forgotten it, nor the feeling that I was being asked to do something to help. I was perplexed and saddened and my heartstrings always tore at me when I thought about those tree beings. I remembered them long after other real-life encounters with people in my life had come and gone, and their faces had been forgotten.

Many a person has had a powerful sense of mission or vocation as a result of lucid dreaming, for our dreams do not only process our subconscious thoughts but may also be vehicles for guidance on a metaphysical level. The passage of years has made no difference to the intensity of my dream of the tree beings, nor has the fact that it was a dream rather than a remembered physical experience. I knew without a doubt that there was a message being given me through their arrival to my conscious mind. All was to become clear some years later through the writing of *An Angels' Guide to Working with the Power of Light*.

During the writing of that book I was given a further glimpse into the world beyond our world, running parallel, and which can be accessed from our current physical reality. This world beyond our world is inhabited by the unseen realms of Nature's angels and guardians. In writing this book I became more deeply aware of this other world that is so close to our reality it can touch us.

Part One

Preparation for the Journey

I knew I was beginning to hear the messages that came from Earth itself via the angelic guardians, the devas and nature spirits.

I longed to help the devas, but my hope felt so small and fragile like a single leaf blowing in the wind. Yet the words I received were filled with such grace. I began to believe that it might be possible that whoever reads these words will feel the beauty and power of the devas' messages as they emanate from the pages of this book.

(Chapter 4: Page 36)

Chapter 1

Hidden in the Hills:
Ancient and Modern Pilgrimages

This chapter describes the recent development of Scotland's wilderness areas. The expansion of industry into wilderness has been mainly driven by the search for so-called green energy sources, which are perceived as urgently needed solutions to fossil fuel dependency. The human impact on wilderness areas is also growing due to an unrelenting tourist industry and the marketing of a national image. This chapter sets the changes that are taking place against a more subtle knowledge that has been carried through landscape, song and poetry from ancient times, and that is still available today for those who have the eyes to see, the ears to hear and hearts that are willing to understand.

As I continued to spend time in Nature's sacred landscapes, I heeded the angels' request to begin a second book on behalf of Nature's guardians, the devas. Messages that I had channelled for others while concurrently writing *An Angels' Guide to Working with the Power of Light* alluded to Earth's healing and Gaia. Around 2011, there was a difference in the messages I received. The request from my angel Ariel became more insistent: I was to go out and send Light for Earth at specific places.

I began to pick up a few fragments of information from the nature spirits directly, such as messages from water sprites at Loch Lomond. Eventually, I was directed to find one specific location outdoors in order to write the main text of this book, which records a series of conversations that I engaged in between 2012 and 2017 with a deva of river and mountain, one of Nature's guardians from the angelic realms.

In the meantime, Scotland had been deemed by politicians to become a *flagship nation* of green energy. Scotland is a small country with beautiful scenery and wild natural areas in close proximity to places where people live; therefore, the visual impact of any development of roads, industry or housing on the landscape is very apparent.

The urgent need for alternative technologies to replace fossil fuels and reduce carbon footprints affects Scotland's remaining areas of wilderness, because such developments need to be sited in areas of low population and with access to open spaces, abundant wind or fast flowing water. New wind turbines are now visible from the roads and from the top of any mountain you can see them springing up in every direction on the horizon. Wind turbine symbols are also appearing across mountainous areas on the latest Ordnance Survey map reprints.

All this is quite literally happening in front of our eyes. The chosen sites for new power line routes, hydroelectric schemes and wind turbines often coincide with strategic sites of ancient human settlements, ceremonial sites and spiritual centres where there has been a strong connection between people and the land.

The great stone circle at Calanais on the Isle of Lewis in the Western Isles is linked to the mountains that can be viewed from that particular point, notably the Sleeping Beauty or Goddess (a hill in the shape of a sleeping woman, called in Gaelic, *Cailleach na Mòinteach*, 'old woman of the moors'). Here, a one hundred and thirty-three turbine wind farm is proposed (at the time of writing), which would then be linked to a huge electric power line running through Scotland to the south. This has come to be known as the Beauly to Denny power line, whilst the plans for the link to Lewis are still being developed.

Corrimony, the ancient site of chambered cairns near Loch Ness, has given its name to a new wind farm on adjacent land. Like Calanais, this is another key spiritual site from Scotland's prehistory. Thousands of tourists visit the Western Isles and Skye every year and include Calanais in the tour. Corrimony is not as well known, but may be linked to the similarly aged four-thousand-year-old Clava Cairns near Inverness.

New large-scale developments overlay the original character and features of places. The developers may see the ancient monuments as unrelated or irrelevant within the geographical area and landscapes in which they are placed. Meanwhile, tourism channels visitors to particular places, such as Clava, in ways that are not in context with the surrounding hill scenery, its outlying cairns and its relationship with other sites that are often further away from the main roads and not so easily accessible.

However, we need to understand that our ancestors were closely linked with the land. Scotland's landscapes and culture are still recognised as having a particularly spiritual intensity. This is experienced through its music, which due to the internet has become increasingly popularised. There is also a strong drive to save the old Gaelic language and Celtic roots. Many people visit these spiritually and culturally important places and keep alive the history of pilgrimages from thousands of years ago.

The Greek historian Diodorus Siculus wrote in 55 BC about an island in the north called Hyperborea, where a round temple stood, from which the moon appeared only a little distance above the Earth every nineteen years.*

This phenomenon can be witnessed at Calanais, where the corridor of stones radiating from its central circle lines up with the position of the moon. Every 18.61 years a lunar standstill takes place as the moon transits over the body of the Sleeping Beauty. The path of the moon is accurately measured by the alignments of stones in the week preceding the event. The moon is then seen to skim over the Sleeping Beauty, following the mountain horizon from her feet to her head, as if to demonstrate a physical connection between the heavenly body of the moon and the Earth. It is believed that pilgrimages to this strategic site date back to ancient times, and they continue today. The next major lunar standstill will be in 2024/25.

I had received many communications from my angel guides describing Scotland as a heartland with its ancient rocks, and the way that people had travelled between the stone circle sites across the land. At the time of recording the deva's (earth angel's) messages, I was stunned to find that this seemed to be verified when watching a TV documentary describing the discovery of a temple complex at Ness of Brodgar, in the Orkney Isles. The carbon dating of artefacts, such as cattle bones or jewellery, has shown that people in prehistoric times travelled and traded from Orkney to other major sites such as Avebury and Stonehenge in Wiltshire, England, and overseas.

Many of Scotland's landscapes have changed due to human intervention and new farming methods. The natural balance of animal and bird life has been disturbed. Bears and lynx disappeared from Scotland in prehistory. Wolves were extinguished and many birds of prey were depleted by hunters in Victorian times. Nowadays, the high number of deer populations and the over-grazing of sheep prevent the indigenous trees from returning. Deforestation over the centuries has caused ancient woodland to be lost by ninety-five per cent.

The upper stretches of Strathnairn (*Srath Narann*), the river valley of the Nairn, are strewn with stone circles and dwellings, many of which have long ago disappeared under the Forestry Commission's plantation areas. These began to be developed after World War I due to the need to re-establish woodland quickly and create an essential new timber industry. The closely planted non-native trees block out light and smother indigenous species. Access roads for wind farms and electricity lines now dwarf the old roads and scenery in the same area and pass within metres of standing stones and circles. Other ancient sites have been ploughed round or submerged in fields over the millenia.

In some places, geophysical mapping technology is revealing the layers of history that lie around the ancient spiritual sites. This method records the temperature of the layers in the substrata of the soil. Where there has been disturbance by human activity, such as building in past eras, the data configures this into images which look like underground maps on the computer screen.

Even as the land is surveyed for new developments, more layers of ancient settlements are discovered. Beneath the area along the A96 road from Inverness to Nairn lies a huge Pictish graveyard. Moulds for pouring metal to make scythes were found nearby on the Black Isle, the peninsula just north of Inverness.

Poetry and Song of the Land

The history of belief and respect for the guardians of Nature, including the fairies and *wee folk*, is embraced within the mythology and folklore of these areas.

Despite the physical loss of wild natural landscapes where people once lived, traces of information about their lives are still preserved within the old place names, and in the literature, poetry, songs and stories that have been handed down through the generations. There are songs of battles, love, loss and celebration that are specific to particular places. In more recent times, there are songs of the longing for home that was felt by those who emigrated or were forcibly evicted when landowners from the south turned over the Highland glens to sheep farming in the mid-18th to 19th centuries.

The music and the songs carry a vibration of the area from which they arise, like the timbre of people's voices.

The names of places have their own particular sound. Many Gaelic poets were illiterate, as the language was originally spoken but not written. Poems and songs were committed to memory and only later collected and documented. Sorley MacLean, considered to be one of Scotland's greatest Gaelic poets and scholars, has been recorded reading his own poetry of the hills in his native tongue. His voice gives a spiritual resonance to the names of those places and hills that were once known and loved by past generations living under their shadow.

Sorley MacLean/Somhairle MacGill-Eain
First verse of poem, *Hallaig*, with English translation

'*Tha tìm, am fiadh, an coille Hallaig*'

Tha bùird is tàirnean air an uinneig
trom faca mi an Àird an Iar
's tha mo ghaol aig Allt Hallaig
'na craoibh bheithe, 's bha i riamh

~

Time, the deer, is in the wood of Hallaig

The window is nailed and boarded
through which I saw the West
and my love is at the Burn of Hallaig,
a birch tree and she has always been*

There are poems and songs dedicated to the beauty of specific places, mountains and trees. Beloved of trees in Scotland is the rowan (or mountain ash) a tree which has always symbolised protection and is also sacred to the ancient Celtic goddess Brighid. There are many versions of her name. She became known as the *Muime Chriosd*, or foster mother of Christ after the arrival of Christianity to the Celtic world. Many Druidic traditions, including those which celebrate trees, were overlaid or merged with the new Christianity. Brighid is also a mythical image of The Divine Feminine, i.e. shapeshifting from the

Maiden to Mother, then Crone.

A song composed in the 18th century by Carolina Oliphant, Lady Nairne, is still dear to many people's hearts and commonplace among Scottish songs and in the piper's repertoire. In Highland glens you will often come across two rowan trees growing by doorways amid the ruins of old crofts. Still rooted in the places where people lived, they will have seeded from original trees planted there as bringers of good fortune and to ward off bad spirits.

Verse from Rowan Tree by Carolina Oliphant
Lady Nairne (1766-1845)*

Oh, Rowan tree! Oh, Rowan tree!
Thou'lt aye be dear tae me,
Entwined thou art wi' mony ties,
O' hame and infancy.
Thy leaves were aye the first o' spring
Thy flow'rs the simmer's pride;
There was nae sic a bonnie tree
In a' the country side
Oh! Rowan tree!

The essence of place also finds its way into one of Scotland's biggest commercial exports. A whisky from Dalwhinnie cannot be copied or compared to a single malt from the Isle of Jura in the west or a Speyside in the east of Scotland, because its taste is specific to the local water that has travelled through the peat and the rock, as well as from the barley often grown in nearby fields. These whiskies literally embody the spirit of the place from which they were made. Any escaped liquid that has evaporated into the air from the wooden caskets is known as the *angels' share*.

There is also a type of commercialism that portrays Scotland in a kind of *false tartan* image or gives a romantic appeal that overlays its true history. As a result, cult followings of films entice visitors to specific locations, thereby creating pressure on heritage sites, adding to what is now known as *overtourism*. I discovered whilst writing this book that this has happened at the Fairy Pools on Skye and at Clava in Strathnairn.

Naming of the Land

Landscape features are named from the ancient languages spoken in past times. They describe a profound knowledge and appreciation of Nature by people who were close to and utterly dependent on their locality for survival, quality of life, needs and aspirations, including their spiritual beliefs.

Unlike the situation in many European countries, most of us who live in Scotland don't understand the significance of the history that is encapsulated within place and hill names of the areas where we live. The names contain meanings derived from the old Norse, Brittonic, Scots and Gaelic languages. Of the four original languages of Britain, only Gaelic and old Scots remain, spoken by about one and three percent of the population respectively.

A lack of understanding of our cultural roots can blind us to the true and inestimable value of our land, together with its spiritual and cultural dimension. For example, the Gaelic word *fonn* (plural *fuinn*) describes three levels of meaning: the land, song and state of consciousness.*

Gaelic hill names are so specific as to describe every hill and crag across the Highlands, a vast array of types of snow cover on a hillside, or a full range of hues within each part of the spectrum. The hill colours are based on a deep awareness of the subtleties of hue, as perceived through layers of atmosphere, water, light at different angles and seeing the hills at nose-to-rockface proximity, or in contrast, from huge distances. Whereas the Monadhliath are known as the grey mountains, the Cairngorm mountain range takes its name from Cairn Gorm, *An Càrn Gorm*, the blue mountain as seen from a distance. The region as a whole is described as the *Am Monadh Ruadh*, the red mountainland. Close up, the granite of these hills glows pink in the evening sunlight.*

It's not always obvious until you're walking in the hills that their names so accurately describe special features. *Bàn* is one of three Gaelic words describing versions of white. *Càrn Bàn Mòr* in the Cairngorms and *Càrn Bàn* in the Monadhliath are scattered with glittering white quartz near their summits; a mineral that was likely to have been highly valued by prehistoric peoples, as it is embedded in the monoliths of the stone circles of the glens.

There are lochans in the hills that can be iridescent peacock blue one day or shine like gold at other times, as at Lochan Buidhe (golden lochan/lake) on the route between Cairn Gorm and Ben MacDui.

In the Cairngorms there are four stunning green lochans. An Lochan Uaine was believed to be sacred to the fairies, who washed their clothes in the water, thus turning it green. From a more scientific perspective, the water is believed to be green due to dissolved mineral content.

Above An Lochan Uaine, the best known of the green lochs, is the hill of *Sìthean Dubh dà Choimhead* (The Black Fairy Hill of the Two Outlooks). The hill looks out towards Loch Morlich, which was believed to be the stronghold of the King of Fairies, Big Donald. There are stories of people being frightened off on hearing Donald's bagpipes, although this might not happen nowadays as Loch Morlich is a busy place with many visitors.

In the Highlands, the landscape was predominantly named by Gaelic speakers. With the decline of the language, particularly after the Battle of Culloden, followed by the clearing of people from the glens in the 18th to 19th centuries, much of the connection between people and their own culture was brutally destroyed.

The mapmakers of the 19th century were able to record many of the names of the hills by coming into contact with people who still spoke the language. Many original sources of names were unfortunately lost and are still disappearing as new map editions sometimes convert the names to a hybrid form, especially the most well-known of the hills. The anglicised name of Ben MacDui, the highest mountain in the Cairngorms, is thought to come from an original form of *beinn mhic dhuibhe*, hill of the son of Dubh (the black one) or hill of the sons of Duff, an ancient family of landowners. Some map versions retain the bh of Dubh, Beinn MacDuibh.*

Myth and Folklore

The importance of myth and folklore for human culture provides background and context for the appearance of Nature's guardians into human perception and cannot be separated from our history. Myth and folklore are the roots and essence of history.

Many hills in Scotland have fairy names because they were also regarded as places of connection between fairies and humans. There are literally thousands of hill names alluding to fairies and fairy stories linked with particular areas all over Scotland. The most famous of these is the poem and song of True Thomas the Rhymer, who rode off with the Queen of Fairies only to return many decades later. This is recorded as happening at Eildon Hill, the magical looking three-peaked hill, that can be seen whilst crossing the border between Scotland and England at Eildon, near Melrose.

The village of Aberfoyle with its Fairy Hill of Doon is located in Stirlingshire in central Scotland. The Reverend Robert Kirk (1644-1692) went there in order to receive communications from the fairy people, the *Sleagh Maith*. He was a notable scholar who had translated the Psalms into Gaelic. This was published in 1684 as *Psalma Dhaibhidh an Meadrachd, & c* (Psalms of David in Metre, &c). He also advised on the complete translation of the Bible into Gaelic, which was published in 1690.

Robert Kirk wrote what is regarded as one of the most significant treatises on fairy folklore, witchcraft, ghosts and second sight. He had gathered this information from his collections of folklore of the Scottish Highlands where second sight, a form of extrasensory perception, is still regarded as relatively common.

Kirk's *The Secret Commonwealth of Elves, Fauns and Fairies* was published under that title over a hundred years after his death in 1815.* It seems incredible that he escaped persecution as a witch, although on the contrary it is thought that he may have seen his book as proof for non-believers and atheists of the supernatural as an integral part of God's kingdom.

Robert Kirk served as the minister of his parish for many years and died on the Fairy Hill of Doon. According to local legend, his body disappeared from its coffin and he was taken to fairyland.

There are many stories of human encounters not only with fairies of the hills but with supernatural beings belonging to the water, such as kelpies (horses of the sea) and dangerous water horses (*each-uisge*) of inland lochs. The famous Loch Ness monster is sometimes believed to belong to the tradition of water horse sightings recorded there, although another theory suggests that the monster is an ancient relic from the age of plesiosaurs.

All the information on 'Nessie', from photographs to sonar images, is disputed, yet the myth lives on and it's hard to drive alongside the loch without the hope of seeing something in the dark waters. My family had once known someone from Drumnadrochit by Loch Ness who actually claimed to have seen the Loch Ness monster. She was so excited that on arrival at a meeting she was compelled to tell everyone of her encounter. This has always puzzled me, because she was a very unlikely person to have invented the story.

The far northeast of Scotland and the Orkney and Shetland Isles have their own traditions of sea beings - the *selkies* (seal people). These shape-shifters can divest themselves of their seal skin and take on human form, often female, to then be seduced by a human male. Only when the selkie finds her skin again can she escape back to the sea, leaving her children behind.

The poignant stories of the selkies and the many stories of humans meeting fairies exist in mythology, music and traditional song throughout Scotland. Often the stories are associated with places of beauty where wild nature is still recognised.

Walking into the Future

Tourism brings people to visit some of the best known beauty spots, while other wild landscapes are unfrequented, being further from the roads and therefore not easily accessible. These places are known only to the local sheep farmers and gamekeepers, as well as people who go to the hills and moors to engage in hunting, fishing and shooting, or to seek solitude amid the beauty and open space. These wilderness areas are now being encroached upon to such an extent that even people in the south of Scotland don't always realise how the wilds of the north have been altered.

When I first read online about the plans to build huge new schemes for wind and hydro power, I thought I was dreaming. It seemed so unreal. I felt shockwaves through my heart when I realised that the areas I had thought of as pristine wilderness - those places I knew from my teenage years when I cycled on the road across the moors in upper Strathnairn or walked in the hills with my father - were now at grave risk.

The Monadhliath mountains, from which the rivers of the Spey, Findhorn and Nairn emanate, are almost legendary for their remoteness yet wind farms were planned there. The area around Loch Ness was to be part of a giant scheme (later to be termed a 'ring of steel') that necessitated developing the wilderness on an unprecedented scale.

The wind farm at Corrimony became part of this ring. At present 363 operational wind turbines have been built, 20 are under construction and 29 awaiting approval or in the application stage. A further 198 wind developments are in the pre-application phase. New hydro-electric schemes are also being planned. This will mean thousands of tonnes of concrete being poured into Scotland's beautiful, wild landscapes.*

Debates continue between conservationists, historians and the people who are affected by these developments. Some prioritise the advantages and profits for local and national economies, and others protest about the visual impact, noise, and disruption to local communities. During the installation of the wind farms, heavy volumes of road building materials are transported through villages and along narrow country roads to the construction site access points in the hills. The companies concerned are often located far afield from the locations in Scotland where their investment is based, and may have no love or knowledge of the land apart from its commercial value.*

I had started to hear the call for help from the devas, the spiritual guardians of landscape and Nature, in 2007 when the research for this book began. At the time of editing my writings in 2019, Scotland officially had no wilderness left.

Although I had read this startling fact and seen for myself the effects of development in the wilderness areas, the following messages which I received from Nature's guardians give great hope. Our current times present opportunities for us to work *with*, rather than *against* Nature, as we step into our role as enlightened caretakers of our planet.

Chapter 2

Angels, Devas and Fairies of the Mountains

In our modern culture, the words angels, devas, nature spirits and fairies may evoke associations with 'fantasy', 'unreality' or 'childishness'. I am the first to acknowledge this as I fought with such fears when revealing my interest in these subtle beings to my family, friends and the general public when my first book - *An Angels' Guide to Working with the Power of Light* - was published.

Several people suggested at that time that I write the messages of the book without mentioning the word *Angel* in order to reach a wider audience.

I was unable to do this, because I had called out for help at a time of crisis and, with my inner hearing, had heard a most beautiful voice. The voice did not make me feel afraid in any way. On the contrary, it filled me with peace and I knew that the messages I received represented a profound Truth. I silently asked who was speaking. The first time this happened the answer was that my guardian angel was present. I could not discount this as I wrote the message down.

I questioned this afterwards, until I was sick of questioning and could find no more reason not to believe it. Belief seemed almost irrelevant at times, because this was my experience and I knew in my heart that I was not deluded. As I continued to scribe the messages in the book I repeatedly checked and asked for the author's identity. I was given the names of known angels. At times I even had to look up some of the unfamiliar names online. The angel messengers never made me feel afraid or asked me to do anything that I didn't want to do.

When I gave talks after writing the book, people from all walks of life would come up to me afterwards to share their own personal angel experiences. They often said that it was something they would never have believed if it had not happened to them. Others emphasised that they came from a scientific background and that it was not the sort of thing they would normally be able to accept. I could have written a second book about other people's angel experiences and how their prayers or requests for help had manifested in the most incredible and wonderful ways. Even children were eager to confide in me. The one thing I noticed about all these people was that it was impossible to discern from their general demeanour that they were in touch with their angels!

I adopted a style of wearing two hats. One was my art teacher's hat and the other my angel teacher's hat. I didn't usually mix the two.

My art teaching background has made me aware of the different paradigms and languages that are familiar to adults and children with diverse gifts and abilities, but I can only describe my angel experience in words that belong to a more metaphysical way of being in the world. As an artist I tend to notice details beyond the superficial appearance of things and ascribe a symbolic nature to our world. I also experience an awareness and a sensitivity to all living things and empathise with their emotional states and feelings, which in turn impacts my own sense of happiness.

I trust that you, the reader, will receive with openness the descriptions I offer of my meetings with Nature's guardians, as I attempt to be as accurate and reflective of the truth of my experience as possible.

My awareness of the devas, nature spirits and fairies had been lost in childhood memories but came to me again through my angels' messages; the same angels that dictated the script of *An Angels' Guide to Working with the Power of Light*.

My personal understanding of angels comes from the

Judeo-Christian religious culture that I am steeped in. Several of the angel messengers' names given to me, such as Michael, Raphael and Gabriel, are from that strong patriarchal tradition. Yet my personal experience of these angels is that they only manifest in name, shape, and form so that we can understand and recognise them as God's messengers, their commission being to protect, help and guide us.

Angels are great powers of Light from Source, that connect with humankind and guard us in our spiritual and soul journeys. They even look after us physically when we ask. They are closely associated with religions but exist independently of all religions. They can reveal themselves as masculine or feminine, as colour, light or presence. Always totally benevolent, they remain true to their blueprint of representing the divine will of a loving God, not a God of fear or a God limited to a purely masculine aspect.

In relation to *Devas*, I had begun to receive extraordinary messages from the angels about the devas through channelled writings for myself and others. Examples of these can be found in the Appendix.*

At first I found it strange that these same angel guides described the devas and fairies as their kin or their brothers and sisters. I had differentiated between angels and fairies in my thinking, whilst interpreting the term deva as being like an angel of the landscape.

When I first began to write the messages for this book I was only aware of the role of devas as landscape angels. Later, I was invited to give talks about angels to the Theosophist Society, which led me to read some of its literature. I discovered that the term deva came into our awareness in modern times with the merging of eastern and western spiritual traditions, through teachings such as those of the theosophical movement.

The word deva comes from the Sanskrit, meaning *shining one* and is the male form, although the term tends to be used generically. In Eastern religions the devas are regarded as caretakers of humans and Nature and have a number of other functions.

While writing this book, I met people from the Findhorn community in the north of Scotland. The three founders of this community had been brought together in 1962 through adverse circumstances, ending up at Findhorn Bay Caravan Park. Following God's guidance, as received through the channelled writings of Eileen Caddy and put into practice by Peter Caddy, they created a community in co-creation with Nature. Eileen Caddy received guidance from God via angels, while her husband Peter worked with others to implement these messages in practice. Dorothy Maclean, who worked closely alongside Eileen and Peter Caddy, had the revelation of receiving messages from the angels associated with plants and landscapes. She termed them devas in order to distinguish them from angels associated with human beings. In her many books she recorded her experiences.

Through the angels' messages I came to understand that, like angels, devas exist in a different dimension yet are connected to the one that we humans inhabit. Their domain is the earth, water, plant life, and the air we breathe. My angels' messages described how the devas care for the nature spirits and the hierarchy of spiritual beings which have had long associations with humankind. These are the fairies, elves, sprites, dwarfs and also the Scottish good folk (*Sleagh Maith* in Gaelic), kelpies and trolls or bogarts of the mountains, to name but a few. They have their counterparts in the rest of Britain and over much of northern Europe and Scandinavia.

I received the following channelled message from my angel guides regarding the name deva:

> The term deva is human-made and understood rather differently by your diverse religions. However, there was always an element or type of deva which connected with Nature and the elements.

The devas are on the same level as the angels of your hierarchy that link with cherubim and thrones... if we use that terminology.

The devas oversee the elementals that are more localised to types of plants, trees, rocks, fires, watercourses. Therefore, they can oversee a large terrain containing rivers, plants, rocks and the substrata, and the air above. However, they do not move out of their region, except by latching on to the aura of a person who is also connected to that place. They have the ability, like the archangels, to be omnipotent, and to be in different parts of their locality at the same time. They can manifest as a powerful fairy, i.e. a queen of fairies. They can manifest as a breeze or shower.

They are always linked to their place because other devas are linked to other areas on Earth.

The devas also link to the divine realms, the realms of your soul star. Therefore you can connect with them in your dreams, or they can come into your consciousness to speak to you.

They may also send a fairy or elf to you to give a message.

They rarely connect with your angels to send a message... that would be like Archangel Michael sending a message to you via Archangel Gabriel. This does not happen because both Archangel Michael and Archangel Gabriel are linked to God directly and can manifest to you individually.

So with the devas, they have the ability to bring messages to you without the need of your angel. But we remind you to have the protection of your angel around you in communicating with them. Your angel may also translate their message for you... as with Ariel who shall translate the communication of your deva for you.*

Besides clarifying my use of the term devas, I would also like to explain my use of the word fairies. In contrast to angels, I had believed that fairies were the tiny beings of myth, folklore and literature, seen by children and some unusual adults but normally relegated to the bottom of the garden, the wild woods, hills and places of ancient history. I had a memory of seeing their coloured lights in the trees in the garden when I was six years old. As I grew up, I hadn't really understood that they had much relevance in today's world, but nothing could be further from the truth.

My hillwalking friend told me that the word *fairy* comes from the French word *faire*, meaning, to do. Those wee dancing fairies of our folklore are also guardians of Nature, working tirelessly!

The traditional role of fairies in folklore is to bring good fortune or grant wishes to those who show kindness and compassion in a given situation. There are also many examples of bad fairies who can cause mischief, or even havoc.

In Scotland and Ireland there are stories of people being stolen away to fairyland, returning many years later with an astonishingly unnatural gift of music. In the borders of Scotland, the magical Eildon Hills set the scene for the legend of True Thomas who rode off with the Queen of Fairies.

My angel guides told me, above all:

Never, ever attempt to connect with a deva or nature spirit without first calling for protection of us, your angels.

I wasn't surprised at the angels' warning. I had heard that Scottish people living in areas where belief in fairies is still strong, also respect them and leave them in peace. At the Fairy Pools on Skye local people do not go into the water, due to fear and respect. However, the place is now a tourist hotspot that is well advertised for its unusual beauty and the possibilities for wild swimming. Given the lengthy queues of traffic on the approach to the site, and the constant streams of visitors, it would now be almost impossible to be alone at the waterside.

The messages I received became increasingly urgent. I was told that Nature's guardians - the devas and nature spirits in their care, including the fairies and *elementals* - are retreating to places that are left to pristine nature and wilderness. This is because their role is inextricably linked to the process of bringing life force to Earth through the raw elements of Nature.

That the devas are inextricably linked with natural landscapes and the process of bringing life to Earth was a revelation to me. I had a feeling that this information could also be understood from the perspective of other sacred wisdom traditions. Many acknowledge the reality of such a life force (*prana* or *chi*), which derives from the natural elements, as in Yoga, Ayurveda, Chinese Medicine, and Shamanism. Accounts of the Native North American way of life are also based on reverence and harmony with our Earth Mother, rather than an imposition of human will resulting in destruction.

I was perturbed to realise that the places of pure nature and wilderness to which Nature's guardians are retreating coincide with the same areas that are diminishing in Scotland, as elsewhere, due to the pressure of overtourism, new industrialisation and general destruction of the landscape.

However, the angels' messages also offered encouragement. Together with warnings about the plight the devas were facing came reassurances that we, as human beings, have not lost touch with the guardians of Nature. Even as they are diminishing, awareness of them is coming back into humankind's consciousness due to our dependence on Nature for survival. I received the following message from my angel Ariel:

> Now, because of the need to respect Earth, love of fairies and recognition of their role in your life brings our image to your consciousness.

People are manifesting images of us by their focus on us. However, as we said before, it is a two-way thing. You cannot have true encounters with us unless it comes from real love and respect for us, and your destiny brings us together.

Chapter 3

Following the Calling

I was part way through writing *An Angels' Guide to Working with the Power of Light* when my angel guides started to urge me to pray for the devas and nature spirits. I was asked to uphold them in the Light.

This meant to visualise sending a beam of white Light, while at the same time holding the intention that the integrity of Earth be maintained. This form of prayer would thereby add a dimension of human willingness to my belief and trust that the purity of Earth's air, fire, waters, substrata and the life it supports would be preserved. I was asked to focus on the places where Nature was being despoiled and to send prayer for Earth's healing.

I had come through a time of debilitating headaches but these had now begun to heal. When I was well enough to revisit the hills and places where I'd walked in the past, the landscape was already changing - much faster it seemed than at any other time in our history.

I was keen to do as the angels requested but didn't know where to start. I reckoned that as the devas were Earth angels who *overlight* areas of land and look after the nature spirits, then the hills with fairy names might give me a clue as to where they could be found. The angels had communicated that the hierarchy of fairies is the closest in consciousness to humankind and that I might therefore seek them in the hills.

The affix Sìth (pronounced 'Shee') which turns up in hundreds of Scottish hill names, relates to the word meaning fairy (*sìthiche* in Gaelic, pronounced *SHEE-yich-ah*), with the plural, *sìthichean*. The word, *sìthean* ('*shee-an*') refers to a fairy hill. Fairy hills were known as places where some races of the fairies have lived and where humans have encountered them. *Sìdh*, also spelled *sìthe*, and its plural *sìdhe*, come from the Irish Gaelic traditions. Hill names such as *Schiehallion* (*Sìth Chailleann*), Glenshee where there is a famous skiing resort, and Campsie are also derivations of the fairy name.

Apart from the word for fairy (*sìthiche*), containing the prefix, *sìth*, the *Sìth/sìdhe* people (*daoine sìth*) are also believed to be a supernatural race of beings, a fairy race sometimes known as the 'people of peace'. The reasons for the connection with 'peace' is mysterious, possibly a human perception of the supernatural effect of their presence, that has stayed with the fairy name through to modern times.*

I had written the script of my angel book on my computer, receiving the messages through clairaudience (which is like telepathic transfer that I normally sense in my right ear) and writing them down quickly. Somehow, I didn't feel that this would work when trying to connect with a deva or nature spirit, such as a fairy.

Like our angels, they exist in a parallel realm, but are based in the physical world of Nature, which is not the way our own guardian angels are connected to us. Angels are a form of divine being that act as both messenger and guardian for human beings. In contrast, devas are guardians that overlight and care for areas of physical landscape.

I was intrigued by the fairy names of the hills and wrote to my angels to ask about the mountain names of Schiehallion (*Sìth Chailleann*) in Perthshire, and Ben Ledi in Stirlingshire.

Dear Raphael, I have checked my books and the name Schiehallion refers to the Hill of Fairies of the Caledonians but the name Ben Ledi may mean Mountain of the Gods. (LeDè in Gaelic means 'with God'.) Can you say more about these names?

The angel answered:

We refer to Schiehallion as a Mountain of the Gods because invocation and worship has taken place there from times before the mountains had names. The history of humans' connection with that hill is far older than the connection with Ben Ledi.
You may say Ben Ledi is a modern mountain-God connection whereas Schiehallion is remembered almost in the way a myth or legend is connected with a place. The connection is ancient.
The allusion to fairies is key to understanding that rites and rituals have taken place there. There is an association of magic... but in times past, magic was part of sacred ritual. Magic and fairies have been devalued and divorced from modern human understanding of religion. Only now is it being understood again. The fairy realms are being recognised and understood as part of the spiritual hierarchy, which in the same way as the angelic realms (where we abide), can be seen, understood, sensed and communicated with by humans. Fairies were so devalued that it has taken longer for their revival into your consciousness - whereas we - your angels - have always been accepted by human-made religions.

We laugh...

Fairies are so close to Earth spirit that they suffered greatly with the destruction of Earth. Only as Earth is saved can they be accepted again. Humans have destroyed what is most dear and life giving.
You as a child believed in and valued them - being close to and loving the Earth spirit. Many children are pure enough in mind (and some adults) to accept them, but in ancient times fairies were acceptable and a fundamental, natural part of the Earth's spiritual life.

We rejoice. There is time yet for the fairy realms to return home - to live in the physical - whilst you, my friends, must raise your vibration further in order to stay. We are helping. It is Time. It is happening fast. We love you all.
Fear is the enemy and must be cast out.

Thank you, Raphael.

I kept the message safe, along with other channellings that I wrote by hand. There are examples of these in the Appendix.*

On the 1st August 2007, I was guided by my angels to go with a friend to Schiehallion, the mountain I had asked about in connection with its fairy name, with the instruction to send Light into the Earth near its summit and to the *Four Directions*.

It was a late summer day. As many people were trooping up the hill, we felt it necessary to be discreet when dowsing amongst the beautiful granite slabs and quartzite boulders near the summit to find exactly the right point from which to send prayers for healing.

We carried out the angels' instructions in blind faith. I had not read any books on the subject of Earth healing or any spiritual subject matter whatsoever, because I needed to be certain that no other information was influencing the messages I was still receiving from my angels as we walked.

I knew there was much history surrounding Schiehallion. In fact, the hill had been a base for an experiment in the 18th century to measure the mass of Earth. Physical sightings of fairies have also been documented there in modern times. These were the type of nature beings who manifest as *good folk* in Scotland (*Sleagh Maith* in Gaelic): the ones who are described as trooping together at nightfall and stealing away vulnerable mortals. Like the Earth elementals, dwarves and gnomes, they also inhabit our folklore and the poetry we learned at school.

> Up the airy mountain, down the rushy glen
> We dare not go a hunting
> For fear of little men.
> Wee folk, good folk, trooping all together,
> Green jacket, red coat and white owl's feather.

from: *The Fairies, William Allingham. Irish poet. 1824-1889**

The angels simply told me to place the intention to bring down the white Light from Source, from God, and send it down through my body and into Earth to assist the Earth angels at that point. I then had to turn towards each direction of the compass and repeat the process.

As a woman in that vast mountainside landscape, I felt my action of bringing down the Light with the intent of helping the devas and nature spirits was rather inconsequential. Nevertheless, I trusted the angel guidance and my companion and I carried out the instructions as best we could. At that point in time, we had no idea that other people were also doing what they termed *Earth Healing*.

My friend, who was a healer, was practising dowsing as research for writing a book on the subject of Earth Healing, so I felt that we were supporting each other. He was dowsing to find the best places, the so-called *power points*, and I was channelling the angels' messages in support of that task.

The second expedition that my friend and I made on behalf of the angel guides was to Ben MacDui in the Cairngorms, a mountain I've climbed many times since childhood. The angels had said that Schiehallion and Ben MacDui are power points and strongholds of the Earth and mountain devas.

Again, we faithfully followed the angels' instructions. The weather was terrible, the sky dark with snow showers and mist, but the angels were insistent that this was the right moment to go. I truly wondered if they were sending us up the mountain to our demise. It was then that we had the experience - as many mountaineers have described - of being in a bubble of clear air with the mist following behind and lifting and clearing ahead as we ascended the mountain. Groups of people, drenched with rain, were on their way down to escape the severe weather above. What was remarkable was that as we climbed uphill we didn't encounter any adverse weather and our clothes stayed dry all the way! The clear air surrounded us right to the top. With no one else in sight, we paced out an area around the summit cairn and sent Light down into Earth and to the four compass directions. The angels told me:

Ben MacDui is a heart chakra centre for Earth.

Over the following months, the angels' messages urged us to pray for the devas, particularly in those areas of wilderness which were being cut through by a new giant electricity power line and its access roads. This has now become the Beauly to Denny power line, which was switched on in 2016.

We were guided to an area north of Dalwhinnie, a place that is famous for its whisky and for holding the lowest mean temperatures in the UK. It lies in the Central Scottish Highlands, just north of the Drumochter Pass and south of the Cairngorm mountains. Here, we followed one of the General Wade roads, a beautifully built track through a glen, some of which was protected by National Trust ownership.

The access roads for the electricity pylon line, which was to transport the power, circumnavigated the boundary of this land. We found wide areas of mud and gouged out land several metres wide. White scars of roads had also carved up the surrounding hillside.

This glen, where the power line was to be routed, was only a small section of the intended line between Beauly and Denny. The completed line was to cross the woods and moors of the wild areas by Loch Ness and Loch Duntelchaig in the north and through to Denny, south of Stirling. The electricity would then be sent on to England and further afield. At this stage we had no idea that this was only the start of the industrialisation of so many of Scotland's wilderness areas.

As we walked along the track through the hills, I saw something in my mind's eye. It was not a solid physical presence, but manifested as a female being - slightly grey in colour and partly transparent. It darted out from the rocks of the river which was a tributary of the River Spey. With a flowing movement rather like an otter, it ran ahead as a wave-like form. I don't know how I knew it was a deva and not a nature spirit, such as a fairy or sprite, as they can all manifest in different forms. Perhaps an inner sensing told me that it was an important being.

Presently we came to a point where we felt we were unable to continue. The air was very thick and it felt as though we were being repelled by magnetic force. A feeling of dread came over me and my legs went heavy as in one of those dreams where you want to run but cannot move. I glanced sideways at my friend who had also stopped in his tracks. It was as if the air pressure was resisting us and there was a bad and unwelcoming atmosphere.

When I stopped to tune in to my angels' guidance, I was told that we were crossing a boundary from one deva's area to another and needed permission as we were not very welcome. Due to the destruction of the land and habitat in that area for the building of inroads for the new pylon line, the devas and nature spirits were apparently unfriendly towards human beings.

As if a door had opened, we suddenly found ourselves

walking forwards. The air around us lightened and cleared. I listened in for my angels' guidance, as I had only a small notebook in my pocket and didn't want to keep stopping to write, which is the way I usually record the messages.

The guidance that came was that the accompanying deva had successfully negotiated on our behalf, but that she could not accompany us further than the next territory, whereupon we would be met by a mountain deva, the guardian of that next stretch of land. We would know when this transition had taken place, as we would see a large boulder up on the hillside to our right, which marked the mountain deva's territory.

We continued on our way, stopping at every point where the building of each pylon was proposed, sending Light down into Earth and in the four directions. After a while, exactly as described, we saw a large boulder on the hillside to our right. I glanced furtively at my companion to see if he would remark on it.

My mind was in disbelief at what my eyes were perceiving, for it was as if my companion was wearing a cloak, and all around the folds of the cloak tumbled and rolled an array of little beings. I hadn't seen anything quite like them before, except in the illustrations of fairytale books I'd had as a child. They resembled the more gothic style of fairy illustration, although the impression wasn't clear. I saw our companion deva running back along the track away from us. She had clearly strayed far from her own territory by accompanying us and was now heading back to the river. As my mind kicked in with analytical thoughts, all the beings disappeared. I said nothing to my companion.

At this point in time, I simply observed the intuitions that came to me and followed the angels' guidance in blind trust. I couldn't yet say whether I could accept with my logical mind what I was experiencing. A few years later I met others who had the ability to perceive devas and nature spirits, and also read the writings of the original members of the Findhorn spiritual community, Robert Ogilvie Crombie, and Dorothy Maclean (whom I would meet in 2016). It was then that I came to understand that my sense of the tumbling nature spirits was a common way for human beings to experience them.

It grieved me to see the shining clear river and the birch trees on the slopes of the hillside, hear the birdsong, and walk through the soft dew-filled grass with its carpets of flowers and deep blue harebells in the knowledge that this peaceful place would soon be a metal corridor for electricity. I felt powerless and heartbroken that in saving our human species from the depletion of natural resources of fuel, it would result in the destruction of wild nature in the very places that were dear to our hearts and to those who have lived there for generations.

At first I wondered if the angels were asking us to support the devas and pray for the demise of the power line, for they had told me through channelled messages:

The devas know what destruction is planned for them.

The angels did not ask us to take sides:

Resistance and anger is a negative energy!
It's necessary to rise above these human emotions. Leave politics out of this and support the devas by prayer!

So, I set my intention for that and tried not to feel anger or hatred in my distress at seeing the disruption. It was clear that a conflict was brewing between conservationists and people who valued their history with the land on the one hand, and landowners and developers who saw the commercial use of that same land as progressive on the other.

I had listened to documentaries and phone-in programmes on the car radio in which people voiced their concerns. I had no idea at the time that the very places where we were praying for the devas were key locations where the wilderness would be eradicated, although I did sense that the excursions to the hills were preparation for a greater work I would be called to do. It was becoming clear to me that my angel guides now wished that I would use my ability to channel messages directly from the devas and nature spirits, the fairies and elementals. The moment when this began to happen took me completely by surprise.

Chapter 4

The Water Sprites Would Wish to Speak to You

It's a glorious October day in 2011 and I have taken a trip out to Loch Lomond. I'm now sitting on a log at the edge of the shore, under a hazel tree, with my feet on wet gravel. Long grasses and bushes of hazel and alder are partly obscuring my view of the loch ahead of me. The edge of the loch has risen to infiltrate the area so that many of the lochside bushes and trees stand with their trunks and roots submerged. A trickle of water from a tiny stream is flowing past me and into the loch.

My angel Ariel is putting words into my thoughts, "The water sprites would wish to speak to you!" I reach into my rucksack for pencil and paper and begin to write as the words come in.

> We are of the water.
> We wish to speak.
> We carry the eternal vibration.
> Water is a carrier of energy on your planet.
> Water is the channel of energy in the same way your blood feeds the cells of your body and is pumped from your heart.
> So, water is the carrier of life force.
> Here it is clear in spite of humans' noisy appliances, and the petrol from boats and chemicals that leach from the fields into the loch water.
> This place is sacred and loved by many.

From my seat on the log I see the tall trees at the top of the hill on the island of Inchcailloch (*Innis na Cailleach*:

cowled woman or old woman in Gaelic. *Cailleach-dubh* also means 'nun'. The hermits of *Cèile Dè* often had island retreats all over the Highlands).

What do you wish to say? I ask the water sprites. *Is there a message from the water?*

> You must pray for us...
> We can tell you that for each beloved place on your Earth there is a counterpart in the spiritual dimension which you call ether. As your wilderness recedes, due to pollution and development (housing, roads, industry) then the physical wilderness retracts and the spiritual counterpart ceases to exist.

Isn't there even a memory of past places?

> Yes, there is a memory but the reality has gone.

Are there many of you water sprites?

> Yes, here there are many, but our population as a whole has retracted and exists mainly in the etheric.

May I ask this? If you can continue to exist in the etheric, then to some humans it may not seem to matter that there is not a home for you on the physical Earth?

> You do not understand! We cannot exist without our physical manifestation i.e., water, rocks, soil and trees, and pure air. Neither can you.

What can we do to help?

> Understand us, respect us and pray for us!

Thank you. I will certainly record your words and pass this on.

And so it was, on the shores of Loch Lomond, that direct messages from these water sprites came to me at last. The import of their words affected me profoundly. I knew in my heart that I had to commit to writing down their messages and keep my promise to pass on their words.

I knew I was beginning to hear the messages that came from Earth itself via the angelic guardians, the devas and nature spirits. However, I was concerned that any messages from the devas and nature spirits of my homeland might be too specific to Scotland and therefore not relevant to other areas of the world.

I longed to help the devas, but my hope felt so small and fragile, like a single leaf blowing in the wind. Yet the words I received were filled with such grace. I began to believe that it might be possible that whoever reads these words will feel the beauty and power of the devas' messages as they emanate from the pages of this book.

It had been necessary for me to practise ways of attuning to the devas and their messages for the purpose of writing the book that my angels were guiding me towards. I realised my forays into the hills to pray for the devas had been such practice, but now I understood that I must go to a place I loved and felt to be *my spiritual home* in order to make my strongest connection with them.

I knew the place instinctively. It was there, between 2012 and 2017, that I recorded the messages from the devas which comprise this book.

Part Two

Entering the Landscape

Occasionally a stronger gust of wind catches the trees and they make a rushing sound like water, their leaves dancing and flickering in the light. The wind sounds in many voices: the wind in the pines, the wind in the birches and the wind through the grasses. Suddenly, another voice starts to speak and I catch the words:

I am the deva that connects with you through your angel Ariel. You had to come here to the moor, this particular moor, to find me. Now we are together.

Your love of us is the key that unlocks the 'permission door'. You then hear us through the door. It is a portal within your consciousness that allows the vibration of our communication to cross.

(Chapter 5: Pages 46, 47 & 48)

Chapter 5

Music on the Moor:
The Deva Immortelle Speaks

My angels are saying, "It is time! It is time to write for the devas!"

It's as if a portal has opened. I feel the devas' call drawing me to this moor and its watercourses. It's August 2012 and I've returned to the moor above Clava to connect with the devas: the beautiful shining beings of Light… the angels of Earth.

As I climb up the hill, a song comes into my mind that my mother would often sing. This was called, the *Faery Song*.* I remember as a child wondering who she was singing about… who were the lordly ones who dwelt in the hollow hills? I hear her clear, light voice in my mind. I feel a deep excitement and joy that the magic I sensed in my childhood is alive!

My quest to find the devas has brought me back to the exact place where twenty-nine years before I'd made some large paintings for my art college show. At that time, I intuitively knew that I needed to complete these paintings outdoors and not tinker with them back in the studio. I needed to be there in the moment, recording the beauty and the light of the heather moor, over the forestry plantations and fields, to the blue waters of the firth and the mountains beyond. At that time, I had tried to convey the 180 degrees of my vision on a rectangle of paper. It was a challenge.

My paintings were made on large sheets of lapping paper card spread on the ground, weighted on each corner with rocks. The paper had to be carried up the moor in rolls strapped to the crossbar of my bike. With small jars of paints in my cycle pannier, paint brushes, sketchbook and packed lunch in my rucksack, I sat astride the large rolls of card and pedalled the long steep climb to the moor from the village where I lived. The summer of 1983 had been hot, and I was able to sit working outside for many hours, as the light was exceptional.

As I stand here now, in 2012, I see again the small gorge which cuts through the moor with its flowing burn and its two pools connected by waterfalls. In Scotland, a burn is a small river. Many are named on maps, or established place names such as Bannockburn, site of the famous battle at Stirling. In the Highlands, many of the burns are red-amber in colour due to the peat content from the surrounding soil, laid down over millennia.

I remember one particular occasion when I'd been painting higher up on the hill. After a couple of hours kneeling on the ground focussing on my work spread out in front of me, I got up to stretch my legs. I left my paper and paints on the heathery knoll and went down to the gorge to refill my water jars and relax on the ledge above the pools.

It had been a warm summer afternoon and I began to drift in and out of sleep up there on the heathery ledge overhanging the water when I heard the sound of a harp playing. The music seemed to play both in my dream, and in the physical reality around me. It was still there when I opened my eyes, jumped to my feet and searched about for the source, but when I tried to work out where it was coming from, the music faded on the wind.

The paintings sold in my art college show and paid the rent of my Edinburgh flat. Years passed. I have forgotten many things about my visits to the moor, but the memory of the harp music has stayed with me to this day.

Moor Visit in 2010

I didn't return to the moor until 2010, after completing *An Angels' Guide to Working with the Power of Light*. I had reunited with the friend who had first introduced me to the place in the 1980s and we decided to visit the moor together, as we had both continued to feel a heart connection with the place. Here we were nearly thirty years later when I noticed we were doing the same thing. As we walked together up the track our paces quickened, and we almost broke into a run in our enthusiasm to retrace our steps to the place that was drawing us like a magnet.

The Forestry Commission plantation of commercially grown conifer trees, planted in the 1980s, had grown to maturity so that some parts of the gorge were now engulfed in dense blocks of conifer trees. On the banks of the burn the native trees had grown up, some fallen in across the water in places where winter torrents had undercut the banks.

On that first return visit my friend and I only had a few old photographs to go by. I was so disorientated by the disappearance of parts of the gorge within the forestry plantation that I argued with him as to its exact location. When we realised we had found the place… right there under our feet, though very overgrown… the sense of recognition was palpable. It was a hot summer day, just as it had been on those earlier visits. Instinctively, I asked the nature spirits for permission to enter their pool and was able to swim there for the first time.

The water was extraordinary: unlike water, more like silk and very buoyant so it was impossible to reach the bottom, which seemed to be some ten feet deep. Despite the intense cold, I entered a world where I felt held and energised with life force of the most pure and benevolent source.

Over and over again I swam as far as I could towards the force of the waterfall, then turned onto my back and surrendered to the water. It held me like a child and gently washed me over to the lip of the bowl-shaped rock holding the water of the pool. Centuries have carved smooth its sides. Beneath the waterfall, the current had undercut a hollow in the rock, like an underwater cavern, completely invisible behind the curtain of water.

Later that evening we arrived home tired but exhilarated. As we reviewed the day's events, we discovered a face in one of the photographs looking out at us from the water of the pool. It was remarkable! I wondered whether the camera had somehow picked up an image of a water spirit from a parallel realm of existence, but its significance wasn't clear at this point. The face belonged to the moor, the water and the memories of that summer day.

Moor Visit in 2011

My next visit was over a year later. Everything seemed different. It was wintertime, I was alone and many things in my life had changed. When I arrived at the gorge I felt welcomed, as if I were a child. This younger sense of *me* clambered down and knelt on the ice and frost and began to weep, warm tears pouring down my face. As they touched the frosty grass at the edge of the pool, they were melting the ice. Then something happened. Where does it comes from, this desire to be creative? In the midst of my heartbreak and tears, I became completely fascinated with the melting ice crystals.

As I reached for my camera I noticed the patterns of lines on the palms of my hands. Through my tears I could see an eight-pointed star and in another configuration of lines a six-pointed star. There were cracks on the ice which stretched across the pool, and they formed stars, just like the ones on my palm. Why had I not noticed before? Was it the cold that highlighted the patterns?

    I began to take photographs of the ice on the pool in the moment, quite forgetting the reasons for my sadness. I became intrigued by the long icicles, and a curtain of ice hanging from the fallen birch tree that spanned the pool as if to hide a secret water world behind. After some time, the following words came to me:

> The devas love you. They wish to help you write their book.
> All is well. You are safe here. You are protected in their haven. You'll hear easily.
> Remember, this place is blessed as it ever was so do not weep for yesterday! Time is only in your imagination; it's not real.
> You age, so you believe it's real. You see the trees age but we devas are immortal and ever sing the song of water and the pool - of rock and shore of heaven. The gates are closed, but you are through in Light. Do not catch cold. Come back soon if you can.
> You are blessed. Blessed. Blessed.

    I could feel the coldness of the frosty grass penetrating the knees of my trousers and I was startled back into awareness that it was time to leave. I couldn't take more messages. It was freezing cold and getting dark so I vowed I would return. I climbed through the prickly frosted juniper bushes, and headed back over the moor to the track, through the winter afternoon light without saying goodbye.

Moor Visit in August 2012

I emerge from my memories of past visits. I've been standing by a small rock at a viewpoint on the heathery rise where I used to paint. As I start to leave, I feel called to make my way over a bog and down to the gorge where the water flows through. This place seems timeless.

I have no idea how the devas might manifest. I don't know where to begin, so I wait on the grassy promontory at the lower pool near the place where I'd heard the harp music all those years before. I focus on a point in the water and then speak into my video recorder, at first checking furtively over my shoulder on the off-chance there might be a passing hiker or local gamekeeper. But the moor is deserted.

I feel a bit silly at first, but my desire to follow the instructions of my angels and to connect with the devas takes away all shyness and I plunge into the challenge. I tell the devas that I've come in peace, with love in my heart, under the guidance of God and my angels, and that my angel Ariel is with me to help me translate their communication.

I wish to thank the devas for allowing me to be here, I say rather formally.

My analytical mind is already questioning how many battery hours it might take to make a video of the pool whilst recording the messages. What if they don't want to speak to me? What to do about the long gaps whilst I wait, being bitten by midges? My face is already burning with midge bites. Despite this, I continue watching the water, feeling mesmerised by its movement and wondering if the nature beings are present. Suddenly I perceive their voices as if in response to my thoughts...

We love you. You are welcome here.

Why do you love me and how can you love me when I belong to the race of humans who have so badly abused the physical Earth?

Put your hand in the water!

It is colder than before when I swam here two years ago. I can't stand to keep my hand in the water. The shock of cold makes me gasp out loud. I wonder why the deva's voice has told me to do this.

At this point, I believe I've lost connection. Recording the conversation in this way seems questionable. After all, there is only my voice asking the questions and then long gaps as I listen for and translate the deva's communication into words. Back home, I will still have to transcribe the words into typed form on my computer.

Tiny black midges continue to bite my face, making it difficult for me to formulate questions and receive the deva's responses. So I pack my camera and climb up the bank, keeping the waterfall and lower pool in view. Soon I find a place to lay down my waterproof mat, where I sit with notebook and pencil balanced on my lap and my back supported by a clump of heather.

The freezing water of the pool has brought me back to my senses. I feel more grounded now, aware of being fully present. From here, on this knoll slightly upstream of the pools, in a light breeze and away from the midges, I can hear the sound of flies buzzing about the bracken.

Then comes the further away sound of the tinkling of the burn: distant, metallic, like the sound of many fairy cymbals.

I can hear the roaring of the wind which sounds like the sea in the young pine plantations. In places through gaps in the tops of the trees I can see the Moray Firth. Beyond the clusters of newly built houses across a ridge of fields, I can make out the woodlands where I used to walk the family dog.

Further away, on the other side of the firth, is the familiar dark shape of the Black Isle with its patches of forest and barley fields glowing gold... and still beyond, the teal blue hills in the haze with Ben Wyvis rising above.

Close around me the moor hums with the sound of bees in the flowers contrasting with the background rattle of the burn. I can see deer grass, common heather with the soft pink of cross-leaved heath showing through in places, pale green patches of lichen and long grass. Further in the distance are patches of bell heather, intense purple on brown purple, bright green ferns and bracken-clad banks leading down to the gorge. Many birches now line the banks of the gorge at the point below where I sit.

Occasionally a stronger gust of wind catches the trees and they make a rushing sound like water, their leaves dancing and flickering in the light. The wind sounds in many voices: the wind in the pines, the wind in the birches and the wind through the grasses. Suddenly, another voice starts to speak and I catch the words:

It hasn't changed much in twenty-nine years, has it?

It feels the same, I answer, *but I'm aware of being older with many events behind me, rather than in front of me.*

I'm not speaking out loud but recording my thoughts as I catch them, writing them down in my notepad with a coloured pen. It feels very natural.

I used to dream of where I would go and whom I would marry and whether I'd have children and if my paintings would become well known. Now I have done these things, been married, had children and lived in other places... still painting, still writing...

Why are you so transfixed by your age? asks the voice.

Do you not know your soul is immortal?

Who are you?

I am the deva that connects with you through your angel Ariel. You had to come here to the moor, this particular moor, to find me. Now we are together. I was there when you came here painting on the moor. I was there then. You were wearing green jeans and…

Amazingly, I am given a clear picture in my head of what I was wearing: green jeans and a stripey cheesecloth top.

The deva's voice continues. It resonates in my consciousness like the voice of a young female: musical, with a Highland lilt and intonation.

You left your bicycle at the farm. You tried to capture us, our spirit in your painting.

I think I feel your presence, but I'm not sure if it's just the happy feeling that comes when I'm out on the moor, doing what I love. Do I feel your presence?

Yes, you always have, but didn't understand it! It is what draws you here… our presences. Some would say you've been bewitched but that is not the case. We have been devalued by humankind. Only people who truly love Nature can sense us. It's why we have come to talk to you. You have been calling on us!

I wasn't sure if you'd hear me from my home in Stirling?

Yes, we hear. When you visualise our places, then we hear you. You have a strong connection with some of us.

Who are you?

> Immortelle of the Waterfall!

What kind of deva are you?

> I am the Mountain Deva of this area. My region extends upstream as far as the source of the three springs that feed this burn and downstream as far as the place where the River Nairn flows through to the sea.

That's a huge area. I'm surprised… I thought you'd only live here. No. Not all the time. It is why some days you feel our presence more than others.

Are you the guardian of the River Nairn?

> Yes, I oversee the whole river.

I feel honoured that you came to speak to me. I always felt you were here.

> We come to speak to you through the request of your angel. You have been given privileges.

I know that, but I don't know why.

> Your love of us is the key that unlocks the 'permission door'. You then hear us through the door. It is a portal within your consciousness that allows the vibration of our communication to cross. The sound of the stream is in both worlds, as we have said.

Why are you immortal and why not humans? Why can we communicate like this? You speak to me like a person! You remember me from twenty-nine years ago. You even show me a picture in my mind's eye of what I was wearing in such detail that I feel as if I'm floating above my younger self in a time warp! Why is this? Why can I hear you now, not then? Why can't I be immortal? Why can't I travel in time? I'd like to be in my twenties again with my younger body, flexible limbs, and not fear ageing, as I do now.

> We hear you mourn for your hair. Ah beautiful hair, the colour of the pool of the Nairn. We hear you mourn for your youth and your lost loves. We are here to tell you that love is never lost.
> It is within. It is the outer skin that comes and goes, as the leaves of the tree.

I understand that… I think… yet even the trees grow old and die. In another twenty-nine years I'll be lucky if I can come here to experience your moor again, to feel the warm earth, hear the burn and its waterfalls, the hum of flies, sound of the wind, perfume of heather, the sun on my face and soft breeze blowing my hair. I'll be lucky if I can clamber down to the edge of the pool. I'll be lucky if I can still see my way.

> Oh ho! You'll see your way alright! You see more clearly now than you did when you came here painting. You hear us!

Dear Immortelle, I understand. Yes, perhaps it is true that my understanding is sharpened and I hear my angels, and your voices on the wind, but my physical body must deteriorate eventually. Maybe I won't live to the age of a tree but I will die.

> Only your body dies. Your soul is immortal. You are connecting with us through your soul body.

    I suddenly stop writing. My awareness moves away from

the deva's voice and I become conscious again of the physical sound of the wind. I love the sound of the wind's many voices. In front of me the birch trees dance. I hear the sound of myriad leaves rattling one on another, and the rushing of the burn.

On the opposite side, the sunlit bank of the burn with the purple bell heather glows and emerges more clearly into my vision as I watch.

An exquisite scent wafts against my nostrils and I breathe it in. I feel the physical world and know I am part of it. I sense the muscles in my back aching a little, the pulsing of blood in my feet, my eyes stinging a bit in the sunlight, and the weight of my body in touch with the ground as I sit on my waterproof mat spread on the heather. I know that I never even thought of using a mat to sit on when I came here to paint in my teens and early twenties.

I am a little taken aback at how much the deva knows about me and my past with her accurate reference to my auburn hair, likening the colour to the Highland river pools that run amber. I am shocked that the deva has picked up on my current worries, such as ageing, but whilst my mind is spinning with these thoughts, I find myself forming a question for her:

Why is one part of me immortal and the other part physical and earthly, and why are you completely immortal, Immortelle?

> *The devas abide in the angelic realm. We are not your angels but are guardians of Earth, of trees, plants, rocks and soil, of water, air and fire. Call us angels of the Earth if you like.*
> *Your angels are committed to you. We are committed to oversee the flow of energy from divine will and through the waters, rocks, plants and fire.*
> *We are a branch of the angelic realm. We do not exist in a physical form but can transcend through many other dimensions.*

We can connect with your consciousness. We can even appear as physical substance but we do not belong to your physical world.

When people perceive devas or nature spirits, when artists have painted them, what are they seeing if you do not have physical bodies?

We appear to you as thought projection of humans.
We have to tell you that the fairies, elves, sprites and dwarves are human-made projections. We only take on form so you can see us at certain times and places.
Life exists moment by moment. You perceive everything in the physical moment by moment. In each of these moments there is a connection between you and your world. At times you see only the outer. At other times you have divine awareness.
The places of beauty exist when you realise them.
When your mind is on other things they do not exist for you. We are here when you are aware of us. When you change the focus of your mind onto other things we are still here but you can't perceive us.
We are aware of you. When you have awareness of us we hear your thoughts. We can only hear your higher vibrational thoughts. We do not hear your thoughts of greed, anger, jealousy, lust.
Your angel is aware of these and helps to lift you out of them. We do not hear them, or only perceive them as white noise as you would term it… like the radio when it is in between signals.
You hear the water as white noise because you are not fully attuned to its higher vibration. When the water sounds in heaven it sounds like music… heavenly music. You heard the elven harp here once, in the sound of the water.

It was because you connected at that point. Your consciousness connected with the Divine. You were drifting to sleep and the sound got through to your conscious mind awareness.
As you walked upstream and downstream trying to find the source of that divine music it always seemed to be in the place you walked away from. It is because it was coming not from one point in the physical but coming to you through your mind. It was your mind that was moving in and out of awareness even as you were walking upstream and downstream.

I understand that now! If I had sat still and meditated, would I have gone on hearing the sound?

Possibly.
Certainly you could not hear it if you tried to attribute it as coming from a particular spot on the ground. By your so doing, by your thoughts attempting to pin down the sound to a physical place you were moving too far into the physical so as to lose the sound altogether.

Now that I can hear you, and hear my angels, would it be possible to go to the bank of the burn and hear that harp music again?

You do not have the power to call it forth.
It will not come by will power. It was a gift from the fairies and devas to you at that time.

Why then?

We were happy you spent hours of time on the moor painting to try and represent the beauty you felt. It was our gift.
We gave it to you then so you would remember it, and

ask us about it now! We gave it to you then as a sign to you now, that you were connected with us then as you are now.

Thank you, thank you Immortelle! I am so happy I came. I am so happy you spoke to me.

We sing and play the harp. You cannot hear us.
You hear only the wind in its lower aspect as white noise.

It would be wonderful to hear that music again but I love the white noise aspect of the sound of the wind and the burn.
Thank you.

I feel happy. I feel at peace. I almost feel immortal here at this moment on the moor, but I know I must go back soon to my commitments. I have been staring at the page so long that when I look up and across to the distant hill it takes time for my eyes to re-focus, so I take a break and wander up the watercourse.

Later that afternoon, sitting above the upper pool on a projection of heather and grass overhanging a steep drop down to the water, I record the impressions coming through my physical senses. The sound is stereophonic. In my right ear, I hear the gurgling of the burn as it runs beneath ferny banks over stones, then undercuts through a narrow stone passage beneath hanging dwarf willows and makes its way to the top of the upper fall, although I can't hear the sound of the fall itself. The deep amber pool below is still and reflective, despite the gusts of wind in the young trees around me.

In my right ear, the gurgling of water echoing through the stony passage contrasts with the sound in my left ear, of the lapping and babbling water as it leaves the upper pool via a miniature rocky staircase towards the second fall.

The sound of the second fall is thundering, almost like cars on a distant motorway. I feel its vibration. It is different from the vibration of the wind.

Here I can pick up three different sound levels. I'm certain a musician/composer would perceive much more and be able to discern harmonies. I wish I had my flute with me as this would be the perfect place to play it.

My recorder cannot pick up the beauty of these levels of sound, nor can my camera show the full kaleidoscope of colours of the moor nearby, or the distant panorama.

When I created large-scale paintings here all those years ago, I had tipped the horizon to attempt to portray 360 degrees of moorland on a two-dimensional paper surface, with all the challenges of painting the pylons striding across the moor with their crossing wires according to the angle of my vision.

Three-dimensional cinematic pictures were not publicly available then. Even now, I wonder how any modern recording equipment can replace the experience of being in Nature, feeling our connection to Earth with the passion of a beating heart. I'm thankful for my eyes so that I can see. I am thankful for my ears and the senses through which I perceive Nature and its angels. Sometimes the angels' voices are like a vibration that comes into my conscious awareness, sounding in my ears like a friend's voice and with all its reality.

The moor feels like a friendly place at this moment, more so than when I first came. I don't want to leave, but I know the midges will make it impossible for me to stay.

I love you.

    You'll come here again!

Thank you.

Chapter 6

Shifts in Consciousness:
Time Travel Beyond the Kitchen

September 2012

Dear Immortelle, are you here?

I'm back at Immortelle's pool again, on a day visit. I'm sitting in the sun, my mat spread over the heather on the opposite bank from where I wrote last time. The bank is steep, almost a small cliff, so that the two waterfalls are now below me, one to my left and the other to my right. I can't go too near the edge of the cliff for fear of falling into the pool below.

In my left ear I hear the roar and echo of the waterfall, a few yards away upstream. The water falls almost vertically into a deep pool, nearly black in colour as it's in deep shadow. White bubbles cascade down and across the surface forming into foam around the edges. The water runs out from this pool and through a small rocky channel then down to the second waterfall and into the lower pool. The higher pitched rushing sound of the lower waterfall is to my right and merges with the sound of the wind in the birches.

It's a month later than when I first came back here to start recording the deva's messages. I only have a few hours before the light fades and I will need to drive home again.

Autumn has turned the purple of the heather moor to pinky orange, the bog asphodel to burnt orange, and the mosses to flaming reds and whites. The deer grass has almost turned from green to brown.

A small rowan sways beside the group of birches overhanging the lower pool. I'm glad of the breeze keeping the worst of the midges away. I inadvertently squash one that lands on my page and immediately start wondering about karma.

I'm terribly uncomfortable. The burning of midge bites is already down my neck, back and upper arms. Even though I've found a place to sit in the glare of the sun on the small cliff above the upper waterfall, I'm being bothered by the midges. I'm too distracted to tune in to my angels yet am captivated by the sound of the water.

Green-ochre birch leaves wave. Spiders' webs gleam from the tips of heather.

Dear Immortelle, are you here?

I'm right beside you!

What do you look like?

> *You should know better than to ask this but I will explain: I manifest as a Light body and continually change form. I dance in the waterfall. I circle through the energy field of the trees. I skim over the moor. I sparkle and flare. This is when you see us.*

Immortelle gives me a picture of one of those fireworks that zigzags over the ground, the type we girls hated at school when the boys threw them down near us to make us run and scatter. I think they were called *crackerjacks*.

She continues to describe how she manifests to humans as a female form. Her voice blends into the sound of the water and trees and I lose her. I'm very distracted but anxious to write more whilst here at the waterfalls. Sitting in the sun, hearing the wind and water, feeling the warmth on my legs, my mind goes blank.

I listen to the waterfalls, the thunderous roar of the upper fall in my left ear, and the higher faster sound that blends with the wind in the leaves sounding in my right ear. An odd thing begins to happen. In my mind I hear the music of J.S. Bach's *Sheep May Safely Graze** with the double flute part. The two waterfalls, the music, the flutes!

I compare the physical sound of the water with the remembered sound of the music. The water is real. It vibrates through my soul and drowns out everything else, including the flutes of the remembered music. Recently, I heard Bach's music on the car radio. As I remember it now it sounds dead by comparison with the present reality of the waterfall, and has no feeling. It's similar to the way writing on a page lacks the vitality of a voice speaking to you.

When I heard the harp all those years ago it didn't manifest the way a tune can get going in your head. It seemed as real then as the water I'm hearing now.

Immortelle, are you here?

> *You humans think that you have knowledge of all things… all things in your environment. You can search online for any amount of knowledge on your computer, can't you?*

I perceive Immortelle sitting beside me… an exquisite female form, like one of those garden statues. Her hands are so beautiful! She cups them under her chin and water seems to flow from her, streaming in lines from her fingers. Then, suddenly, she's gone and there's only me here, sitting on the bank. Just when I assume she's gone, her voice cuts in… from somewhere above the nearest tree.

> *Humans know nothing! Your knowledge is empty. Knowledge alone will not save your planet.*

What is the best thing we can do, Immortelle?

Send Light! Why aren't you doing it!? You don't need to understand the way it works. Just do it!

Thank you, Immortelle. I'm sorry.

Immortelle speaks differently from my angels, I realise. The angels are always patient, loving and so forgiving that it feels as if the existence of that word is not necessary in their realm. The words that come into my consciousness from the angels do not carry any particular feeling of human character, apart from the remarkable exceptions of their great humour, laughter and singing.

In contrast, Immortelle's voice comes into my consciousness in a way that feels almost human, even though she is a divine being and from the angelic realms. It's as if she has more personality, and when she speaks on behalf of Nature's realms, I begin to sense some of her indignation and impatience with the human race.

Although she directs her comments at the human race in general, her question - *"Why aren't you doing it?"* - brings me up short. I think of all the times I have forgotten that the nature spirits need our help in the form of prayer. For years the angels have asked me to pray on behalf of Nature, and some of my visits to the hills of Schiehallion and Ben MacDui were specifically for this purpose. Now, a few years later, this nature guardian, the deva Immortelle, comes to me with the same request.

At this point my mind drifts away from the conversation. When I slip into thinking and self-analysing mode I am less receptive to hearing the deva's words and cannot pick up the incoming messages. I shift back again to awareness of my physical surroundings as I look out over the view on this glorious September day.

I see the Beauly Firth from here so clearly, the hills beyond, the roofs of farms above the folds of fields. I sketch a horizon line across the page. Drawing was always easier for me.

In the changing light the moor has turned to orange gold. The deer grass remains green at the root, but its stems move through yellow orange to burnt orange; yet it gleams with pure white strands as the light hits, and it waves and ripples in the breeze.

I hear the wind in my ears, disturbing the quietness. It feels as if I'm the only person on the moor.

At that moment noise pollution cuts in! Beyond the distant sound of water and wind I hear the roar of traffic on the A9 trunk road to Inverness and the bleating of sheep.

The deva's voice softens, as if she understands my thought processes that have taken me into feeling remorse.

We love you. We are happy you have come here. You are welcome. Come again. All is well. This book will be easily written. We'll help you all the way.

Three hours down the road and I'm home, sitting at my kitchen table where I first took down the words of the angels' message seven years ago. It now feels comfortable and normal to be writing to my angels and recording their answers.

Impressions from the day are strongly on my mind. I still feel the peace of the moor with its colours and shining light, the views, the firth, the Black Isle and mountains in the distance. There are so few days with such a view. I'd never seen it like that before.

Dear angels, will you help me with this book?

We are delighted to help. We applaud you for your trust.

I feel the presence of my angel Amber. I've never physically seen her, although a psychic friend once saw her standing beside me. We were in my kitchen. Amber was robed in white and had massive wings like those of an archangel. Under her robes she wore a garment, the colour of tiger eye or amber, and there was a belt around her waist.

My friend's description delighted me. It was exactly as I had imagined her even though I know that angels take on many forms and often tell me that they are *shape shifters*. It seems that the devas are also shape shifters.

I know that my guardian Amber often stands in my kitchen, in the same spot on the floor. She's here now and I feel her presence. The only way to express the feeling that arises in my heart is to write. I form the words from the feeling, *Thank you*.

Sometimes, in the presence of my angel, I feel as if I can travel through time and although I am in my kitchen sitting at the table, the memory of the pool comes back strongly.

In my mind I am on the moor again. It has changed completely. Perhaps it's been frosty as my breath is forming light steam in front of my face. The moor has turned to red, with purple-brown-red of bracken, purple of last lingering heather flowers, and orange-brown tips of deer grass. The birch trees have turned to gold: pure gold, brown-gold and green-gold hues.

I sit at the lower pool on the grassy promontory of the further bank. The colours of the water are so intense that I feel I am looking through a lens with yellow-green filter. My coat is soaked. The mat I'm sitting on is soaked. I'm uncomfortable holding my pencil with numb hands, feeling the cold rising up from the ground. Occasionally leaves fall, spinning, from the small lichen-covered birch overhanging the pool.

On the further bank is every imaginable shade of green: light green of *blaeberry* to deep blue-green of moss that's spread over the rocky bowl of the pool's basin.

The peaty Highland water is thunderous. Near me, to my left, is a higher pitched sound as the water exits the pool laughing and murmuring, while a fountain of gold bubbles jump and play. In my right ear is the larger sound, the thundering tympanic roar of the waterfall as it enters the pool.

I kneel on the deep green wet moss, lean forward and cup both hands under the water at the edge of the pool. Ochre birch leaves float across the surface, some stream below the surface. The icy cold hits my hands hard and the shock of the water makes me gasp out loud. I can't bear to keep them in the water for more than a fraction of a second.

I hear a deeper vibration beneath the sound of the water. It seems to come in waves. I hear it and feel it as a pressure on my eardrum. There's a metallic sound to it and, up on the surface, a slapping sound as the waterfall impacts.

The surface of the pool is perturbed, full of movement and bubbles. It's not the dreamy still pool that I'd seen on my previous visits in past summers.

As I await the deva's voice it begins to rain. Oh so cold as the raindrops fall on my hand and on the page. I pack up and make my way back through woods in the waning light. Then the memory fades out and I'm back at the kitchen table.

The strength of these impressions is sometimes alarming to me. In this case even though I still have the impressions in my mind of the glorious day as it was a few hours ago, this visit to the moor within my consciousness seems to take place within the time frame of a later point in the same autumnal season.

My angel explains the need to practise how to travel between the realms safely. It would not be safe to attempt to speak to a deva or nature spirit without this knowledge of how to move in consciousness, and without keeping my awareness open and calling on the protection of the angels.

Chapter 7

We Will be Here as Long as the Rain Will Fall on Earth

Message received on 14th February 2013

I am happy to be here. I feel so blessed!

The page on which I am writing is suddenly flooded with soft light.

I hear the lower fall roaring in my right ear. On exiting the pool, it falls again over the rocky shelf, the sound of the plunging and bubbling water in my left ear. It's as if a speaker picks up the sound of the waterfall on my right, and one on the left records its exit from the pool as it slides into a small rock basin and throws up bubbles like a jacuzzi. A spray of water hits my face, ice cold.

I have asked for connection with the devas here, through the permission and guidance of my angels. I have told them I come with love in my heart, under God's guidance, and under the protection of angels. I tell them that I wish to listen to and record their words. I ask that they tell my fellow humans how we can heal the Earth.

As I look up from the page my eyes are blessed with a symphony of yellows, greens and brown-golds of the moss wall under the birch that hangs with lichen. The base of the rock pool is brown but gold grains and amber light gleam on the surface, whilst small bubbles bob down to the rim, where a fast stream of water exits.

I feel bathed in the most healing light, filled with life. It's calm here even though breezy and cold at the top of the bank and out on the wider moor.

We love you. We have called you. We are happy you are here. We are as happy as you are to have you here. We give you a bouquet of sensations for your eyes and ears. The colours and scents, perfume of moss and leaf. The many-layered sound of the white water falls, the swaying tree, sentinel over the pool, where your angel stands guard also.

Our raison d'etre is joy - through creation. Through manifesting this joy we bring life force to Earth. We make the trees grow, and every rock, animal and plant could not grow and evolve without us and our love. We work tirelessly. Joy and love is our natural state.

You only sometimes feel that. When humans experience deep connection with the Divine - when they experience their own truth, their true self, and experience that reflected and manifested around them, then they are co-operating in making love. This energy brings abundance, life and peace to all around.

This is how you reach your highest vibration, and from this state of being, healing happens. Love heals.

It is our job, and also our joy to manifest and proliferate this vibration. If we did not, the plants would not grow and all life would cease.

The deva gives me a memory of myself with a group of people. One of the women had spoken of her visit to a village in France in the 1990s, where during World War II the whole population was obliterated, apart from two young boys who had been away for the day. The dead bodies of the victims had been thrown into wells to rot, so that any survivor who went there would be unable to drink the water. The woman who described her visit said the amazing thing was that the place was still silent. It was devoid of life. Even birds no longer sang there.

The deva tells me she is using this example to show that

plants and Earth do not give life without being imbued with divine spirit. The devas are active in supplying that flow of life force, to maintain its purity.

The atrocity in the French village caused the Earth's vibration to fall so low that the devas could never return. The pollution was not only physical, but also spiritual.

> The most important quality we need from humans in order that we can co-operate and survive, in order that we can continue to evolve, and in order that humans can exist on Earth, is RESPECT.

The deva's words come to me in the form of telepathic communication and I want to catch the meaning and interpret them as carefully and closely as I can to her original intention. As she says the word respect, I simultaneously hear the words transformation, creation, evolution and synergy. I struggle to make a sentence of them, but the deva doesn't wait.

> The Earth can exist without the human race! God is here without the need of the existence of humans!
> However, humans cannot live here on Earth without us - your devas. We are from the angelic realms also. We are Earth's angels, if you like.
> We are older than your angels. We came from other planets to Earth when Earth was in its infancy.
> Your angels, archangels, principalities, thrones came to serve as guardians of humans. The cherubim and seraphim of God are manifestations of God. You may think of them as God's chakra and aura... if you were to see God as a physical manifestation in any way.

The deva gives me a picture of God sitting on a throne as depicted by Byzantine artists, with rays of light emanating from a boat-shaped mandala (aura). Immortelle does not give the complete list of the Nine Orders of Angels as developed by medieval Christian theologians.

> *We are of the order of thrones, principalities, archangels and angels. We are connected to Earth, not humans. We are as old as the Earth.*
> *Immortelle at your service!*

I feel I ought to check who is speaking, and as I do I see the graceful being, Immortelle, the deva of the waterfall and of this stream and the wider moor and mountain area served by this particular water-course. She shows herself sitting cross-legged like a yogi and holding a flower in her lap. Her dress takes on a grey silkiness as she hovers a few centimetres over the surface of the pool as if sitting on an invisible cushion.

Suddenly the cheeping of four coal tits and a cerulean-coloured bird like a blue tit, but with a very high crest, interrupts my writing. They flutter onto the branches of the birch tree on the bank, coming close and seemingly unafraid. Listening to their song above the thundering pool, it's hard to move out of this moment and to return to writing.

Taking down the deva's message requires deep focus. Immortelle has gone and I'm now only aware of my close team of angels. The birds had broken into my awareness, as if they'd transited with me from a higher awareness to where I am now. I felt myself come right out of the vibration I'd been in, returning into current awareness of my physical surroundings. The birds were in both worlds. Like me, they belong in both worlds. They came back with me as if guiding me.

It's freezing cold in the shadow of the sun by the pool. I can no longer sit in the same position, with my back unsupported. Although the sunlight glows on the bank opposite and reflects back on me, I'm not feeling its warmth. So I pack my notebook in my rucksack and clamber up out of the shadow and into the light on the bank that skirts the upper pool.

Message received on 15th February 2013

I revisit the pools the next day. I'm amazed as I've never seen or heard them like this. The whole of the lower pool is white and turbulent and the fall that feeds into it is a raging torrent. The stream of bubbles forms a path right through the pool to its exit point over the lip of rock towards a new waterfall which has replaced the quiet slipway of water that was there before.

The upper pool is thunderous and the dark water swirls in the basin like a cauldron, creating banks of froth and enormous bubbles banked up under the rocky overhang.

Dear Immortelle, thank you for speaking. May I ask - How am I to convey this information to people in a way that doesn't seem self indulgent, over imaginative or even delusionary?

Here I am, a fifty-something year old woman sitting by a pool, writing in a notebook... a conversation with a deva? We speak of God, of seraphim, cherubim, thrones, principalities, archangels, angels... These are beings who walk the corridors of the world's great spiritual faiths: the entourage of deities, ambassadors of gods and goddesses, manifestations of the Divine. How dare I even speak of them? Who will listen to this? Who is this book for?

Others have written about devas. Devas seem to be appearing now in spiritual magazines and the New Age repertoire. Why do you need my take on this? Who is this book for?

> We wish that you write this book because of your lifelong love and connection with us, because of your desire to help, because of your active involvement in our destiny. Your prayers for us are heard. We have called you through your angels to come here and write this book. It was first necessary to scribe the Angels' book. This has paved the way for your connection with us. You've come to us through your angels and with a pure heart, asked us for permission.
> You are not writing a treatise on the types and kinds of

devas, although we do speak of our physical manifestations.

So what is this book to be about?

It is about the function of the devas and how and why we connect with humans. The purpose is to gain your respect and co-operation in bringing the Light to Earth to heal.
This cannot be understood by explanation of words but must be heartfelt.
Though this book that you are now writing is manifesting in words as given by us and translated to you by your angel, the sense of the words will resonate with anyone who cares to read it and to learn how to help us. All is well.

My mind recalls the *Flower Fairies* books I was given as a child which my father had read to me in his deep gruff voice. I think of the current resurgence of images of fairies on cards, books and posters.
The deva picks up on my thoughts.

Coffee table books! Pah!

She nearly spits out the words.

How dare humans connect with us and speak of us as little dancing fairies as if we were your pets that come close to you when you offer a bowl of milk or a pat on the head!
We are great powers of Light and we can snuff you out in a moment if we so wish. We can obliterate humankind for good and many devas now wish this to happen.
Those of us who remain true to Source suffer humans' abuse and pollution and continue to repair and heal all

that we can. We are from God. It is God's will to allow humans to learn through mistakes. We cannot go against God's will for if we do, we transform into a form that is not pure. You would call it evil spirit. Those devas that have debased themselves and become evil spirits live in a self-realised hell and they wish humans to join them there and that all will self destruct.

From that lower vibration they cannot feel joy, only pain. They have moved so far from their identity that they lose their power to work with Light.

Our contract is to work with God as angels of Earth. We cannot break our contract and remain true to form. Angels are angels and cannot break their contract or they cease to be angels and become agents for the devil.

We do not wish to speak these dark words but it is necessary for our explanation to you of who we truly are. We have been debased and abused by humankind, segregated from your angels and cast out from your religions. Yet we are of the true religion and part of the angelic realm.

You cannot live without us. We cannot emphasise this enough. You may pick up your rucksack and go back to your car and back to your life, but you know full well that you are dependent on us for your life. Your car runs on fuel from Earth. Your home is made of stone, wood, glass and plastic. Your health and happiness comes from the need for love and joy and for your blood to flow.

You have separated from us. You kept the angels in your churches for your angels cannot leave you. We now need to come back into your consciousness for you humans to survive. We need your co-operation.

Thank you, Immortelle.

We thank you, star child.

Dear Immortelle, do I have connection with you?

Here I am!

May I ask you - I'm confused because previously you said you were the deva of the waterfalls here, but you also said you are a mountain deva. You said your territory expands out to the River Nairn and to the sea at that point at the town of Nairn.

Yet somehow in my head I imagined you lived here, only on this small part of the moor. My feeling had been that mountain devas would be separate from waterfall or river devas. How is it that you are both? Did I make a mistake in hearing you?

The sense of the deva's words come to me rather than the individual words themselves, as she is communicating with me telepathically.

I see in my mind's eye, a picture of the River Nairn and its tributaries. Then she shows me the link between this particular tributary and the mountain and moor. She emphasises that her realm is from here to the sea, then adds that this place is where she frequently hangs out.

You are confusing your idea of mountain as in mountain deva with earth. You associate mountains with rock and earth. You think of water as separate, and in some ways it is. However, as you know, water is the life force of planet Earth. It's a carrier as your blood is a carrier of life force from your heart through your veins and the arteries of your body, giving life.
Principally, I am of the water, but this mountain is where I live - where I am from. I am both mountain and source, water source of this area. It is not the tributary alone, not merely the watercourse that I overlight, but the surround-

ing earth it feeds. I am of the Essence.

The sun has come out and light falls strongly on the page where I am writing with one of my soft drawing pencils. I feel differently from yesterday and more in tune with the deva. Her words and the sense of them are totally believable to me at this point. I ask in my mind what happens upstream of her area.

Another deva, she explains.

Thank you, Immortelle. I feel as if I understand this.

> We also work with hierarchies, as you do, in some ways. The water sprites that humans have catalogued as being part of the elemental kingdom are different from the devas that over-light the tributaries. These sprites do stay in their own streams and pools.
> Some never move far from their pool but play continually there, tumbling down the falls but going back to their pool continually. So each pool or bend in the river has its own sprites. They are very loved. They are pure. Today you have seen what fun they are having in the torrent.

She alludes to the stream of bubbles I had seen.

May I ask then, to me the river seems to be roaring and angry today with much tumult. I felt a little afraid crossing it in case I fell in and was dashed on a rock. The water is deep black and swirling, the banks swollen and tree roots are being undercut and anything that falls in is swept away.

I stoop and peer over the cliff edge to the upper pool, still roaring and white with endless streams of bubbles continually forming and swirling into a side pool. Further down I can see the stream exit round a bend and out of sight, white with bubbles.

The deva continues…

We do not express anger as you do. Humans project their emotions on us.

The tree is undercut, falls into the pool over time, decays and is carried away. Its physical form transforms to carbon and will form the peat of the moor in time, or feed insects or fish, or form rock. It's of no consequence. The tree has then changed form and its life force feeds another. The devas or fairies of that tree will move to another tree and nurture a new growth. It's a continual cycle. We do not weep for the tree as it has played out its life and generates new material for the life of other forms.

What we abhor is the disrespect of humans and their greed. They wantonly cut the trees, pollute our watercourses and cause us not just to move on, but to die or mutate to a lower form.

We spoke earlier of evil spirits. Humans' evil work creates mutant devas that have shrunken forms of their true image… debased, disgusting things.

You see, we cannot persist, we cannot flourish in humans' low vibrational world inflicted on us.

I think of the beautiful Highland woods being torn down. My mind wanders away from the deva's words. It takes energy and focus to hear her. I think of all the wind farms, new housing, roads, industrial areas, pylon lines and great swathes of land cut through, and tarmacked.

Even here, this part of the moor is very near civilisation. The pylons cross the moor. Over the burn a few feet away and beyond is the Forestry Commission plantation, and beyond that fields and houses. Above and around me is the grouse moor. All is manmade or land that is managed, apart from scraps of natural woodland and places where only the wild trees can grow, clinging to the edges where sheep and deer can't reach them. New pine seedlings are growing on the moor, perhaps from seeds blown there by the wind. They'll soon block the view at this point on the moor looking west.

The deva catches my thoughts and says that this is progress and that one day there will be a natural forest here and people will enjoy walking beneath the trees.

Will the pools still be here?

How much have they changed in 29 years?

I stop to consider this for a moment. I've compared the photos of then and now. Twenty-nine years ago was a very hot summer when the waterfalls and pools shone blue in the light with the rocky basin exposed and no fallen trees across them.

Hardly at all!

We will be here! As long as the rain will fall on Earth...

I think of the layers of history and the beliefs that have been held by the people who have lived in this area. Throughout time, Immortelle's burn has flowed down from the mountain to the River Nairn.

It's hard to walk in this area without tripping over history. Tucked into the layers of hills are stone circles, hut circles that were ancient prehistoric settlements, old churches, the tumbled down walls of small farm holdings called crofts, their field systems often submerged under the inaccessible blocks of forestry plantation.

The Gaelic name for the River Nairn, *Uisge Narann*

or *Narainn*, translates as Water of Nairn, which perhaps came from a Pictish word or older source suggesting the pure spirit of flowing water. Another version of the name, *Uisge Nearne*, describes it as the water of alders. To this day, these trees grow abundantly, some to a great age and maturity on the banks of the river's lower reaches.* Strath and glen are anglicised from *srath* and *gleann* meaning valley, with strath being a shallow, wider valley and glen being a deep valley.

Strathnairn, the valley of the River Nairn, had a turbulent history and times of depopulation. The 4000-year-old Clava Cairns down by the river, the beautiful late 19th century railway viaduct that spans the valley there, and the Culloden Battlefield area are all within a short distance of each other.

Inverness was once a Pictish stronghold and the names of places, such as nearby Daviot, are Pictish in origin. Further up the strath there are carved stones and rock art from that era. Later, Gaelic culture infiltrated Strathnairn. The people who named many of the hills, even this hill and this burn, were Gaelic speakers, though the burn's name no longer appears on more recent maps.

This land would have been natural woodland in those times, with lynx, bears and wolves roaming. Travel would have been dangerous. Clansmen from the Highlands traversed the wild terrain to fight in battles in other parts of Scotland, and cattle drovers also made the long journey from here through passes in the hills to Comrie in Perthshire, or Falkirk in Central Scotland. It's hard to imagine that now when driving or walking along the quiet single-track roads past farms and fields.

If you walked from here towards the A9 without turning off towards Clava Stones you'd pass farms, such as Castletown. I've always wondered about the name. The farm is one of several local sites that are examples of fortified dwellings or castles from medieval times, some of which are now on privately owned land. In the past, people were loyal to their landlords and church leaders but were also at the mercy of those in power.

Overlaying this history, Culloden casts its shadow. Centuries of clan system and warfare culminated at the Battle of Culloden in 1746, when rival clans joined forces against government troops. The bravery of the young men of Strathnairn and neighbouring Strathdearn is legendary.

There is a prehistoric stone in the woods at Gask near Inverness, and a church wall at Dunlichity near Farr in upper Strathnairn, where there are spine chilling sights of stones scoured with the marks of many swords sharpened for the last time, before the men went into battle.

At Culloden, a generation of young men was wiped out, and all through the area innocent people were massacred, even if they had not supported the Jacobite cause. It is said that families fled to the hills to hide from the Hanoverian troops, only to suffer hunger and cold. I've often wondered if they came to hide here, at this burn, on this very hillside.

Once I believed I had seen the ghosts of soldiers. As a teenager, I often walked the family dog through Balloch woods up to the railway, and along a path under one of its arched bridges into the Forestry Commission area. From a small hillock near the path I could see over the top of the railway embankment in front of me and watch the sunsets over the Black Isle and Moray Firth to the north. One misty day I had decided to go no further into the woods as I could only see a short distance around me.

I was about to turn back when I noticed that the dog's hackles had risen, her ears flat against her head. I looked behind me and saw a line of figures on horseback in the distance moving along the main forestry track uphill from where I was standing. The whole line of horses and riders turned off in a southerly direction, moving slowly disappearing into mist. At first, I thought they were the local riding school, but then wondered why they would be out on such a day. The point at which they were turning off the track didn't make sense, either. They'd have had to go over a ditch of brambles and barbed wire fencing to get to the fields around Viewfield Farm which is adjacent to the battlefield area. The dog's terror unnerved me. She bolted for home and I ran after her all the way.

A few weeks later, when recounting this experience to an elderly neighbour, I wondered whether I had possibly seen ghosts of the Battle of Culloden. The small hillock viewpoint was called Gallows Hill when she was young. She also showed me places where her grandparents' generation had had illicit whisky stills in the fields near Chapelton Farm, as there are many natural wells in this area. Nearby was the site of St. Mary's Chapel, possibly a relic of an old Celtic church. Using an old 1961 Ordnance Survey map revised from a 1904-05 edition, together we explored the local woodlands searching for wells. I remember so clearly the taste of the water which was believed to have healing properties. We took some home in a bottle. Some of the documented holy sites were destroyed or lost after the Battle of Culloden and have long disappeared or been infiltrated in recent times by natural woodland, new housing and road networks.

One particular well in the area is famous. It is one of two Clootie Wells, the other being on the Black Isle to the north. I remember an ancient Scots pine tree growing beside it, its lower branches covered in strips of cloth (cloots or clothing) that people had hung on it in order to ask favours of the nature spirits of the water. The tradition is that the cloth would be soaked in the well water and as it dried out and rotted away in time, the healing power of the water would be dispersed to the person who was being prayed for.

It's possible that the name, St. Mary's Well, was transferred to this clootie well from the one hidden in the woods near the site of St. Mary's chapel at Chapelton. This well has other names too: Culloden Well and *Tobar na Coille*: Well of the Wood. It may also have been known as *Tobar na h-Òige*: the Well of Youth, a name which seems reminiscent of *Tír na nÓg*, the Celtic otherworld.

Not far away, and closer to the main battle site, is a well with a long association with the Battle of Culloden. This is known as the Well of the Dead (*Tobar nam Marbh*). There is a Blue Well (*Tobar Gorm*) nearby, marked on the older maps. Some of the well names suggest an older history of Celtic celebrations of Beltane predating the Battle of Culloden.

Traditionally Beltane (1st May) and Samhain (31st October) are times when the dead and ancestors are honoured, when spirits can be seen and the gates to the afterlife open. There are records of people visiting clootie wells on May Day into the early 20th century. In the 1930s there had been an upsurge of interest in St. Mary's Well, with several buses a day transporting people there from Inverness.*

The second of the two clootie wells, known as the Black Isle Well (*Tobar Fuar*: the Cold Well in Gaelic), has become better known in recent times as it is now a stop off point on the main tourist routes and easily accessible from the road.

As children we knew little about the history of the wells when we explored the woods in the 1970s. I remember being overjoyed to discover water avens, not realising then that it was quite a common plant in the damp Highlands ditches. There was also the heady scent of the conifers, broom and flowering currant at the side of the tracks in the late spring, and we filled our mouths with sweet wild raspberries in summer, taking the extra home to make jam.

We saw the strips of cloth on the trees around St. Mary's Well simply as being a custom going back to times when people believed in pagan gods, nature spirits and fairies. Nowadays, the custom of leaving cloths near the well sites has become popular once again and there is concern about the amount of synthetic materials that are hung from the surrounding trees as older cloots rot away.

My sister, brother and I once saw a beautiful woman near that place, walking along the same track where I'd seen the horsemen in the mist. She was fair haired and dressed in what looked like a long coat or cloak of fine white fur. She stared at us as she passed, and we felt awe. She may have simply been an unusually beautiful local person out walking, but ever after that I secretly feared going there in case she reappeared. Instead, I took to walking the Cullernie Woods to the east, near Feabuie (*An Fhèith Bhuidhe*: the yellow marshes), where there were old crofts, and areas of native trees on the edges of the forestry plantations, where the gloom of the Culloden battle-field area didn't reach. From there I walked as far as Dalcross which was then a tiny airport and is now Inverness Airport.

I pause in my thoughts and come back into the present, taking in the peace of the moor. I can see towards Culloden Battlefield and Visitor Centre through a gap in the trees below my seat in the heather. Beyond are the dark woods above Balloch village and, in the far distance, the blue of the firth and the Black Isle.

It's hard to imagine what life was like after the Battle of Culloden here. Following the battle, a whole section of society left in the Highland Clearances from the mid-18th to mid-19th centuries. During this period of eviction, people were either forced off their lands to make way for sheep farming, or left through poverty or choice to find a better life.

The large houses where landowners lived in past centuries still stand at strategic points along the Nairn River. Some became hunting lodges, bought as Highland country residences by the wealthy or were developed for tourism. The farms of this area such as Daviot Mains, known as Daviot Dairy, must have been built in more prosperous times of the late 19th century.

Down the road from here, on the way to Clava Cairns, was the old Clava school attended by some of my friends. The rural schools had the reputation of providing good education in the 1960s, but at the time when education for all was being implemented in this area in the late 19th century, the only teaching offered was in English. Children speaking in their native tongue were brutally beaten and the playing of traditional music was banned.

This final repression of Gaelic culture must have been so severe in people's memory, that even in my own generation, a few friends who had Gaelic speaking parents were not taught their own language as children and had to re-learn Gaelic at university. Nowadays the situation has turned around. The language and its music are taught again in local schools, and are thriving especially in this area.

The old Clava school is now a private house. From there, down a steep brae (hill) towards the Clava Cairns enclosures, the view across the fields is of the magnificent Clava Viaduct.

It was completed in 1898 and was built by Murdoch Paterson, director of the Highland Railway, as a direct link from Inverness to Aviemore, and south to Perth. It's the longest viaduct in Scotland with its one-hundred-foot wide arch over the river and twenty-eight subsidiary arches following a curve spanning the Nairn valley.

The building of the railway must have had a massive impact on the area. A temporary line had carried the local red sandstone from a nearby quarry at Leanach to the main site. Along the railway line networks of small bridges and arches are still visible, which allowed farmers to move their cattle from one field to another. When driving in the area or even walking in the woods, you pass under these beautifully constructed arches and bridges. I have often wondered whether the local people and barefooted children stood in the fields to watch the work in progress. Old photographs show the viaduct half built, covered in scaffolding and the workmen walking along precariously high planks. There must have been fatalities.

Steam trains were still running when my parents came here in the late 1950s. We could see the viaduct from our house at Nairnside, and nearby Culloden Moor station was still open. Inverness was a small Highland town then, but by the time my family had returned to the area in the 1970s the North Sea oil boom had started, bringing work opportunities and development. We were what some people might have termed white settlers, but I never felt anything other than a deep sense of belonging here in the place where I was born. New roads and housing were in process of being built around our village and since then the development has continued. Inverness has become known as the 'fastest growing city in Europe'.

Two world wars claimed so many lives, as is evident by the sheer numbers of names on war memorials in villages across Scotland. Strathnairn, which had been losing its population through the centuries, was a quiet rural place when I attended high school. However, since the late 1990s the area continues to become more densely populated due to a surge in housing development, especially around the village of Farr in upper Strathnairn where community life has revived again.

I think how different the land was at the time of the building of Clava Stones, millennia before all the documented histories. In essence it looks the same as it did when I used to sit in the field nearby with drawing paper spread over the ground, and not a soul in sight. Nowadays, continuous streams of visitors converge on the roads nearby the Clava Cairns. You'll find drivers, unaccustomed to the tiny single-track roads, stopping to check maps when their satellite navigation (GPS) aids don't work.

From here where I sit on my heathery perch, I can see in the distance new houses gleaming in the sunlight on the horizon - houses that weren't there when I looked down from the moor in the 1980s.

Chapter 8

Message from the Source of Immortelle's Burn: It is Time for Humans to Co-operate in Earth's Healing

16th February 2013 (the third day of my visit)

I make my way through the plantation and up to the moor. It's a dull day with soft light. It has rained overnight.

As I approach the edge of the trees I can glimpse the moor beyond, then out of the trees I pick my way through the bog and down to the pool. The first impression is of that of the timeless sound, the roaring of water. I carefully skirt the bank by the overhanging birch above the vertical moss wall and climb down to a ledge of moss and grass beside the lower fall. For a time I sit spellbound, watching the flow of water as it pours over the moss-covered rockslide, the force of the creamy water as it enters the pool and the stream of bubbles shooting under the surface and emerging some three-quarters of the way along the length of the lower pool. Before slowing, they break into larger bubbles, some of them popping and others reforming and bobbing over the lip of the pool edge and down the rock steps to join the stream below.

Clear memories return of bathing in the lower pool when I first returned here in 2010. I was with the same friend who had introduced me to this moor years ago. I remember discovering the rocky ledge beneath the curtain of the waterfall and that the wall was undercut below into a perfect bowl shape, smooth to the touch. Below this wall was no moss, only smooth rock. As long as I shall live, I'll never forget that as I plunged into the black peaty water it didn't feel like water at all, but more like silk and very buoyant. The cold of the water engulfed my senses yet I felt totally healed and at peace.

I had swum repeatedly from the curved lip of the edge and across to the base of the waterfall, using all my effort against the current as far as I could, then relaxing onto my back and floating with the water to the curved shelf. It was unlike any other spiritual experience I'd ever had.

Although so cold, I hadn't wanted to leave the pool. The incredible feeling of the force of the current floating me back to the shelf and the silken texture of the water made me feel real; the life force of the water and mine were as one. I felt an extreme joy of being in the moment that I can't compare to any other experience.

I hear Immortelle, who rouses me from my memory of the water.

Immortelle! You're here!

I know it's her because the words come into my head. They're not like my own thoughts but come from an outside influence - in the same way the angels' words come to my consciousness.

I think of the ways in which she speaks differently from my angels. I've noticed an obvious way to tell the difference. The deva's voice emanates from my left side, whereas my guardian angel Amber's voice comes from in front of and a little to the right of my vision, as do all the angels' voices.

My awareness comes back to Immortelle. She's referring to my experience in the water.

You were being reborn.

Do you mean this in the sense of, say, a born-again Christian?

Immortelle laughs a peeling laugh. The feel of the laughter vibrates somewhere on my left.

You humans use water as initiation. You have not lost your connection with the true purpose of water. Water gives life. Bathing in our pool was your initiation into our world. You had asked permission. You silently acknowledged us as you entered the water and in a spirit of gratitude and appreciation.
You pretend to have only recently discovered us yet you knew us as a child. You accepted us as part of God's kingdom then.

It was then I remembered playing on our swing that hung from the old larch tree at the bottom of the garden at Nairnside, across the moor on the other side of the Nairn valley. My family lived at Nairnside until I was four years old. I believed in both God and the fairies of the unseen realms, all of which I could find in the garden. The warm energy of the larch tree felt like that of a friend.

I sometimes saw fairies in the form of little lights like sparklers in the trees. I continued to see them up until the age of seven. By then my family had moved to a place near Dundee in the Sidlaw Hills (Gaelic: *Na Sidhbheanntan*, a fairy or sacred hill name referring to the prehistoric cairns on those hills).

Later, my experience of connection with Spirit expanded within a more religious setting when I attended the Episcopal Church with my mother and sister. In Sunday school I was taught the story of Christ's crucifixion. During the service, when staring up at the images on the church walls, my small heart went out to Jesus, wondering if he could be set free. Later we joined the Religious Society of Friends (Quakers).

I loved the freedom of playing in the beautiful gardens my father had created on the edge of moorland, both at Nairnside and later in the Sidlaw Hills. I recall running from one group of trees to the next, feeling their energy fields pulling me in or letting me go, similar to the way a bubble on the water pulls its energy field away from an adjacent bubble, then merges with yet another or pops itself free.

I thought God was a kind of gardener personality and the energies to be the spirit of the garden itself.

Well, you weren't far from the truth! exclaims Immortelle, in response to my thoughts.

My mind comes back into the present. I think of the layers of history and the beliefs that have been held by the people who lived around here.

Immortelle continues to speak and refers to the chambered cairns at Clava, a mile or so from here:

> *The men who built the stone circles were as intelligent as you are, only more so because they worked from the power of their hearts and were in tune with the seasons. Their intellect was in balance with their hearts.*
>
> *People who lived after them thought they were giants or in league with giants. People who came after assumed the circles were places of foul deeds and sacrifice.*
>
> *They were places of worship in a sense. They marked the power points on the land, the spiritual power points and minor chakra points of Earth's life flow.*
>
> *They were in alignment with the grid of power that surrounds the Earth like a web, and passes through the Earth's centre.*

Message from the Souce of Immortelle's Burn:
It is Time for Humans to Co-operate in Earth's Healing

Immortelle shows me a diagram of a web-like structure, but I can't take it in and the image fades from my mind. She presses on, despite my difficulty in concentrating.

> *The circles are star charts and are links to the system you mainly call the zodiac. The people who built them knew they were from the stars. They plotted the significant points at these stone structures.*
> *They were in connection telepathically with other communities around Earth, and also with the entities you call angels. They connected with the angels and the guardians of the stars. The people who built the stone structures were star children who were fully aware of their evolution from stars and lived in hope of their return to the stars at death.*

May I ask, are you angels also guardians of the stars as well as guardians of humans?

> *Yes, there are angels that oversee the movements of the planets and are linked with each star system.*

Last night, I saw a most beautiful starry sky through the skylight in the bedroom of the place where I was staying. I haven't seen a sky like that for years, because of the light pollution where I live, or because of wet weather.

> *Yes, there are few places left in Britain where the skies are clear. There are patches of clarity over the hills and mountains and away from cities.*
> *Your angels govern the stars. You forget this because of your ego. You think they are only there to serve you but you are part of the cosmos!*

Thank you, Immortelle.

The voice of the deva fades into the roar of the burn. Though sunlight crosses my page, I'm aware of the cold breeze of the moor that sways the trees. There's no sound of wind in the leaves to mingle with the sound of water. The only leaves that remain are the dead birch leaves strewn on the moss amongst the heather.

I feel so peaceful that I want to stay here forever but I know the cold will bring me to my senses. My angels are already prompting me to move. They won't let me catch cold. Ariel encourages me to walk up the hill towards the source of the burn, telling me that more will be revealed and that my angels and the deva, Immortelle, will accompany me.

I smile at the comical picture conjured in my imagination: of myself, a tall human carrying a rucksack, Immortelle as a Light body whizzing about in the air, and three enormous angels behind me holding their robes up out of the peaty bog! Hoping no one will see us, I finish my coffee and slip my writing pad into my rucksack.

We thank you for your effort to connect with us!

Thank you, Immortelle.

I set off through heather and bracken, skirting the edge of the burn where I can and following an old track past the clump of trees further up the burn. Here the ground opens out into a huge bowl-shaped valley filled with grass and impenetrable dead bracken. In places the burn meanders through the landscape.

I follow a ridge of higher ground until the track peters out. Here the whole moor around me is waterlogged and it's nearly impossible to proceed further without sinking into deep holes.

I've been jumping from tussock to tussock for some time, so as not to put my leg into deep peaty holes in between

Message from the Souce of Immortelle's Burn:
It is Time for Humans to Co-operate in Earth's Healing

the heather and grass. Making my way carefully across frozen patches of snow, I come into the corrie (or *coire* in Gaelic), formed by ice and rocks scouring out a hollow shape on the mountainside during the last ice age. I'm tempted to press on to the top of the hill that lies beyond and try to assess how long that might take. There's nothing but heather and peat and a row of fence posts further along. The winter light is beginning to fade and I need to allow time to get back over the rough ground.

An underground stream churns and echoes below me. The splashing sounds are like a giant water cistern. In one place a flow of water rushes into a hole amidst green grasses and disappears underground. I place my mat on the ground.

I sit for a while amid the water and wet here at the source of Immortelle's burn, praying for the devas and nature spirits. I know this is a most significant location. It is not the source of the main River Nairn; however, it is part of the same ecosystem where the rains come down from the local mountains, filter through peat and rock to rise to the surface, then join forces with other streams and burns and flow down to the sea. This particular tributary, whose name still survives in Gaelic on some old maps, carries the essence of the sacred River Nairn. I was to make the journey to the source of the Nairn a few years after completing the writing of this book.

The February sunshine has been welcome, and I've tried to capture on video the views which stretch miles to the distant coast and mountains on the opposite side of the Moray Firth. I can see as far as the hills of Glen Affric, Ben Wyvis, the Sutors of Cromarty, and eastwards up the coast of Scotland as far as the lighthouse at Portmahomack, and the conical peak of Morven. I feel minuscule as I take in the magnificent view. It all makes me and my attempt to write about the devas seem very insignificant.

It's not insignificant!

I hear Immortelle above my thoughts.

The one message of this book for all who read this - and even if one person only were to read this book, it would make a difference.
Even if you have no belief in the angelic kingdom of Earth, we have one message for you: Respect Earth! Your life is dependent on this. Your joy is now dependent on this.

Glancing up from my writing, I see the distant plume of steam from the wood processing plant, a familiar landmark on the firth near Inverness.

It seems very clear to me the devas and nature spirits have retreated to the wild woodland, forest, moor and seas, where they hold the Light and generate more.

It's hard to pick up Immortelle's voice. I am distracted by the view, taking photographs and drawing diagrams of a distant standing stone for later research. The lighting articulates all the detail of distant landmarks. I feel as if I have the vision of an eagle as I sit here on the soaking peaty ground, a morass of grouse moor created by the Victorians who once managed the land here. Clava Moor used to be one of the most famous grouse moors in Scotland.

It's not insignificant! Nothing is insignificant! One prayer from one human creates Light. Never think you are too insignificant.
Please go to the source of your nearest river and send Light to the water. If you cannot get to the source of your river, then stand on the bank, just where you are and send Light from there.
We know when you pray and we receive your Light. It's time for humans to co-operate in Earth's healing.

Dear Immortelle, I am privileged to be here at the source of your

Message from the Souce of Immortelle's Burn:
It is Time for Humans to Co-operate in Earth's Healing

stream from where I can see across many miles of heather moor, fields and woods, past houses and farms and down to the Moray Firth where the dolphins play!

The dolphins are connecting with humans. They are messengers of Light.

I sense the enormity of writing this book. I have no idea what to write. Our task as humans to save our planet seems a near impossibility. The news we watch and listen to in the media is beyond awful at times. Areas of pollution seem irreparable, and our technologies are so advanced now that I don't see how we can go back to living in simple dwellings.

And yet, as I gaze at this fabulous view on this clear February day and take in Immortelle's messages, I feel a great excitement, hope and determination to communicate the messages of the Earth's voices, from the immortal ones, the angels of Earth and the nature spirits.

The February sun is descending in the sky. I need time to get back, so I get up, pack my bag and head down the hillside as fast as I can over the frozen ground.

I have always loved running. Now I start to run down the moor over the frosty ground, leaping the heather tussocks as if I was in my teens again. The good thing about heather is that it forms a soft bouncy surface for falling into.

As I pass by the pools the winter sunset is catching the edges of the heather in pink and orange light, the hills beyond turning deep cerulean and purple. I don't stop running until I get to the gate by the wood. Leaving the moor and entering the plantation there is very little light remaining. The only sounds are the cracking and groaning of swaying trees and the occasional fluttering of a pigeon. Below the woods is the distant gleaming water of the firth, and Ben Wyvis floating above in the soft sunset.

Chapter 9

Sacred Commission

1st April 2013 (2 months later)

The call to visit Immortelle was insistent. It was a beautiful spring day, the sun slanting in and falling across the kitchen floor as I mopped. I became engrossed in watching the little patterns of foam as I listened intently to the radio.

For some reason, I'll always remember that moment... swirling the mop across the linoleum, and the anticipation building at the thought of leaving the house and driving north again. My plan was to stay with my hillwalking friend at Burghead on the coastal peninsula beyond Findhorn, arriving late afternoon. I would go from there the next day to spend time on Immortelle's Moor. I wanted to go straightaway, but leaving things tidy in the house and cleaning the floor made for a sense of completeness.

The floor of the old Victorian flat, though sturdy, isn't quite level in the kitchen. There are the familiar corners where my two sons' marbles had often rolled. I remember all the games they used to play, the places they would hide around the house. They were rarely apart, playing harmoniously together inventing games, many of which required rolling dice and logging the results in notebooks and on small cards, exquisitely designed, with drawings added. There were numbers and calculations everywhere and many notebooks filled with them. Their world was frequented with imaginary personages who played all the different parts in the games. Each had names. Memories came so clear of their fair heads close together as they worked away on their current game.

Football fascinated them both and after much practice

they were skilled enough to lob a small foam ball from the kitchen right through the hall and into their bedroom, a feat which required great precision as the ball needed a specific trajectory - an inch either way and it would hit the door jamb and not make the goal. That was before they grew up, became tall and darker haired and started following the local Stirling Albion matches or playing *footie* with friends for hours after school, once their homework was complete.

Late one evening, we tried Michael Jackson moon-walking, laughing loudly and possibly disturbing neighbours in the flat below when a kitchen stool crashed to the floor.

I often thought of the how we spent the hours, happy in each others' company... the deep mix of joy and sadness a parent feels... that they are not there any more, and the house never feels quite the same again.

There came the day they left for university. My mother helped with the packing, sneaking boxes of her rich fruitcake in with their possessions to 'keep them going'. Later, when we had all had parted company, I headed for the car park by the sea to watch the sunset before driving home. On leaving my car and walking swiftly to the edge of the dunes, I tripped over a low wire fence and nose-dived down onto the beach below. Luckily it was a soft landing and a friendly Labrador came running along, licking my face. The fall seemed to take away some of the pain of parting, and brought me to my senses.

When they come back, the house fills with talk about the latest football match and news of friends. Their lives have diverged now, but when together they're as close as ever. We congregate in the kitchen and as they each explain their work projects, my brain feels as if it's being stretched beyond its limit trying to understand the mathematics involved.

I come out of my reflections on the times that we have had here in this household and move back into the present. I stop in my tracks. On Radio 3 the music of polyphony is being discussed in quite spiritual terms. The layers of music are described as being piled up. The sound is multilayered and exquisitely detailed, worlds within worlds of sound. I think of the waterfalls, of Immortelle, and tears begin pouring down my face.

I finally back towards the kitchen door, twizzle the mop and squeeze it in the drainer, then hurry downstairs to empty the bucket in the garden... take out the compost, go back into the house to pick up the last of my bags, lock up and, with great sense of freedom, drive north.

This journey is one I will never forget. The mountains of the Cairngorms, rising majestically, appear like floating islands above the surrounding scenery. The more recent housing developments on the hinterland around the mountains catch the afternoon sun. Every old larch tree by the roadside appears to be waving branches filled with light. The ugliness of new building and the mess of roads seem immaterial.

Coming over Dava Moor I catch glimpses of white mountains to the north, beyond the Moray Firth. Later in the evening the sun sets like a huge crimson fireball over Findhorn Bay.

Next day: I drive back from Burghead to Clava to work on my writing of the deva Immortelle's book. The sky is hazy and clouded, but beyond a clearly visible line stretching across the firth it is deep turquoise and the snow on the mountains glows golden in morning light.

As I reach Culloden Moor the hills appear, floating above breaking clouds, with the moor on the edge of the line between cloud and clear skies.

The sun breaks through, lighting the path to the moor. I pick up a piece of mica from the ground, shining like silver. Today I intend to ask Immortelle about the Earth's crystals. I feel a bit unprepared and wonder if it might be best to simply wait with an open mind and see what she says.

Approaching the pools I sense something different. The water is quieter, while the level has dropped so much that the pools and rushing water pouring into them are almost unrecognisable.

In the place where the water passed through the gorge before, it's now possible to climb down the bank and stand on the green mossy edge, which is no longer underwater. A large promontory juts into the upper pool, reminding me of the photographs I'd taken during the drought in the summer of 1983, when the water level was as low as it is now and the rock basin of the pool was exposed to light.

The slope of the waterfall seems less steep in both falls now, with the water falling quite calmly beneath a skin of ice and the most exquisite icicles. A curtain of ice, torn through and melting, hangs from the twigs of two broken trees lying fallen across the pool.

On the lower pool there are no large bubbles floating

through, but in an eddy of the burn below the lower pool a perfect circle of ice turns slowly, like a large eye watching the exit.

Shafts of sun within the water highlight, for a moment, the vertical shelf below the curved lip of rock at the edge of the pool. Here the water must be ten feet deep.

I hesitate to write these descriptions. It's difficult to manage pencil and paper when I'm crouching or kneeling among the frosted grass and slippery rock, but the deva encourages me to do this now and not wait until I'm home to write.

It takes a while to settle in. Singing under my breath, I wish I'd brought my flute to play at the water's edge. In my head is a Quantz flute concerto.* This would be the perfect music to play today!

Where the sun has warmed it, the grass underfoot is quite dry and the water and pool seem as peaceful as they are in summer. It occurs to me that I've made the effort to come here to write but the deva might not be prepared to talk to me.

They are not like angels although they're from the angelic realm. They're not committed to humans like our angels, nor under any obligation to communicate with or help us. My presence with them is purely at my own risk. Or is it, I wonder?

I lift a shard of ice from the edge of the pool as I wait and hold it up to the light. I'm shocked to see the beautiful form of a woman in the etched lines of the ice. The lower torso and legs are perfect and it's hard not to see the figure as a woman.

My analytical mind kicks in. I try to see it simply as a pattern on a piece of ice, but this is impossible. It's a fact of science that humans recognise faces in everything. It's basic learned behavior. I know this from discussions with one of my sons when he studied psychology. But this is a complete figure! The form is more perfect than anything I've seen in a life drawing class. I admire her back and arms, and above her shoulder blades are wings stretching up. These are not like angel wings as depicted in art images, but more like a kind of funnel of light.

Immortelle! Is it you in the ice?

She laughs. I carefully place the now melting ice back into the pool and watch it sink below the surface as I reach for my camera to record it. It seems silly. Immortelle isn't the ice or trapped in the ice, but has somehow projected her image there.

The sun is going behind the clouds. I wonder whether I should stay or drive further west and seek the sunlight on the Moray coast. My mind is blank and I have nothing to ask.

The voice of Immortelle breaks through like sun through mist.

Blessed be! We are happy you are here. We've called you. We've made it all possible. We light your life. We light your path. We uphold the vibration of the spheres - we're of Earth, the divine aspect of Earth - and so are you! It's why we connect with you. You love us and we love you. Blessed be. Our voices are in the water, in the wind, in the birdsong and ether. We're here and we're there. We come to speak to you. You've been privileged. It's been your charge to write for us, through the guardianship of your angels and guides you come to us.

This mission is sacred. We'll help you. Have no fear.
This place is your connection point with us. It is also a confluence of streams of energy where the mountain meets water and connects with the vibration of Earth.
It's a chakra point of Earth. Not far from here as the crow flies are the sacred stones of Clava. Humans have positioned this monument in line with the natural energetic pathways that converge here on the Moray Firth coastline. The stones show a pattern of stars and connect with the Pleiades (Seven Sisters), and there are other galaxies that are represented by this sacred symbol, Andromeda, Pegasus, Orion the Gateway.
They believed this point on Earth to be sacred. They were correct. The vibration here is pure. If you think of music, the vibration sounds a pure note not a harmonic.
If you think of mathematics, then you may think of magic numbers or those that cannot be divided by multiples.

You mean prime numbers?

Yes! The world's greatest mathematicians and astronomers will materialise these calculations and find a point, a place, a position on a map that rings true. It is attuned to the divine vibration. This place is one.
It is why you connect with us. You were born here, on the other side of the Nairn valley. You came here for a purpose, born to a family that didn't belong here but had come here by a series of synchronicities and events to make this place their home. It wasn't their natural home but it is your home. You were called here, destined to be born here, to grow up on the moor, destined to return here in your youth, and again in your maturity. You have kept your promise and we charge you with the task of writing our book.

Dear Immortelle, I feel rather self-indulgent though - making these trips here, driving up the A9, burning fossil fuels only to be in a place I love, by the water, with my sandwich and a cup of thermos tea.

Other people are at work, earning good money in offices, as I sit here talking to you. I feel as if I'm taking holidays and writing about myself. I feel anxious; I'm not earning and I have bills to pay. But when I'm with you, I'm at peace. When I wrote the Angels' *book, I felt like that too. I couldn't imagine others reading it. It was my journey of healing to take down the angels' words. They'd promised I'd heal my headaches, pain and anxiety, and that promise was delivered. Through writing the book I was healed. I hear from others who've read the book of similar experiences and miracles happening. Now that I'm healed I'm worried about wasting time or being self-indulgent!*

> You are much mistaken to speak of self-indulgence. You commit to a life where you must trust in abundance for your next meal to be there and to be able to pay your bills and heat your house.
>
> You commit to coming here in all weathers, and when you are not here (physically that is) we hear your prayer for us.
>
> So do not underrate yourself any more. You do not understand the importance of this mission, yet you make efforts and sacrifices to be here writing for us. Not many of you humans make this effort and it comes from deep belief, respect, love and sensing of the real world that does exist, here, and there, and everywhere.
>
> There are songs that describe the love of a man for a woman, but we can tell you that when you give your heart to a man, woman, animal, plant, thing, or place you are only sensing a part of the love that is everywhere. You are 'in love' not knowing that you are in love all the time, for all that you can be, do and have is given from Source,

from God, and is given freely.

The Beatles song, *Here, There and Everywhere*,* is blasting through my head. It seems incongruous within the scenery of the Highland moor. The deva continues.

Humans seek to control and destroy. Do not limit your love. Do not place limits on yourself. Your soul is from love, the eternal Source, from God.
So, you are drawn to people, places and events, and they are drawn to you to manifest, and make manifest your beliefs and desires. When your beliefs and desires are in tune with the flow of life, then your manifestation takes place more quickly and abundantly.
As you let go of your old ways and outmoded beliefs then you manifest new reality. When this happens you may think you are dreaming and wonder how you got so lucky? You are already abundant. You must believe it and it is so. Do not limit your beliefs in any way, for you are all of God.

Dear Immortelle, I know you are immortal but I cannot pretend to be. Each year I come here I'm older and one day I won't be able to come here. I'll age and die. It's not nice seeing ageing and deteriorating of our faculties and of those around us of the older generations, those loved parents and grandparents, and those we see struggling along with their shopping.

I suddenly find myself packing my notepad in my rucksack and leaping up. I walk swiftly over the moor and back through the plantation without looking back or saying goodbye to the deva and nature spirits at the pool, which is very unusual for me. I am so certain of where I am going that my legs take me back to the road in only a few minutes, nearly running. I fling my rucksack into the boot of the car and then keep walking along the road. The small collie pup from the farm runs to greet me and pads along beside me for a while, but I don't stop and he turns back to the farm. I turn in at the junction of the road to the old school at Clava and head downhill.

There is no feeling of stiffness or tiredness in my legs at all. I feel young and as light as a feather. I have no plans for what I am doing, yet have complete certainty. I stride into the field with the outlying cairns at Milton of Clava and circle them several times, sending Light to Earth and to the four compass directions.

The cairn here was badly damaged in the past and many stones lie scattered, but a large monolith of the surrounding circle is still standing. In past times pagan monuments were destroyed or other Christian churches built beside or over their foundations on the same geographical power points. Here at this outlying group of cairns, it's believed there may once have been a Chapel of St. Bridget, a version of Brighid, dating from the times when Christianity was spreading and taking over the older religion.

I walk along the road towards the wooded enclosure surrounding the three main cairns, circle around them in the same way and send prayers for Earth.

The structures of the Clava Cairns form great circular mounds about forty metres apart, each held by banks of kerb stones, an inner and outer ring, infilled with smaller stones. They are aligned in a north-east to south-west direction. Roofed at one time, they have been open to the sky for millennia. Two of the cairns have passages leading into their centres, but the middle one has no entrance. In Victorian times they were ransacked, and old photographs show them half buried under the ground with the early archaeologist pioneers standing posed for the camera in their tweed woollen breeches, overcoats and sturdy boots. Much work was done to preserve the cairns after this point, and they were eventually placed under national protection.

Immortelle has spoken of these three cairns being aligned to a pattern of stars above and to the moon. What is generally known is that they are also aligned so the light enters the chambers exactly at the moment of the setting winter sun. Looking across from the eastern-most cairn, towards the west at winter solstice, it looks as if the setting sun is balanced over the furthest cairn.

The middle cairn of the group of three has no passage-way running into its centre; however, there are lines of stones going out in rays and linking with stones in the circle surrounding it. The unique feature of many of the chambered cairns in this area is that they are also *ring cairns*, each with a surrounding stone circle. Some of the monoliths of the circle are huge and have been calculated to weigh many tons. One of the stones is split and has come to be known as a *praying hands* stone. Here at Clava, the tops of the stone circles are of varying height in line with the angle of the sun as it moves through the seasons. The banks of flat kerb stones around the circles also follow this pattern, being larger to the south-west. Many are cup-marked and the stones that infilled the banks were originally graded in the colours of local stone: smaller whiter quartz to the north and redder sandstone colour to the south-west.

I was to receive a message from my angel guides in July 2015 whilst at Avebury, which also seemed to allude to these particular stones at Clava:

> The circle within circle represents the womb, the creative aspect of Mother Earth without which the crops would not grow. The alignment of different stones pointed to the important conjunctions of the stars - at certain times, such as solstice, and lunar months. Larger stones pinpointed the spot from which the alignments must be made.

Immortelle has already revealed to me that the Clava Stones also represent a moon circle, as at Calanais on Lewis, in the Western Isles. I'd heard about other moon circles in Strathnairn. Nearer to Inverness than Clava is the great stone circle of Gask, which contains a huge monolith of almost three and a half metres in height by three metres in width but only twenty centimentres in depth.

I believe there are many links with planets and constellations. I have spent evenings with star maps and Immortelle's messages spread on the table in an attempt to discover some of these.

Although much visited in recent times, the stones still hold their mystery. At this stage though, as I am walking around them sending Light there is only one other person in the distance and it is still possible to spend time alone among the stones. I have no idea at this point just how busy this ancient site will become in the next few years due to the cult following of televised films and overtourism.

I walk on to the bridge over the Nairn where the brown water flows tranquil and to the Clava Viaduct up the hill where I used to cycle years ago on my way towards Cawdor or Craggie. From here I walk along the top road back to my car. I can't believe how fast I've been walking or why I have been compelled to do this.

I start the car engine and glance in the mirror. My face is different! I look younger by far. I stare at the young woman in the mirror. She is me, but more confident. I like her! She's beautiful, her hair plastered against her cheekbones from the light mist. The youthful illusion lasts for about ten minutes as I keep my eyes on the road and focus on the traffic. When I look again, I am back to an older version of myself.

Chapter 10

Midsummer, Magic and Manifestation

I visit the moor again in the baking heat of July 2013, at last free of other commitments. My plan to be here at midsummer has come to nothing, although I had watched a TV programme about the summer solstice and the different places where people gather to celebrate. There was a gathering at Calanais on the Isle of Lewis in the Outer Hebrides, and also a few camera shots of people here at Clava Stones. I had turned up the volume and was listening closely for any details that might throw more light on the information given to me by the deva Immortelle.

A notable archaeologist was interviewed and seemed to be about to say something significant when the TV camera zoomed out again to people in the crowd dressed in gothic-style clothing who had travelled from other countries and parts of the UK to be here. Then the view changed to the Calanais Standing Stones at Lewis and the camera panned through the crowd there. There were no shots of the sunset as it was a misty day, nor any mention of the history of the pilgrimages to view the phenomenon of the moon skirting the sacred mountain, that of the Sleeping Beauty.

Mention was made about the stones being markers of the phases of the moon, but nothing further. I was very excited that this at least confirmed what Immortelle had told me. At this point in time, the information plaques at the site describe the function of the cairns at Clava as burial chambers, which conflicts with the information received from Immortelle who has described them as being linked with the stars.

Back on the moor on this July day I settle for a while with my feet in the cold water of the sill of the lower pool, sitting on my trainers to prevent the damp from seeping through my shorts. I listen to the splashing of the water down the rockslide and staircase entering the lower pool and watch the shimmering ripply surface expanding out towards me, reflecting the light. To my left, the curved vertical wall of rock plummets deep beneath the surface of the water, perhaps by six to nine feet like the side of a well. Buzzing flies that skim and circle over the pool are bothersome. I don't feel connected at all to the devas. I'm not hearing them.

My angel Ariel tells me to cross to the other side. I'm too hot to feel hungry but drink a little of the water I've brought, then check my mobile phone for emails. I've come all this way to be here to write but there is nothing to say, and I feel as if I'm wasting the opportunity by not picking up the deva's words. Checking my mobile is a waste of time and has put me into a different mode of thinking.

Ariel tells me to wait. The sun is hot and it's hard to write on the glaring white page. Suddenly the voice of Immortelle cuts through my thoughts. I recognise the deva instantly.

Your time here is not wasted! If you learn anything in this life it is to know that time is in your hands and that everything is a network that brings you to the right place at the right time. You could not be here if you weren't here at the right time!

I don't feel right, Immortelle! I don't feel at peace, even though these weather conditions are idyllic. How many days of the year would it be possible to head out here and not be frozen, wet, or midge bitten?

Length of time matters not. The connection here is made at a different level than your immediate physical surrounding. The gap between your physical self/surroundings and the Higher Self and emanation of this place as it co-exists in the etheric - is what gives you pain of separation and longing. When these come together you are at peace.

The shining light and warmth in Scotland and England at this time gives people a shock, especially in Scotland - as it's so different to the usual conditions. Does it change the reality that we are used to?

Is that why, when hot weather hits Scotland some of us feel a bit out of sorts and frustrated? I don't feel right. I'm frustrated I don't feel connection with you and my mind keeps wandering. I have a lot of conflict in my heart. I don't know how to write this book or where the script is going. I have little knowledge of fairy folklore. I'm surrounded by a material world and the constant struggle to live in it - to make enough money to live now, let alone in the future. It's all very well to bask in the sun, and just be in Nature. I'd love to be free to come here any time and wander on the moors and in the mountains indefinitely, but we have to be practical. We have to be social and work within our networks and meet our obligations to friends and family and earn our crusts.

You felt that the Angels' Guide book was a personal journey and were afraid to get it published. Now so many people tell you they love that book, n'est-ce pas? So we must beg you to trust us your devas to keep writing, keep pushing through the veil to hear us, we make it possible for you. You must not worry what others think!
You are protected in Light by many angels, and we mean, many! If you could see them now you'd be shocked how many - a veritable consort - and you think you are alone as you sit there on your mat on the wild moor, all alone! We laugh!

Well, Immortelle, I'm tired of worrying what people think! I'm tired of worrying how to find time to write this book and how to do it. I'm tired of feeling so weird about it and having to be secretive *about the true nature of this book. I wish I could just be normal and have a normal life and not have to hide my true self any more!*

Believe us, there are many of you feeling like this! Many will identify with this book.
We require you to complete it. We desire that you push through your self-criticism and doubt. We require that you stop punishing yourself when you feel out of kilter with your actions. We require - we absolutely require you to help us.

Immortelle, many have written treatises on fairies, devas and esoteric knowledge. I know nothing! Nothing! Nothing!

I look up from the page and see that everything is bathed in grass green, moss green, a million greens: heather stems, moss, bracken, ferns, the juniper, the birch and rowan trees that overhang the rippled dark pool, which shimmers with light and reflects green and the sky.

Over all is the sound of the waterfall as it enters the pool, and the soft bubbling sounds as the water exits over the shelf. Clouds are forming in a deep cobalt sky.

The angst I felt in my solar plexus is softening now. I'm coming back into myself. My mind releases. I feel that nothing matters - nothing at all - everything is as it is.

This, says Immortelle*, is your reality! We thank you for coming here to complete your task. You have elected to be a scribe for angels and devas. This agreement was made in past lives. It is a miracle you are here - that you made it through eons of time to be here now.*

The sun warms my back. It feels pleasant and relaxing here. I do feel physically very present. I stop writing and pour a cup of tea from my flask. I'd intended to ask the deva what to write but instead find myself blurting out:

I don't know if I like the idea that I elected to complete this task eons ago in a past life! Why did I think I was so clever! I don't think I like the idea of a consort of angels and Ascended Masters watching my every move. What about my private life! Is there no privacy? Am I ever alone? And is it the same for everybody?

Some more than others, Immortelle says in a secretive tone.

What about free will? Where does that come in?

Where does it go out? she retorts.
Child star. Humans were given free will. They abused it. Free will is the last gift that was given. Now it's in the balance.

Dear Immortelle, for so long I've wanted to come back to the moor. Ironically, today I don't want to be here. Part of me wants to run away home and when I am home then I want to come back. I don't know where home is any more. When I am there I want to be here. When I stand on the moor and look across to the other side of the firth, I want to be there at Rosemarkie or further north at Dornoch or go and climb Ben Hope. When I'm on that side of the firth I can't help staring over at the Culloden hills on this side.

When I'm on the Cairngorm plateau at Ben MacDui I want to be over the other side at Cairn Toul, Angel's Peak or Braeriach. Why do I always want the thing that's on the other side or the path I didn't take?

You are driven by many forces.

I lie on the mat in the heat, too tired to take in what the deva is telling me and unable to process the information. I don't like the concept she is explaining to me and allow myself to drift into sleep, then jerk awake, feeling as if someone is standing beside me. I turn. There is nothing, only the tree overhanging the pool.

On the way back over the wet peat bog a very strange thing happens. Amongst the bright gold yellow spires of bog asphodel, the white of cotton grass and pale pink of cross-leaved heath, I come upon some flowers with large pale yellow petals. I bend down carefully to have a look. They don't belong to the natural flora here. They look like arctic poppies, but the centres are more like that of a cranesbill. I carefully pick a couple of heads being sure to leave many others and place them in my water bottle for the car journey home.

In the evening I spread all my mountain flora books across the kitchen table and pore through the diagrams for hours. I search online until my eyes are sore. I begin to wonder if I will ever identify them? I have never seen them or anything like them in the Highland bogs before. In my heart, I begin to believe that they are some kind of manifestation from the fairies for me. As a young child I particularly loved the small bright yellow tormentil flowers and these are rather like a giant version.

I feel badly because earlier today on the moor, I found it hard to tune in to the devas. I had switched on my mobile to check messages, which is something I am learning that we should never do, as it opens their sacred places to the same energy of pollution and darkness that we humans are linked to through the internet. Yet, here are these remarkable flowers. I put them in a vase with some other common flowers of the moor, harebells, heathers and purple vetch.

In 2013 I returned only once to Immortelle's pool. During that visit I took some photographs at the pool, trying to capture the faces of the water spirits as they manifested on the surface of the water. Then I set off walking in an easterly direction. The moor had turned to autumn greys, purples, reds, browns.

I didn't stop to take more messages, though I could hear Immortelle's voice in response to my thoughts and prayers:

We hear you clearly. We safeguard you.

Chapter 11

Where Is Your Heart Connection?

March 2014

It's been over six months since the last time I was here. Winter gales, floods and months of rain have passed. It's overcast today, unlike yesterday which had been a blue dream of a day. I had hoped for the same when I set out, but after four hours of driving to get here the scenery looks unremarkable and grey. The only thing that particularly stands out for me is where the trees have been bulldozed alongside the A9.

The hills of Culloden sit quietly under a hazy mantle of light. As I pass the beloved fields, trees and switchback roads, I feel disconnected. Reaching to open the car window as I cross a small bridge over the River Nairn, a flood of birdsong brings everything sharply into focus. I'm back.

As I reach the summit of the hill before diverting off the track to go to the pools, all seems white-washed, bleached and quite unlike the last visit when everything was in glorious technicolour.

I ease my way down the vertical banks and peer over the pool. It's gentle and quiet. The water level is lower than usual, so I easily cross to the opposite side, where a grassy spur juts out beside the rocky bowl. Here I lay my mat, pour a cup of thermos tea and begin to write. I've no thoughts in my head or even any wondering if Immortelle is here to speak.

> *We are happy you're here. We're happy you've come back even though you're tired.*
> *Your world is changing fast now. Many are healing. Many*

are following their heart path. Many are dying, going with the old world. They cannot accept the new.

The grassy spur on which I am sitting is covered in dead leaves from the overhanging birch tree.

Who speaks to me?

Why, it's Immortelle at your service. We've been calling you.

Yes, I know. You make my life difficult at times. I so long to be here to talk to you that it makes it hard to focus on my life and work back home. I fear my heart will detach itself from my body. I'm sure if I didn't have the people I love and my children to keep me attached, I'd split, or have to come and live here near you.

Child, part of you does live here! You do not need to split yourself and you do not need to come and live here for that part to dwell here.

What part of me is that, then?

A part of your soul! And, we may add, having part of your soul here does not affect your operation in the physical place you live, with the physical people you encounter.

Is this true of many people… that parts of their soul are in different places from their bodies?

In a word: yes.

So, what does it look like to you, Immortelle, from the perspective of a deva who is not in the physical dimension?

We see you as rays of light and amorphous shapes that glow. You particularly glow when you are happy, feel good, feel at home. You are glowing now, even though you are tired and not particularly happy at the moment.

Immortelle, may I ask? What about people who live in one place all their lives, or people who go back to their roots where they grew up or even people who emigrate or have a sense of home in a foreign land?

We are happy you've asked. They go to the place where they're required to live, expand, evolve their consciousness. This may be done by living in a place other than where a person grew up, or they may be called to another land.

Chapter 12

Gaia: Her Kingdoms and Hierarchies

13th April 2014

Eight years have passed since I started to write the *Angels'* book. I remember the experience of the car being bombarded by white feathers on 10th April 2006 and that same evening asking the angels what to write. They told me to go into my living room, log onto the computer and start typing. That was the start of chapter one. There was no transcribing to do. The text was there right from the start and the angels asked me not to change a single word of their messages. This request caused a few worries in my conversations with the book's editor, but she agreed to be strict with my grammar and lenient with that of the angels!

Writing this book about the deva Immortelle is not so easy. It takes time to plan the visits and pack as if preparing for a hill walk: waterproofs, boots, gaiters against the ticks, balaclava, scarf, waterproof mat, notepads and pens, thermos and sandwiches. Then I must walk uphill through the woods and bog, clamber down a steep bank through juniper bushes by clinging to clumps of heather, find a crossing point on iced or mossy rocks, and finally locate a place to sit or kneel near the water from which the deva's messages emanate.

I arrive at the pool mid-afternoon on this April day after a slow journey and then circling the whole of Culloden Moor looking for a place to stay the night. The angle of the sun strikes the lower pool at the edge where the water exits, the sound of the water merrily churning over a small rockslide. In my right ear I pick up the roar of the waterfall entering the upper pool a few metres away. Leaving the upper pool, the water descends through a rocky channel before dropping down the second waterfall into the lower pool. Standing beside the lower pool and looking up into this rocky channel from below, I can see all the way through, as if looking through a telescope, towards the white chutes of the upper waterfall in the distance. It is perfectly framed in my centre of vision.

Across the pool, the sparkling sunlit bubbles are drawn towards the exit. They pop as I try to capture the image reflected in them with my camera. One of them floats tantalisingly close and as I press the trigger I see again the ancient face of the spirit of the pool. I think I've captured him on camera. The bubble is balanced on his nose as if he's performing a trick for me. I have no fear of him. My angels have told me that I'm protected here, as my connection with this watercourse and its deva is strong. Had I arrived here earlier the sun would have been shining full over the length of the waterfalls, illuminating the entire amber basin of the pool. But now only the curved shelf shines beneath the surface, whilst the centre of the pool is a deep sepia brown, with reflection of green moss and light shining over the surface.

I'm troubled about repeatedly writing these descriptions of the pool each time I come, but the angels assure me that it is necessary in order to connect with the nature spirits here before they will speak to me.

The sun is gradually edging away, throwing the pool and grassy promontory into shadow on this side of the bank. To keep warm enough to write I need to cross back to the other side and find a place in the light.

Hallelujah. We are happy you came.
We are happy to help you. Have no fear.

Dear Immortelle, are you here? Is it you?

We light. We shine. Our music is on the wind. We cause

the trees to grow, the water to flow, the moon to rise, the sun to burn, the Earth to turn. All hail, mortal one. We see you. You're shining.

Who are you? Is this Immortelle speaking?

I soon realise that this is not the voice of Immortelle, but an encounter with the elementals who look after Earth, Water, Fire and Air.

We are of God. We mean you no harm. We are the elementals connected with this watercourse.

Then I'd like to ask you: how do you have the power to make the sun burn and the Earth turn, as you have said?

We are of the Essence. We connect with your planet at this point but we are beyond. We are from the angelic realms. We are connected to cherubim. We are of God.

I keep hearing the word cherubim. I don't understand the function of the cherubim or how it relates to the devas and elementals of this place. I am totally perplexed as I don't understand what I'm writing.

The same power that drives the sun, that turns the Earth, that flows through the wind, the water, that grows the tree, that breaks the rock, that grows the crystal, that powers all things... is lovingly taken care of by the elementals and guided by the devas.
The elementals and devas are also of God - as you are - and they are governed by the cherubim of God. You have connected with cherubim.

I am afraid in my mind, though I feel peaceful in my heart.

There is no need for fear. We are guiding you. We reassure you that this book can be written.

Where is Immortelle?

> Immortelle is translating the messages for you. She's downloading them in a way you'll understand.
> She'll only give you a voltage that you can take. You could not withstand a higher energy than this.

Is the voltage like electricity?

> We say it's a form of divine electricity. It's the spark of knowledge sent to your consciousness and is turned into words.

What is my greater task? What is this book about?

> We describe the function of the angelic kingdom of the devas.
> You see how the water bubble reflects the sun and also the landscape and the tree, and you see yourself reflected there. When the bubble pops you cease to be in that moment. It's passed. You see your reflection and the reflection of your surroundings in all the other bubbles within your view. You see that in every particle of water you are reflected - in every particle within your vision.
> We say that you are of the stars and carry light. That light is in your heart and shines in your soul. Your eyes are like the camera lens. They capture a moment of reality. Those who would look into your eyes would see themselves reflected there and they'd see beyond to your soul.
> We remind you that it's your brain which believes your eyes and makes up many 'stills' of your world. You believe this to be real because you can feel it.

However, it's all remembered. It's all memory. The water is never still. It's a living, flowing force of Nature and your brain has encapsulated it into a thing.
And so with the grass, the plants and the trees... they are constantly growing, though rooted in one place.

What about when the water freezes? Then it's so solid, it's not moving and can be walked on.

In this case, the water has changed form and become crystalised. However, the crystals are moving and growing or retracting and melting as the temperature changes. And all is governed by the sun, and the sun, your sun of your galaxy, is part of a greater rhythm. It's a fireball. It's burning up.

What happens when the sun dies?

Another sun is born from the debris. We are telling you that all is connected. The devas govern us - the elementals who care diligently for each plant and each organism.

There was a pause and the voice changed.

Who is speaking now?

Immortelle at your service!

Dear Immortelle, I was told that you were downloading information from cherubim in a way that I can understand.

Yes, child. As you see there are greater powers than human, there are greater powers than devas.

So, you too are downloading information from the greater powers of cherubim in the same way I download information from angels and from you, with the help of my angel Ariel?

May I ask why don't you download through angels too? I have often seen diagrams to explain the connections between God, man and angels and they explain it in a hierarchical form, thus:

God
Seraphim
Cherubim
Thrones
Dominions
Virtues
Powers
Principalities
Archangels
Angels— — —Man
Elementals

These diagrams show God at the top of the tree, and the elementals at the bottom with the angels and archangels in ascending order. Where are humans in relation to all this?

She gives me another diagram telepathically.

God   *Pan*
Gaia
Seraphim
Cherubim   *Devas Elementals*
Thrones
Dominions
Virtues
Powers
Principalities
Archangels
Angels   *Human*

> As we have explained to you before, we are of a different branch of God's kingdom than angels. Angels are guardians of humans. We are guardians of your planet. We connect with cherubim as you connect with angels. We are a form of angels, dear one. We are plant angels and rock angels as we've said and we have to remind you we are as powerful as any angels of God and we are more ancient than all. We came from a place before your universe was born. We are connecting with you because it's our mission to make it known to humans that you must co-operate and help save the Earth.
> If this Earth dies then the entire universe is thrown out of balance.
> Humans are only visitors here yet have had the audacity to destroy the very life they depend on.

Why are we humans even tolerated here if you are so powerful you could snuff us out and thus prevent the carnage we're causing?

> You're on your last chance. It's God's will that humans will grow up to be as angels and come to Light, and peace will reign on your planet - on our planet. We love you.

I think about the deva's words for a moment, wondering how peace can ever come to our world when wars, violence and persecution continue, some of it in the name of religion or from a belief in a God not of love. How can we humans ever grow up and be as angels? A question forms in my mind:

I need to ask you directly, why is it that some people like me abhor and don't understand violence and cruelty and other people commit acts of violence. Is it our karma at work?

> You cannot hate anything when in alignment with God's power.

I recognise the presence of my angel Amber telling me to rest, so I climb up the bank above the shadowed pool to find a place in the sun from where I can see over the tops of the trees to the blue firth. I sit with my back against a rock facing the sun. There's an icy chill in the air when the sun goes behind a cloud.

I admit that I hate the biting midges. I hate the sensation. On the way to Immortelle's waterfall earlier today I saw an official sign on a gate with a warning and detailed information about ticks and how to guard against being bitten. I don't regard ticks as lovable creatures but respect that they have a purpose here.

Do ticks, midges, flies, beetles and all insects have a guardian or angel equivalent watching over them? Do I attract bad karma by killing them? Or do they attract bad karma through biting me? Is this a silly question?

> *Midges, ticks, beetles are all of the animal kingdom and a vital part of the plant kingdom also. Ticks are parasites and weaken their host by injecting poison. This ensures that the weak do not survive, leaving room for the fittest animals to proliferate.*

What of smaller forms such as amoeba and fungi?

Dear Immortelle, I have many questions arising such as, do small life forms have angels too? What sort of angels look after animals? When is it wrong or cruel for humans to kill animals and kill our environment? Is it cruel when an animal kills another animal, bird, fish, worm, insect, or when a cat kills a bird? Is a human seen as a predator in the animal kingdom? Where does hate come into the equation? You couldn't say a cat hates a bird?

> *Hate is a word that evolved with human consciousness to*

> describe the response to strong prejudice.
> Only humans have free will. However, the dog or cat has a brain and a will but its will is not free. So its angel is there guiding, but the animal is living in the present where it is influenced from some memories, but it doesn't consciously plan its future.
> All animals are under Pan. The nature spirits, including elementals are also under Pan. Pan is operating from Source, from God.

I asked if all life - snails, bugs, beetles, flies, midges, ticks or amoeba - had some form of guardian angel.

> We hear your question. We explain that all creatures that breathe have a Light body. This Light body is cared for by an elemental.

Can I go back to asking about the amoeba? Does its Light body guide it as the dog angel guides the dog?

> No, the amoeba and early animal/plant life forms are collectively looked after by the elementals.
> You may call them fairies.

So fairies look after amoeba, early plant forms and insects collectively?

> Yes.

I'm thinking of the Ten Commandments taught by Jesus as recorded in the Christian Bible. There may be equivalent laws in other religious texts, but one of the Ten Commandments is 'Thou shalt not kill'. I would imagine this refers to killing other humans. Where does killing become immoral? Is it wrong to kill a dog or horse for food? Is it wrong to kill an amoeba or squash a tick?

> *People say that 'Nature is cruel'. Does a mouse feel pain? Does the tick I just crushed on this page feel pain?*

Humankind has been given dominion over animals and over the Earth. There will come the time when many more of you become vegetarian.

You experience the dog's Light body as being like an angel because you are not a dog and cannot experience it from the aspect of being a dog. So when people have come to you to help call home their lost pets, it is through the angels of the people concerned that the animals have been rescued. Their angels connected with the animals' angels or Light bodies - be it dog, cat or bird.

Angel Chamuel connects with lost animals. Gabriel connects with all mothers, including animal mothers.

Animals that connect with you humans, especially pets such as dogs and cats, can perceive your angels. They also see when in spirit and can teleport to be with their owner.

Animals that have been domesticated - cows, pigs and many farm animals - are sensitive to angels. Cows are most sensitive to angelic presence. It's why many people stop eating meat. It's why bovine disease has proliferated - because of the disrespect and abuse of humans towards these animals.

What about wild animals - wild boar, deer, horses and fish that we eat?

They're under Pan. They are not concerned with humans and their divine connection. They're under their own divine connections that link with Pan.

So the elementals that look after the plants are also caring for the insects that feed on the plants?

All creatures, including humans, that have souls and consciousness, have a Light body in the etheric. These Light bodies depend on survival from Source, from God. All creatures that have a brain have a guardian in the etheric. Only humans have free will.

At this point I begin to think of the young farm collie pup that had followed me up the path on the way here today. I told him to "Go home" and he seemed to understand and ran back to his master driving the tractor in the field.

So you say that a dog has an angel in the etheric then?

He has a soul, a consciousness, but does not think in the way a human thinks and has no free will.

~

We sing! We laugh! We uphold the eternal vibration of the spheres. All is in perfect harmony. All is well.

This message of the elementals enters my mind and I hear the sound of the harp, both gut stringed and metal stringed. It echoes through the sound of the water and wind over the moor.

Sunlight fills the pool and turns it to amber and gold. The bubbles slip over the rocks in a downward staircase over mossy banks. Soon this water will join the River Nairn and flow out to the sea, to the firth of dolphins, and transform again into vapour, into clouds and rain. What I heard next was Immortelle's voice. So I asked:

How far do the vapour and clouds travel, Immortelle? Does the same water drop arrive back in the original stream it left? How long does the process take?

The journey is never ending - the clouds travel halfway across the Earth, then release the droplets that soak the soil, filter to the streams and flow to sea.

Immortelle, I wonder if our favourite places, which look the same, year on year, are carrying droplets that could have originated from the Arctic, the American continent or from the East.

Yes, that is correct. The physical shape of the land creates the shape of the watercourse but the water is multicultural.

I never really thought of it that way before.

It's the deva of a place that gives it its essence. That is our raison d'etre. We bring together and harmonise all elements to create a vibration. You are attracted to a particular vibration. As we said before, people are at home at the place they grew up, or they go back to their roots, or they may put down new roots in another place so as to evolve their consciousness - or they may hold memories of past lives.

If everything gets so mixed up, with our streams coming from water from across the globe, movements of animals and people across continents, then doesn't everything lose its identity?

The identity of a place on Earth is created by the devas and elementals that govern the region. Full stop.

I can hardly imagine this but without the devas and elementals, would the place appear just as a picture that carries no particular feeling - a 'dead' scene?

Yes, without us, there is no life.

Are photographs, calendar pictures, film recordings of places 'dead' or do they carry something of the original place? What if the photographer has enhanced the image? What of manufactured computer images of landscapes, film sets for instance that switch between landscapes in Scotland and New Zealand?

> If a person has a connection with a particular kind of place or if it's a particular place, a spot on the ground that has been captured or photographed in a movie, he or she will pick up on the essence of the place. It is not as powerful, of course, as being there in person, but through the skill of the photographer or artist who connects to the place in person, the image is transferred and carries the spirit of the place to the degree that the photographer/artist has been able to carry it.
> You, child, are a carrier. In your paintings you seek to catch the essence.

Yes, it's what I was trying to do all those years ago when painting here on the moor. I always felt that I fell short of achieving this. I felt constrained by the size of the paper on which I needed to convey the vastness of the landscape. Putting a 360-degree view on 2D paper is a perpetual challenge.

During the spoken part of the art college final degree exam, one tutor commented that my small landscape images of the moor transferred a sense of joy. Others commented that the large paintings I had made by laying the paper on the ground carried the joy.

I couldn't understand how someone else looking at that landscape of a bleak grouse moor with electricity pylons had managed to see through the image to what I saw and felt when I painted it.

You painted from experience. You painted from life.
You can always tell a painting that's been done from life, painted outside, n'est-ce pas?

Yes, I can tell. As an art teacher I can tell if my students have worked from life or copied from a 2D image. They're different skills.

Working outdoors you have to edit the sensation into colour, shape, line, form. You're not simply copying. There's too much. And it's all moving and changing. To paint a moving subject would be impossible. Even if the lake is frozen, the light changes and the colours change. On the moor the wind blows the grasses and each plant has a million components. We have to edit the image.

The person who copies has to be true to the marks the original artist made. So they are learning how to edit and make marks. It's more of a dry technical skill, whereas the artist who is working from nature is recording and translating.

I wanted to ask you - where you have a professional copyist for example, someone who forges an original master painting - what is the difference in terms of essence? Does the forger or copyist pick up on the essence of the original?

The forgery is a lookalike. Depending on the skill of the artist who copies he or she may be able to pick up on the character of the sitter if copying a portrait.

And if a film has parts that are mixed from different locations or computer generated, how beautiful can they be?

As beautiful as the degree to which the artist is connected to Source.

This leads me to consider how to navigate between the times when we feel the inspiration coming from Source and the times when we don't.

What about the days when I'm not really engaged in my life, when I'm simply going through the motions? What of these days when things seem an effort and I feel despondent?

Yes. It is the function of your angel, child - to guide you back to your true form, to your joy. Always follow the joy.

Is this why I am here now writing this book sitting with the sun on my face and hearing the water?

Yes. You were called here - even to the point where the weather has allowed you to be outdoors. Your angel Ariel guided you and your devas were calling you.
We urgently need your perseverance to write this book. Do not denigrate it as being unimportant. Your housework will always be there for you. There'll always be other things to do. We require that you prioritise this.

I am privileged. I'm also daunted. How will this book help with Earth's healing?

You tell our story in your own words. It's coming from your direct experience of being in Light. It comes from *true connection, love and devotion. Yes, we know you'd love to walk on the shore at Rosemarkie and to walk free in the sun and visit other places of devas. We are happy you stayed here.*

That reminds me of something else I wanted to ask. It's about the extent of your region. Before, you said it extended downstream to where the River Nairn enters the sea. You said there were other devas upstream. Do these govern the other tributaries and the land they flow through? There are much more spectacular waterfalls on the hills above Barevan, a little further downstream. Are there other devas governing these falls?

No the waterfalls in the hills above Barevan are also my domain.

I wait for the implication to hit home. Is Immortelle saying that she's the main mountain deva governing all the waterfalls of every tributary from here and downstream?

YES!
Child, we need to explain to you this way. You are often asked if particular angels such as Archangel Michael make themselves known to many people as that angels' omnipresence, or whether there are millions of Archangel Michaels?
We explain to you that your angels are like drops of water from one sea, composed of the same essence.
Angels are like one water, water from Source that carries true spirit.

Thank you, Immortelle.

I'm still finding it hard to believe that the deva Immortelle oversees other waterfalls as well as the small ones here. I have such a sense of belonging here and although the other waterfalls are far bigger and more spectacular, I don't feel the same sense of belonging at those places. Perhaps we're all connecting with the elementals in the places we love, just as Immortelle described.

The sun has moved on and is beating down on the bank where I'm sitting, the warmth striking through my clothes and burning my face and arms. The waterfalls and pools are in shadow below the banks, black and deep. Contrasting with the dark, reflections of sky and clouds pass across the surface of the water. I move back into the moment and become aware of my physical body. I thank the angels and Immortelle for speaking.

Until next time! The thought comes that, like the water, I'll transform one day and return, perhaps in another place, in another form, in another body and in another time frame. For once, this thought is strangely reassuring.

Part Three

Be Still and Listen

When I've had a long day out in the hills I've noticed that after a few hours I can finally tune out of my thoughts, step out of my ego and fears, and become at one and at peace within my surroundings. Normally, without these forays into Nature's peaceful places, it's harder to still my mind's endless chatter.

We humans are given such a gift of life and yet we seem to forget. Or through circumstances we move into heaviness and fear. We forget how to trust and how to be joyful like a child, despite all the beauty and love around us. I speak for myself, though.

(Chapter 13: Page 138)

Immortelle:
Our raison d'être is joy. Life runs on this power and this power is within you. Do not be distressed by the thoughts of your mind tuned to the dark happenings of the world. Keep turning to the Light as a tree grows always to the Light.

You have good reason to feel optimistic, child. Happiness is also your raison d'etre and you must now choose happiness. Happiness and gratitude are the only qualities that can transcend and transform the dark as your angels constantly tell you.

(Chapter 18: Pages 170 & 169)

Chapter 13

Rosemarkie and the Fairy Glen: A Question from the Sìthichean

14th April 2014

I have been staying near Cawdor, a place known for its castle, set within lovely woodlands, that has remained within the same family lineage for generations. From my room at the front of the house I can see the Moray Firth gleaming in the distance. Beyond the ancient church I can see the shape of a hill covered in trees, where the remains of a Roman fort lie, built perhaps on the site of an old Pictish fortress.

In the 1980s, the same friend who had first introduced me to Immortelle's moor drove us here in his orange Volkswagen Beetle. We parked by the church, walked beyond the walled enclosure along a path between fields and crossed the River Nairn when we came to stepping-stones. We wound our way through the woods on an old path, then climbed the hill to its stony top. The view of the Moray Firth from there was stunning.

I've tried to go back there a few times in recent years but have been unable to navigate my way from the church as the path is overgrown. Nor could I find the place to cross the river, though I searched in vain for the stepping-stones I'd remembered. I ended up having to balance on slippery boulders and wade through the river. On reaching the foot of the rocky hill it was impossible to fight through thorn trees. I still have blood stains on my map from the cuts made by thorns as I attempted to reach the top of the hill.

It seems there is no longer a path to the summit. I asked

the owners of the house in which I've been staying about this, but as they had only recently moved to the area from the south they knew nothing about the history of the fort hidden in the trees.

Last night when I looked out of the window there was incredible light spread like a mantle over the fields and woods. It was so bright that I thought the house had exterior flood lighting. The light cast into the house was soft and magical while a huge moon shone through a south-facing window. I've never forgotten the intensity of that moonlight. Perhaps because there were no streetlights the luminosity of the moon appeared extraordinary.

Back in my room I could see far beyond the lit up garden and distant woods and fields to the lights of villages and isolated farms twinkling all along the Moray Firth. I could see the radio mast with its vertical line of red lights on the hill near Rosemarkie on the Black Isle, on the opposite side of the firth. As my eyes became accustomed to the darkness, I could just make out the black shape of Ben Wyvis on the skyline.

I decide to leave early in the morning and drive via Inverness over the bridge to the Black Isle and visit Rosemarkie, before returning to Stirling. Rosemarkie is a traditional small seaside village where to this day, local people from Inverness and its surrounds take their children on summer holidays. The orange-coloured beach is full of fossils from the old red sandstone sea cliffs. The neighbouring village of Fortrose, with its ancient ruined abbey, was once a busy fishing port. It's said that people could cross the harbour from one side to the other simply by stepping from the deck of one boat to the next. On the edge of the Black Isle peninsula, a little further along the coast, lies the old medieval town of Cromarty. It is situated at another strategic point where the two Sutors, names of the sea cliffs to the north and south, form a narrow gateway into the deep long channel of the Cromarty Firth on the north side of the Black Isle.

In World War II this area, including the small village of Nigg to the north, was an important naval base. The docks were later expanded and developed for the oil industry in the 1970s. Recently, it has become a base for refining crude oil as well as developing renewable energy, and it is also used as a port for the largest of the modern cruise liners stopping off to bring visitors to the Highlands. This is possible because of the depth of the harbour.

Nearing the time of this book's publication after COP26 (UN Climate Change Conference) in November 2021, the funding has been granted for the multi-million dollars development of a giant factory here in order to build the largest state-of-the-art wind towers to support 18 megawatt capacity nacelles. The offshore factory will boost Scotland's contribution to renewable energy. Further funding is to become available for a second tower factory and floating steel platforms which require hundreds of metres of extension of the harbour and deepwater quayside developments.*

Ancient Pictish history still feels part of the landscape around here. The extraordinary and beautifully carved cross slab stones once situated on the cliffs are now housed in the churches of the small villages of Nigg and Shandwick. More of these crosses are also found in small museums at Hilton of Cadboll and the old early Christian monastery site of Port Mahomack.

At a place called Chanonry Point, half-way between Rosemarkie and Fortrose, a peninsula of land points like a finger towards a similar peninsula on the Inverness side. These peninsulas create a narrow channel between the outer and inner Moray Firth. Old maps show this was a ferry crossing point. To the west of this gateway between the two peninsulas is the inner Moray Firth basin.

The inner Moray Firth is still a haven for dolphins, despite its proximity to the recent oil industry at Cromarty and the dangers for all marine creatures ingesting plastic washed in from the North Sea. Meanwhile, the area of Rosemarkie and neighbouring Fortrose has attracted visitors for dolphin watching, which is putting huge pressure on the local area in terms of the influx of cars and motorhomes and subsequent lack of parking spaces for residents.

One positive aspect is that a new kind of relationship between humans and dolphins is developing. The local bottle-nose dolphins and other large sea mammals, such as harbour porpoises and mink whales, are so well observed that much scientific data is being collected in order to understand them better.

From Rosemarkie Beach the Fairy Glen goes up into the hill. Robert Ogilvie Crombie, who was involved in the Findhorn community in the 1960s, described in his memoirs his encounter with the fairies here when he re-discovered the place. The Fairy Glen has also attracted considerable attention in the last few years. There are two waterfalls and two pools here that are much bigger than those on Clava Moor.

I feel excited to be here again in such a special place and make my way from the beach to the path that follows the stream up into the Fairy Glen. Feeling a strange mixture of gratitude and reverence, I walk quietly through the woods by the waterside, taking in everything, including the flowers and the clean pure air.

The babbling water flows down from the hill until it reaches the sea at Rosemarkie Beach. Overhead, the canopy of green trees is reflected in the water. I continue upstream until I reach the top waterfall and then, as no one is about, I climb beyond the top of this waterfall and find a quiet place to tune in. The energy here is palpable.

I ask for connection with the devas of the Fairy Glen through my angel Ariel.

> Awakened one, we greet you. Your consciousness has opened to us and we reach you at this place. All is of

God. At the eleventh hour, Earth ascends. In these times we manifest Light and hope to many. Tell them our true story. The children need you and we need them for the glorious future. We are all around you now. This is our retreat. We are here when the cars have gone. We're here forever.

Do not fear writing our book. We shall see that no harm comes to you, and success is imminent. Be at peace now. Follow! It is made easy.

Thank you. Who spoke to me there?

Moziel.

Thank you, Moziel.

    I clamber back down from the top waterfall of the Fairy Glen. I feel that the fairies and nature spirits have retreated up above this waterfall, and in the small glade with the old rowan tree I was in no doubt of their presence. Since childhood I have always believed that rowan and hawthorn trees are beloved of fairies.

    I make my way quietly and with great reverence back through the glen and down to the beach, a place I love. Here I walk along the shore as far as the caves and back, only stopping to explore another rocky gorge, from where I can see a waterfall in the distance. The banks are steep, almost impenetrable, mossy and slippery, and many dead trees have fallen in. I feel that I am disturbing the peace of the nature spirits by sliding about on the bank in my trainers. Not wanting to fall, I turn back. Then I hear the words clearly:

Why is your heart so heavy?

    I don't know who is speaking but I feel it's a fairy

presence. I have a sense that this communication comes from one of the Sìthichean, or perhaps even one of the fairy race known in Scotland as the People of Peace.

I am sorry for my heavy heart, I say out loud.

There are no more words. The question to me had been simple yet resonates deeply and challenges me. As I walk back along the beach, I become more aware of my physical senses. I notice how the heaviness in my body and heart seems to mirror the weight of thoughts in my mind. When I've had a long day out in the hills I've noticed that after a few hours I can finally tune out of my thoughts, step out of my ego and fears, and become at one and at peace within my surroundings. Normally, without these forays into nature's peaceful places, it's harder to still my mind's endless chatter.

We humans are given such a gift of life and yet we seem to forget. Or through circumstances we move into heaviness and fear. We forget how to trust and how to be joyful like a child, despite all the beauty and love around us. I speak for myself, though.

Back at the car park at the sea front I notice a family walking towards the beach. A young girl runs over the grass and cartwheels ahead of her parents. As she stands up and waits for them, I can see her aura shining. The only way I can explain it is to say that she stands out. The other members of the family also have auras but theirs aren't shining like hers. I know instinctively she is an enlightened soul and wonder where she has been and where she will go in her life.

I have seen children like these in the school where I taught… children whose light actually shines brightly around them. Sometimes, they would linger at the door thanking me for the lesson, not wanting to leave the relative peace of the classroom. There was recognition between us. I wanted to help them further, but talking about spiritual things was beyond the remit of the art lesson I was there to teach.

I start thinking of my sons and their generation of young people and the gifts they have come here to bring. A sense of wonderment comes over me as I begin the drive home.

Chapter 14

Messages From the Water Elementals of Clava

22nd July 2014

I don't make it back to the pools to write more of the deva's book until a boiling hot day in July. I've been on a trip to Lewis to visit my hillwalking friend. The weather is exceptional. On my return, after staying the night at her cottage at Burghead, I detour by the Findhorn Community Park to drop off more *Angel* books at the Foundation shop.

As I drive back by way of Cawdor to Clava the landscape shimmers in full summer haze: gold barley fields and green of woods, and the old fort near Barevan with its hill now impossible to climb because of the impenetrable thorn trees. It feels as if the nature spirits have barricaded themselves there and are not friendly to any human who tries to enter their realm. Beyond the edge of the coast a sea haar, the local Scottish sea mist, is building up and rolling in.

At the pool… and on the grassy promontory, a flying beetle lands on my arm and stings hard. I brush it off, drop my manuscript on the grass, slip down to the edge of the water and splash ice coldness over the pain. A small pimple of poison emerges in front of my eyes. So I move further into the sun away from the midges, among the bracken where tormentil shines in the long grass.

I call to my angels to help me write. It's not easy writing and waving off flies at the same time. But it feels right to be here by the water, enclosed in a magic circle of greens from the overhanging birches and the mossy banks that enclose the amber pool. The water is much reduced, the pool two thirds of its usual size, the mossy banks exposed. The exit is a narrow stream, easy to jump over. The waterfall enters at one side of its rocky chute and is only a fraction of its normal size. It slaps onto a small step before entering the pool from which the outflow water churns down rocks towards the woods below.

No bubbles flow across the pool, though the surface ripples flicker with lime-green and deep green-brown reflections. Amber lights shine from below where the sun strikes through, catching the rocky walls.

The shelf looks different. Hairy dull-green moss grows out from the curved lip and waves beneath the surface. One purple foxglove petal bobs by the edge where it's stuck in an eddy. The curve of the birch tree trunk above flickers with reflected light from the pool, its branches of green leaves lit with sunlight. The sky is too bright to look into.

I feel surrounded by the benevolent presence of the moor, the circle of trees, the gorge, the grass and scent of bracken, like tobacco. Although I'm bitten and annoyed by flies, I feel peaceful.

> We're happy you're here again. We've called you. We've much knowledge to impart. We've heard your questions and delight to answer.
> Yes, we wish that you record these descriptions of this area, this valley, moor and aspect. Yes, we wish you to speak of your connection with this place, past and present. For how else can you convey your love of us and the beauty of Earth?
> We do not give you dry knowledge in the form of facts, tables and graphs in the way a scientist displays his work. We cannot separate ourselves. You seek to measure matter, which is… immeasurable. You seek to count the uncountable. Mathematics is not science. It is a language that seeks not to measure but to express the beauty of the universe, which expands.

I try to catch what the water elementals are describing.

Be at peace. We are helping you. You connect with us here, yes. Believe us. We are here. We are not your angel, Ariel. We speak through Ariel. Ariel safeguards you.

Will we destroy Earth? Even since I started writing this book there's been much destruction. Some years ago, the angels asked my healer friend and me to walk the path of the pylon line between Beauly and Dalwhinnie and to pray for the devas. It wasn't a practical action but we wished to pray for the nature spirits that had been displaced from these wild areas.

Now, the forests of giant pylons are there. Great swathes of land have disappeared under access roads, scarring the landscape. More have been designated to be built in these magical and special places, cutting through wilderness - the last wilderness areas of Scotland. In particular the Monadhliath has been affected. This is the great wilderness area from which Immortelle's tributaries emanate, and also those of the rivers Findhorn, Ness, Dulnain, and Farigaig that run down to Loch Ness. It feels as if nowhere is sacred. Is nowhere safe for the devas and nature spirits? The most wild and hidden places are under threat.

From the tops of the Scottish mountains wind turbines can now be seen everywhere. They've sprung up in the last few years. Ecologists and conservationists place their arguments on both sides of the equation and it's all very confusing with the green energy industry growing because of the targets promised by politicians.

Meanwhile, many landowners have become gratuitously rich, and pollution of water by chemicals seems to be a growing threat whichever energy system we are to use. Sorry for my rant, and I am not against green energy which we need, but against the manner in which it is implemented. It grieves my heart to see this destruction happen to fragile and beautiful places during my lifetime.

You must hate us for the atrocities we commit to Earth?

What do you have to say?

> We are devas of God. We do not hate. Hate does not exist for us, only love. When our physical counterparts that make up the body of Earth are poisoned and destroyed, we must retract and move from your consciousness. We go elsewhere. This leaves you bereft. It leaves Earth depleted.
>
> We need humans to love Earth and connect with us, work with us. Then we can return. There is hope. It's why you're called here. Others are also working diligently to find a way forward.
>
> There is a missing link. This link is your link with God, and your connection with us in your consciousness.
>
> Humans have separated God from Earth, have debased nature worshippers, have plundered the goods of Earth without appreciation or acknowledgement of Source. Divine Source! For the Earth and all its material aspect is of God. We are of God.
>
> Would you eat excrement? Would you give a child dirt to eat? Humans are destroying the very life force that is necessary for their own survival.

What can I do to help? What is the message you wish me to write?

As I look up from the page where I've been writing, a light show of green catches my eye. The moss of the further bank is lit up and shines, casting its reflection in the water. Light dances across the page where I write. All my senses seem heightened and a scent of flower perfume catches on the breeze.

I know that the devas want me to write about our connection with Earth and to explain that everything natural is divine, is alive, has an energy field and is in connection with Source. Even the biting midge, even the grain of sand, the amoeba in the pool and the places beneath Earth that are never seen by humans are of God. Somehow, I've come back to this place at this time to pick up on my connection point with the deva of this area.

Thank you.

> We're happy you came here.

Chapter 15

The River Elementals of the Upper Findhorn

July 2014

Sometimes my angels prompt me to do something that isn't on my plan. When I trust and follow the guidance I often realise the significance of it afterwards.

I had stopped at Alvie campsite in the Cairngorms and slept in my tent, with the intention of returning to the pools the next day and taking down more messages. I packed my tent up again in the morning as I planned to stay at the campsite at Moy for the following two nights.

While on my way back up the A9, the angels direct me to turn off at Tomatin and to take the road to Coignafearn which runs through Strathdearn. Strathdearn runs parallel to Strathnairn, and in between them lies a band of outlying mountains of the Monadhliath. The River Findhorn runs down from the Monadhliath at Coignafearn, through the strath, where it crosses the A9 at Tomatin and then flows northeast towards the Moray Firth at Findhorn. The proposal is to build a massive energy substation by the river in Strathdearn to meet the electricity demands of the new power structures in the area.

I pull in off the road to read a large notice board:

"SAVE STRATHDEARN. You are standing at Garbole, where a huge electricity substation is planned with a network of power-lines throughout the glen and across the surrounding hills. The landscape is industrialised and the wildlife put at risk.

THIS IS THE WRONG PLACE FOR SUCH DEVELOPMENT.

PLEASE HELP STOP THE DESTRUCTION OF THIS SPECIAL GLEN AND THE WILDLIFE IT SUPPORTS. Take a leaflet. Take action. HELP SAVE STRATHDEAN." Websites were given at the foot of the notice board.

I park further on and make my way down to the wide river and, sitting in the sunlight, I feel a great peace. I had become aware of the devas of the Findhorn River before now, at a place of exquisite beauty called Randolph's Leap, but here the Findhorn is in its upper reaches where the streams flow down from the mountains.

It's a wild landscape and I'm wondering how the vibration of concrete, metal and electricity will impact here.

The riverbed is full of glittering light and bubbles, churning and chattering over its stones. Looking upstream and to my right, the hills are clad in natural trees. I feel their presence as they dance with light and flow with energy. To my left, the hills are covered with forestry plantation and the feel is sterile as if the energy is blocked.

Dear devas of the Findhorn River, I come here with love in my heart and at the request of my angels and Ariel my guardian. Do I have connection with you?

Behold! We are of Source and we greet you. For all is of God and all is sacred. We are of essence. The water here carries the essence of the mountain and wind and rock and soil, all elements in balance, contained within our droplets. Nature has consciousness. Here the rocks are most ancient. We connect with past and present and we are infinite.

Dear water spirits and devas, does time go backwards into infinity and forwards into infinity?

Yes of course!

Does it meet?

You are one point connecting with us at one point. One point of connection here, now, but your soul is immortal and we are infinite. And yet, humans have been given a brain and a memory and use it to destroy us. Evil is planned.

Can this be stopped?

Yes, if not by humans, then Earth will self-destruct.

Please help us!

You were called today and we wish you to return over the hill to Daviot so you shall see the confluence of the Findhorn and the Nairn - both are sacred - where the wilderness meets humans' cities.

Thank you.

I drive over the hill on the twisty single-track roads to

the area above the village of Farr. The raw natural beauty here grabs my heart, and memories come back of cycling in this area years ago. This is a place of wild moorland with many small lochs and stunning views. The River Farigaig runs westwards from the Monadhliath, crosses this area and drops down steeply to Loch Ness north of Foyers. The Rivers Dulnain and Nairn flow in parallel to the Findhorn in a north-easterly direction to the Moray Firth coast. The largest body of water in the area is Loch Duntelchaig, which along with Loch Ashie and its smaller connected Loch a' Chlachain form the water supply for Inverness and connect with the River Nairn. Some of these lochs are also protected sites and form habitats for rare breeding birds.

I'm already in shock after seeing the signs in Strathdearn about the proposed substation by the river where the elementals spoke to me. As I come over the rise the white blades of a huge wind farm come into view on my right. I don't realise, at this time, that it has been built as one of Scotland's new flagship wind farms.

Finding a place to park near the small lochan of Farr, I walk back up the road. It's intensely hot and bubbles of tar are melting. The verges are full of flowers, but as I reach the edge of the wind farm area I see that a whole swathe of land has been gouged out. There is an unnerving vibration which makes me feel queasy and I have a sense of not being welcome. After a time I take some photographs of the metal corridor that cuts through the beautiful scenery and down to Inverness and then head back to my car. The song, *Where Have All The Flowers Gone?** by Pete Seeger, often sung by my mother, comes softly to my mind.

As I walk back down the road I feel a strong presence walking beside me on my left. It's invisible yet vividly present. At first I think it's one of my angels, or simply a feeling of my higher self but neither of these seem right.

I recognise Immortelle! She has shape shifted and now

walks beside me like a light and shining presence. I don't know why she is accompanying me. This is also her realm, where the rivers Findhorn, Nairn and Dulnain flow down from the Monadhliath mountains and over the moor near Inverness. Here at this place of confluence the scenery is being gouged out. So Immortelle's region is being destroyed! I do not know, at this point, that another large wind farm is being built in the mountains at Càrn Ghriogair, the source of the rivers Nairn and Farigaig.

I stop by the loch and watch a family in a rowing boat swimming from the boat and shouting loudly to each other amid shrieks on encountering the cold water. I don't want to intrude. Surrounding the loch the area is filled with rhododendron bushes, a beautiful yet invasive species in Scotland that is gradually taking over the natural flora.

By the time I reach Clava it is late and I don't have much time to communicate with the devas there as I need to get to the campsite at Moy, to pitch my tent before dark.

Dear Immortelle, I am here under the guidance of my angels and Ariel. I ask for connection. Am I too late? I feel that I've delayed coming here though I've been taking in much information. I'm here at last but I only have an hour or two.

We are aware of these dark feelings, child, and the heaviness of your mortal body. We surround you. We love you.

The book shall flow like the river - it is fully time to write. We heal you. You feel your life is uncertain? One thing is certain, your path with us is true. Follow. Follow. Follow.

Spumes of bubbles explode on the surface of the small pool into which the lower pool flows. The main pool is rich amber and covered in shining bubbles. Some reflect sunlight.

I can't write more at this point. The midges are biting my eyelids and stinging my arms. When I brush them off my face, their black bodies cling to my hands. I put my manuscript and pen in my rucksack and climb back up the bank, then follow upstream to a heathery cliff overlooking the stream.

I feel the presence of Immortelle again. She oversees this burn from its source and down to the pools and falls, and away through the woods, carving through rocks, joining the main river near the Clava Viaduct and thence through woods and fields to the sea town of Nairn.

I pack and make my way to the campsite where I spend an uncomfortable night. It is normally peaceful and pleasant - one of my favourite campsites - but there has been a flood and the kindly owner has allowed people with tents to pack in along a verge beside motorhomes. The next-door neighbours pitch very close to me, and their children and dogs keep nosing into the meal I am cooking on my camping stove. On the other side, the neighbours talk long into the night, while their dogs bark. In the morning I rise early to get away.

I can't face braving the midges at the pools so I drive thirty miles south to Glen Feshie in the Cairngorms to walk up to Càrn Bàn Mòr and the peak of Sgòr Gaoith (The Peak of the Wind), overlooking dramatic cliffs and the remote Loch Einich.

I have a stomach pain through having lain awake half the night and not having eaten a proper breakfast. I think of turning back several times but somehow keep going. I have my flask of tea and digestive biscuits in a small tin, and the salt and sugar in these seem calming on my stomach.

Soon, I am walking along the rocky edge of Sgòr Gaoith summit. The mountain is really living up to its name today. A wind rises, making it difficult to hang around the precipices, so I head down.

On my way back, not trusting my instinct of stopping to check the map, I follow a group of people circumnavigating the wrong way round the lower hill of Meall Tionail (Hill of the Gathering or Assembly). It is so windy that I don't want to go back up the mountain to correct the error, so the walk ends up in deep bogs and heather terrain circuiting an outlying hill, Geal Charn (White Hill).

The path ahead in the distance alongside the Allt a' Mharcaidh River (River of the Horseman or Rider) is miles off course, although in theory it would be an alternative, forming a huge circular route over rough terrain. I head for it anyway. Finally, I reach the Allt a' Mharcaidh and begin to follow it downhill, but completely in the opposite direction from my original plan.

A couple of hours later I'm still by the river that flows down to the Rothiemurchus Forest, jumping from one side to the other and squeezing past tree trunks. It's a totally wild place with huge rockslides and waterfalls, sandy bays where the river turns, and undercut banks on the opposite side. It's difficult to walk here and my legs are already shaking with tiredness. My body is crying out to lie down on the soft sand under a pine tree by the water.

Fear kicks in. "What if I never get out of here?" What if they find my car the next day and report it, or someone realises that my tent is empty? My imagination begins to create pictures of worried relatives receiving police visits. My mobile phone battery is low and the screen isn't responding to my cold fingers.

Deep down, I know I am safe. If I lay down by the water, I will be rested by morning and can continue. It's summertime after all, although it wouldn't be a good idea to lie in wet clothes. I clearly experience the energy of fear raising its head like an ugly dark spectre. On the other hand, I can feel my soul and all the love of angels around me. What to choose? Risk being out overnight, or push on?

Immortelle! Where are you? Surely you won't let me be swept away over the rocks of the waterfalls here, but then you don't belong here. This is a tributary of the River Feshie! Maybe the deva of this river is not as friendly!

 I can hear my angels telling me to check the map. Presently, I catch sight of a bridge ahead. With tremendous relief, and almost in tears, I head for it, climb onto it and sit down to rest. I get out my map. What I haven't realised is that the track coming down to the bridge is on the edge of my map. Unknown to me, as I have been walking beside and through the wild river, there has been a track only a few metres away up the bank all the while.

 I now set my compass and walk along forest tracks in an easterly direction until I come to the road by the Gliding Club, a familiar landmark on the road to Achlean. I have a few miles to walk back to my car, but a kindly man gives me a lift and points out on the map where I went wrong. I don't feel embarrassed, only relieved, but am concerned that I have soaked the seat of his car with a puddle of river water streaming out of my clothes.

 I head for Glenmore Lodge (Cairngorm Mountain Centre) to treat myself to something to eat, because they have rather excellent chips cooked in olive oil. I talk to the people at the desk, and they tell me that if I had phoned them they would have been able to check my location and talk me back to the correct path.

Chapter 16

The Lady of the Lake:
The Elementals of the Lake of Menteith

September 2014

September brings a Scottish Indian summer. I feel the call to go north and write more of the deva's messages. I await my chance to escape duties.

I've been teaching art at a local school where I try to find a connection point with the children. They are wary of a supply teacher. Some are bright eyed and totally engaged, some look for the first chance to create trouble, and others are tired or withdrawn.

I've learned that a percentage of the families rely on food banks and that there is a problem with children spending time on screen for too many hours. Some are privileged, loved and fully supported at home, some are needy, while others are spoilt materially. But they are all precious souls.

Throughout my teaching career I have introduced children to the beauty of Nature through art, pattern-making, design, observational drawing, and colour. Although I have always emphasised teaching children about the natural world, it has not generally been on the curriculum. Nowadays, everything has turned around and outdoor education is implemented by law in Scottish schools.

I ask the children to put up their hands if they know of a tree that is special to them, or a place they like to go. Have they ever climbed a tree?

A forest of hands go up. I show them an easy method to draw a tree, but I want them to draw the tree from being *inside* the tree. They all want to tell me their stories, some of which involve scrapes and falls. I quickly refocus on their connection with the trees. I've brought a variety of different leaves to show them, and I plan to tell them the names of the trees. A group of children are keen to copy down the names and seem to enjoy sorting the leaves and identifying them. They engage fully with their drawings, and search for ways to describe the leaves in pattern and colour.

In another class of seven year olds we make cardboard models of birds. They are a simple, three-part design with body, wing and tail shapes that slot in. I have templates and pictures of birds. Most children go for blackbirds, robins or blue tits. One child wants to draw a baby golden eagle and improves the template shape by turning it upside down.

"I am sorry, I don't have an illustration of a baby golden eagle," I say. "Would you like to make it an owl instead, as I have an owl photo here?"

"But I know what a baby golden eagle looks like!" He then proceeds to design a young golden eagle with surprising knowledge of the markings on its plumage.

I am encouraged by the children's enthusiasm for Nature. I had thought they lived on cartoons that were pre-designed by professionals, sometimes very crude, ugly or commercial. However, it is clear that many children have little confidence in using a pencil as a tool for drawing or scissors for cutting, and they need to learn the basics.

I sense an energy, a desire to connect with Nature. They want to tell me about their pets, even the one who seems to have little love and support at home catches me as he leaves the class to tell me how much he loves his dog.

After a day of teaching I head out with rucksack and manuscript to the Lake of Menteith, a local beauty spot renowned as the only lake in Scotland. Here, within a serene body of water, sits an island with a 13th century priory, made famous by a visit from the young Mary Queen of Scots and the writings of Sir Walter Scott and his poem *The Lady of the Lake*.

At the fence by the shore there is a sign warning of the danger of blue algae and asking visitors to keep away from the water and the white scum floating on its surface. The water is a glass-like sheet, shining like metal under an aqua-white haze of sky. The beach looks larger than I've seen it for many years now that the water level has dropped in the late summer drought.

I place my mat on the ground and prepare to sit and wait to see if any deva here will speak to me through my angel Ariel. It was here at this spot that I first heard Ariel's voice.

"Thank you for picking up the litter," she had said to my amazement, as I had no idea that angels would comment on such everyday things. Later I learned that Ariel is the angel of the environment, protector of wild animals and fish and of the natural realm of devas and elementals.

> God's infinite power touches every stone, grain of soil, and every plant. The portal from this place is overhead though you cannot see it when you look up. You're sitting upon a crossing point of ley lines. The monks' voices have fallen silent now. They prayed here for five hundred years. The vibration of their prayer exists in the ether as a memory, in the water of the lake and in the stones. Here is Heaven.
>
> Keep writing and believe our words however insignificant this seems! You are here today as a witness. Your soul connects with those who went before. You've been here in past lives. Yes. We thank you for coming.

Who is speaking, may I ask?

The deva that oversees this Lake.

What do you wish to say?

Humans are poisoning us with fish food. The lake is out of balance. Too much food - too few fish. The water's toxic. We are not a plaything. Too many fish are introduced and fed here. The wild population is overwhelmed. Water is treated as a dump and holding pen for fish which did not come from these waters originally. The natural water is in peril. We need humans' co-operation to rebalance. We need time. We can be restored. No more fish food. It is throwing the system out of balance.

I am sorry for our misunderstanding. I remember seeing a photo in the local paper a few years ago where the edges of the lake were completely green with algae. Was this the same problem?

As I write a fish leaps out of the water, creating ripples that seem to spread out as far as the eye can see across the lake. The smell of petrol lingers from a passing boat and its vibration echoes across the water as the motor starts up again. I know of keen fishermen who love going into the wilds and spending the day on the water. I never associated them with causing pollution.

Some of them understand and do not disturb the balance. Others don't make the connection with us.

Thank you for speaking.

Chapter 17

Now It is Time for Healing!

February 2015

I'm back at Clava Moor. Soft clouds hide the view of the firth. The air is freezing and after walking a short distance along the road towards the hill I need to turn back for my balaclava. I quietly retrace my steps along the muddy track where last summer the flowers had poured over the verges. Now all is empty and still.

As I turn from the track over the moor and bog towards the pools, something feels different. Logs are strewn on the heather. Reaching the edge of the gorge the torrent of the burn thunders through the two falls and roars through the lower pool in a white cascade, but my attention is focused on a pile of birch logs, newly cut with an outer layer of gnarled lichen-covered bark. The old birch tree on the rocky spur by the bend below the lower pool has been hewn down. Its branches are scattered everywhere on both banks.

I put my hand on the rough bark of the stump and it still feels alive, like a body. I feel my heart thumping in my chest and my throat tightening.

I wonder why this tree has been taken when there are so many in the plantation. The thought occurs to me that the person who took the tree may return and take others by the pool, as well as the sentinel tree where the devas rest. These trees are also filled with gold magical light, all full of lichen, insects and life. And it would mean nothing to that person.

As I stand listening, spray cools my face. A fountain of white-gold bubbles plays below the exit of the lower pool; the force of the water rushes down and bubbles gleam in the light. The mossy ledges under the leaning birch have gone, leaving the bare red sandstone exposed.

I come with angels. I come in peace with great love in my heart for this place. I come with Ariel and speak through Ariel. I wish to speak to Immortelle. I pray she is still here and will speak to me. And why have they cut down the tree?

The water, expanded now with snow-melt, gleams with light and is transparent and filled with myriads of bubbles. A large one floats towards me and I see myself in it with my turquoise walking jacket and pink scarf.

"Write your description, child," say my angels. I'm still in shock about the tree. I've forgotten to bring my mat and the grass and sphagnum moss are so saturated that there's nowhere to sit. The thought crosses my mind to fetch a log from the cut tree but even the small ones are too heavy for me to lift, let alone carry precariously along the edge of the torrent. So today I stand to write, leaning my back on my rucksack against the vertical side of the bank.

Child, there are no coincidences. You have not wasted your life with illness, tiredness, or procrastination! So think back with happiness, not with sadness. Do your hear us?

Yes, I hear you. I think you've picked up on my sadness about your beautiful tree being cut down. Yes, I am so grateful to be here again and to have survived to this point, but a part of me - a big part of me - only wants to go forward in order to write this book.

We are aware of your desire to write. We can reassure you of this: you are in time. Your sentinel trees above the pool are protected. They won't be cut.

> *Much of human action is pointless to us. You see Nature as one of us. You feel our pain, even many of the country dwellers don't see us this way. That's why we wish you to write.*

My rucksack, containing the first notebook of my writings for the devas and thermos flask, suddenly tips forward towards the black pool. I manage to catch it in time.

I still don't understand about the tree. It seems such an effort for someone to come here with a chainsaw and then leave without taking most of the logs.

There are many things I want to ask you, Immortelle. I want to ask more about the stone circles, and the star people you spoke of before, the people who worshipped here. I want to ask you about the infiltration of the pylon lines, wind farms and hardcore roadways built into the infrastructures of the wilderness to service these installations and connect with major routes. I want to ask about the effects on the devas and the purity of the landscape.

> *Alas, your fears are not unfounded. We are polluted not only by chemical waste and poison in the air and water, but by the vibration of metal, wire, and impregnation of ground-up rock taken from another source. And most of all, human intention to take, to plunder, to rape, to get what they want for life… whilst our intention is to give to life.*

From where I am now sitting on a spur of heather, moss and dead bracken, I see a shaft of sunlight in the pool which is some twenty feet below me. Under the tree float the bubbles.

If my eyesight was good enough or excellent like the eyes of an eagle, would I see the image of myself sitting on the bank, reflected in the bubbles down there? Does the fact that I can see the bubbles in the distance mean that I am in them? Or is it possible to be at an angle where I see the bubbles but not be reflected in them?

> As long as you see them there is a direct line of vision from your eyes to the bubble, however small or far away. Therefore, if your eyes were as perfect as the eyes of an eagle you would see yourself there. If someone closer could take a look they would see themselves there and you in the distance as a tiny dot. So your vision of things reflects your belief they are there. You see beauty because you believe or know or feel it. You feel our words or presence, as with your angels. You do not have any need to see or be shown our image.

If I did not believe in myself, would I not see my reflection in the bubble or mirror?

> That would be a hypothetical situation. Because you believe in yourself you exist on different levels. Mainly you experience the physical. This is the area that has been intended for you to experience. We need to tell you that you are believed in by God, your Creator. It's why people refer to God as Creator; however, humans were sent to co-create, thus you all shape your life and your experience.
> You do not believe your eyes can see an image of yourself in the bubbles from this distance away. When you do, you'll see yourself.
> You do not believe you can hear the water from afar. Too much else is interfering with the vibrations that reach your ears, yet you know that dogs hear miles further than humans. The dogs in the house that you passed on the way here heard you and barked, even though they were indoors - but we digress.
> We wish to explain within this book, that humans chose

to believe in themselves in preference to believing in the Spirit integral within themselves. They chose to believe in the physical body. They turned away from their spiritual nature, believing the power was only physical, yet the power comes from Source, only from Source.

So humans came to believe they would grow old and die, and therefore felt the need to accrue material wealth by dominion over other humans and over Nature. Their beliefs became their world and became true for them. They saw their generation grow old and die, or being attacked and killed by other individuals. They built towers and guarded them, built armies and hoarded their gold, sought the strongest soldiers, the most beautiful women, the best artists, servants and slaves in the race for power and the greed for a better life. This belief in civilisations demonstrating power of dominion became true for them. Yet all the while there were those children from the stars whose awareness of their origin is a belief in the power of love and Earth Mother. They knew the secret of gratitude and that love heals - that all is given of God, the Earth provider.

They were always persecuted because they held the true knowledge and the true power.

This description would fit the history of Scotland, Immortelle. Even within a five-mile radius of here are the Clava Cairns, many stone circles in the vicinity of the River Nairn as well as the hut circles throughout the river valley and between here and Cawdor.

I'm scanning in my mind through the layers of history: the standing stones and circles, cup marks on the rocks that mark the circles or lone standing stones at the head of the loch near Duntelchaig, the remnants of the castles of Daviot and Castletown along the River Nairn, then the farmsteads, still standing, the old field systems still visible, the Battle of Culloden with its graves and ghosts, the land reforms and hunger marches, the coming of the railway and the Clava Viaduct, forestry plantations, pylon lines and wind farms that now mostly dominate the landscape and the newly-built houses shining in the sun.

Immortelle, I don't think my knowledge of history is good enough to describe this and as I am trying to write this I find myself going into my logical brain and fear of getting it wrong. I worry that I can't hear you!

> We did not connect with you to give you a history. We are here to give you Her story: the story of your Divine Earth Mother. Now it is her time, and she rises again in true power.
>
> Many star children are here again, here to unite against the forces of evil to bring true awakening to this power, where all can be manifested. All that is not from God, from Source, can no longer proliferate.

Why did God/Mother Earth/Divine Source (whatever you mean by true Source) allow humans to live in the way you've described earlier, by taking rather than receiving in gratitude?

> Humans always had a choice, as you do now to sit in the cold and hear our words. Humans were given imagination, creative imagination, to make their world a joyful place to live, but they used their creative imagination and turned from Light. They always had choice. Now they come into conflict because they destroy the very life which is given them. Just as a child wantonly breaks his favourite toy in a rage, it is human beliefs which have caused their own pain and destruction.
>
> Now it is time for healing, for the Divine Feminine to rise up. Without this transformation you cannot live here any more, nor ever again.
>
> There is no future where the planet is blown up or poisoned to death to become uninhabitable, and people

simply migrate elsewhere to Mars or another solar system, because you are of Earth and Earth is unique.
Humans look for planets that could support water, support life. They overlook the value of what is already given. You are already given the possibility of healing the Earth.
There is no possibility of life as you experience it, happening in another cosmos, in another time.

I've been aware of TV and radio programmes about people believing that there could be other universes, other Earths or Earth-like planets and parallel existences. I've begun to take on the belief myself. You spoke before of consciousness being here where I connect with you and being real in the moment, and of the possibility of moving my attention to another place of consciousness. So why would it not be possible for other Earths elsewhere, which we can travel to in the future?

All is true. However, if Earth is destroyed there is no other possibility. Other possibilities die with Earth.

My angel's words intervene...

Some of you are from planets beyond this galaxy, which are yet to be discovered. You often wonder, because of this awareness of your planet, how you shall get home eventually. Your angels reassure you that you will get home, and that there are others around you also from your home planet. You've had many lives on Earth also. The survival of your home planet depends on the survival of Earth. It is all connected. Many people are feeling this. They are coming out of their fear to do what they were sent to do on Earth for Earth's healing. Your angel Ariel imparts this information, and Immortelle is here.

Thank you, angels. Thank you, Ariel. Thank you, Immortelle.

Chapter 18

Our Raison d'Etre is Love ~ Our Raison d'Etre is Joy

Another visit in February 2015

I am back again, sitting above the upper pool on the nearside bank with the lower pool to my right. I had forgotten when setting off in the afternoon sunshine that the moor would be flooded in light but that the watercourse would be completely in shade. So I position myself above the upper pool with the sound of its thundering waterfall in my left ear and the higher sound of the water as it leaves the lower pool in my right ear. The two sounds remain as separate and distinct as the different voices of the angels.

I feel the vibration of the water flowing beneath my feet. Only one hour until the light goes behind the hill. I feel incredibly peaceful despite the angels' dark words and my heart feels happy, buzzing, excited.

Our raison d'etre is love and we see, hear and feel those of you who are praying for a better world, where the lion shall lie down with the lamb... a world where children shall not live in fear, where man respects woman and woman respects man and all respect the lives of their children and know their blessing. Gratitude shall lift up your hearts to healing and salvation and world peace comes at last.

Dear Immortelle of the waterfall and mountain, do you feel our gratitude?

> Yes, we believe in you. We believe in the potential of humankind to live in love and kindness. It's why we wait and hold the vibration despite human atrocities.

Are you speaking of human abuse of the natural world, such as I saw yesterday: the quarrying, pylons, roads in an area of exquisite beauty?

> Yes.

Dear Immortelle, what happens to you when the upper reaches of the sacred rivers Findhorn and Nairn are filled with concrete and metal and the vibration of noise pollution of electricity? Can you remain here?

> We need to make it clear to you that human abuse is most final to us when they destroy the planet for their own greed.

That is clearly happening here in Scotland and throughout the whole world. All our resources of fishing, whisky, and education are becoming asset-stripped. I've heard that the Isle of Harris is one of the only places left to catch wild trout whilst its tweed suddenly becomes a fashion commodity.

> Yes, your fish are a barometer that measures the toxicity of water. We are of the water. Water can be healed! You know this. By the thoughts of humans, by the prayers of humans.
> We wish you to record this message: that if you pray for the water, the water can re-energise and re-align. Yes, then the wild fish can return and proliferate. No need for fish farms.

I'm afraid it's a big industry, Immortelle, and we who pray are probably very few. So much is destroyed.

> Your world is changing. We are of the angelic realms. We can see beyond your limited vision. We are beyond human's control ultimately. We continue - we are of Essence - we continue beyond humans. If the Earth is destroyed we retract and move to another realm.

Dear Immortelle, near the start of this book, when I was speaking to the nature spirits at Loch Lomond, they said that if we destroy the devas' places, then they will cease to exist even in their etheric counterpart. You also said yesterday that we humans couldn't simply trash the planet and find another, because all is dependent on planet Earth.

> You have not made a mistake in taking down our words. Earth would be destroyed. Our sacred places destroyed and forgotten and the etheric counterpart made extinct, but we would divorce from our physical counterpart, etheric counterpart and continue as angelic vibration with no home, if you want to think of it that way.
> Remember we told you at the beginning that we devas are in the realms beyond human. We are in the same level as your etheric body. Our physical counterparts are trees, rocks, soil, fire, water and air. If you destroy the trees, rocks, soil, fire, water and air, we will be forced to retreat from our etheric body and leave forever, and never to return or go to find another planet. We would be like homeless angels. We are more invested in your Earth than angels, whereas angels are invested in humans.

What would happen to angels without humans? Were there angels before humans came to Earth? Angels that governed the stars and planets, perhaps?

> Yes, this is where humans have drawn their hierarchy from. Angels of God being seraphim, cherubim, thrones, principalities, archangels and angels - the last group being angels sent by God to watch over humans.
> Yes, without humans, these angels would be homeless in a way.

Angels don't die do they, or cease to be angels?

> Angels are closely connected with your universe - we are manifestations of God, like parts of God.

So, if we humans destroy Earth, we upset the devas, interfering with their purpose.

> Yes, you have interpreted this correctly.

Wouldn't you all just go on without us though? I think I asked this question before in the context of humankind destroying Earth and the universe and God and the angels continuing without Earth. Now I am asking if the angels can go on without Earth and humans?

> It is forbidden. Ask no more.

I feel very joyful today, Immortelle, even after the sadness yesterday of seeing how more wild natural habitats have been destroyed round here. Last night the stars shone through the skylight of my room and when I opened the curtains the sunlight fell over the folds of the hills. I had a great desire to run to the hills, the moor and your waterfall. As I drove along in my car past the old villages, it felt much the same as when I used to cycle here as a teenager. The shape of the landscape, the fields and old trees glowing in spring light, the purity of the air and the lichen growing on the old birch trees.

> You have good reason to feel optimistic, child. Happiness is also your raison d'etre and you must now choose happiness. Happiness and gratitude are the only qualities that can transcend and transform the dark as your angels constantly tell you.
> As humans feel appreciation and experience gratitude, they raise to a higher vibration in keeping with Earth. They can no longer destroy what is life giving.

We are far from being in this state, dear Immortelle. The evil is apparent every day in the news. It seems there is even a war against innocent children. Children are being abused and killed. Little girls are being violated and barred from education. There are abuses against people who only want the freedom to live their lives. People who fight for these rights are being persecuted. One feels powerless to help. What can we do?

> You are not asked to do more than you are able to do. Those who are called to help know who they are. They heed the call and they go. They are supported.
> Yes, there are great acts of heroism. However, no one is asked to measure themselves against anyone else. You are all asked to do what you can. Do what comes naturally and follow your gifts. Most fish don't fly and most birds don't swim. Do what comes naturally.
> Follow your hearts in all that you do and pray for each other and for the world. Your prayers from the heart are more powerful than you can ever know. It is heart by heart that people connect with their Light and the true power.
> The forces of evil know this. They fight for the power. They strike at the heart: they repress women, they kill

your children, they cut out the heart but love is greater than fear. Good is greater than evil, and hearts may not be broken. The heart of God is not broken and Earth's children shall live again. The only way to live is to move into happiness and gratitude. This brings life to you and all with whom you connect. Happiness is contagious!

Our raison d'etre is joy. Life runs on this power and this power is within you. Do not be distressed by the thoughts of your mind tuned to the dark happenings of the world. Keep turning to the Light as a tree grows always to the Light.

The deva's words come in waves. I always know when to stop writing because it's as if I've suddenly unplugged from her high vibration and am aware of my surroundings again. I have been writing higher up on the moor at the rock by the pine tree with a crooked stem, which marks the place from which I made the large-scale landscape paintings many years ago for my art college show.

My thoughts are interrupted by a loud roaring sound coming from one direction. It's so loud that at first I mistake it for a helicopter or forestry truck along the track many metres beyond the gorge on the other side.

I pack up my notepad into my rucksack and make my way over the bog towards the sound. I stop at a promontory of heather a little higher upstream than the pools. Looking down, I see that all the sound is emanating from a small white waterfall flowing beneath rocks and through a cleft.

Making my way down along the wet mossy ledges and clinging to an old tree, I follow this water into an enclosure of ancient birch trees. I find myself looking into a pool I hadn't ever noticed before in all my wanderings up and downstream.

I feel privileged to enter this enclosure, picking my way down to the edge of the water. This third pool is quite hidden by the trees and steep banks. The ambiance of the nature spirits is very powerful here. I sense I'm permitted to be here looking at their hideaway, and yet I also feel I'm only being tolerated. Perhaps Immortelle has given me permission to see this green realm and has told the elementals of this spot to let me pass through.

The shelf of the pool is curved like the others below. The black peaty water forms a cauldron possibly six feet deep, maybe more. The water slides into it, swirls through and exits through a broader channel to the other pools below.

Thank you for letting me be here.

Holding on to the old birch tree I climb back up the bank. I wait here in the twilight for a while, listening to the water and enjoying the companionship of the nature beings. I remember the song my mother used to sing, the *Faery Song*,* in which the fairies are described as having limbs whiter than moonshine.

My mind then clears. No particular thoughts arise. I wander back upstream and out of their realm.

Chapter 19

We Need You All to Stay Strong and Be in Tune With Us

Remembering Our Past Connections with the Land

March 2015

I've completed a block of art supply teaching and am free to return to the area of the River Nairn so as to work on my book. I have found a place to stay near Cantray, on the other side of the river.

From my accommodation I can see across the river valley to the hillside that is so familiar to me. The weather is exceptionally clear and bright, with every detail on the landscape visible in the low angle of the spring sunlight. I feel impelled to check the features that I can see against the map in order to try and piece together where the layers of history converge with the present-day landscape. I set off walking miles on old tracks near the river with the map in my hands, trying to understand the alignments of the ancient ring cairns and standing stones in the fields.

The air feels pure, the sky is an incredible shade of azure blue and the birds are calling in the woods by the river. After following an old path up the edge of a field with its line of weathered beech trees, I walk out over the grass to a magnificent solitary standing stone. As I put my hand out to touch its weathered, mossy face, I hear the hooting of an owl close by.

Stepping back, listening, I wonder if it is a short-eared owl, as they hunt by day. I feel as if I am in a spell and allow myself the luxury of wandering, following no particular plan but where my instinct calls me, passing the old mills by the river. Eventually I cross an ancient bridge to the other side, where the old military road joins the one from Cawdor.

Here, I remember a place where I used to stop with my friend on our cycle runs in the 1980s. I had made a large painting in a fold of fields on a hillside there at Cantraydoune. There is a pile of boulders on a ridge overlooking the nearby road and adjacent to that road is a twelfth-century *motte* or mound, the base of an ancient fortification.

My friend had waited there at the stones, on the ridge overlooking the landscape below, reading his book in the summer heat, while I worked on my painting some distance away, out of sight in a fold of the hill. Walking past some cairns on the way back to him, I felt a pressure as if I was being pushed. I stumbled and dropped my box of paints on the grass. The place felt magical and at times, inspired both awe and fear.

We asked the local farmer about the stones. He laughed and told us that these were no ancient stones at all. The 'boys' (Highland term for 'lads') had placed them there one day, using a fork-lift truck! We thought about the farmer's story for a long time but couldn't quite believe that such a vehicle would have the capacity to lift these huge boulders.

Once, on a beautiful summer night, on the way home from Cawdor Tavern, my friend raced ahead on his bike as we passed the stones which seemed to glow in the moonlight on the ridge above us. He left me struggling to keep up. When we reached the turn-off for the Clava Cairns we slowed down, feeling that we were now on 'home territory', before climbing the next hill alongside the River Nairn. I had to resort to standing up on the pedals of my old 3-speed bike to make it up that hill... the same one where nowadays tourist coaches descend, brushing the twigs and branches of trees on either side as they bring people to view the nearby Clava Cairns. Finally, we headed back down the hill to the village where I lived at that time.

On this visit in March 2015, I decide to return on foot to the place of the stones at Cantraydoune. While walking along the lanes and roadsides, I hear the owl call again as I turn off the road and find my way up the track near where I had painted in the grassy enclosure within the folds of hills. This time I walk further, keeping to the path to avoid going directly through fields.

Over a small rise I come to a ridge littered with similar piles of boulders near the area of the prehistoric dwellings described on the maps as 'hut circles'. Clearly the story of the 'boys' and the fork-lift truck was only a story. I can now see a surprising number of these formations of huge stones in this small location. The sheer quantity of these remains, placed there by humans in ancient times, seems to explain why the area still holds such atmosphere.

Standing here on the hillside and gazing towards the Moray Firth, I feel in awe that I am looking out on the same landscape as people who had lived here three to four thousand years ago. As I wonder what their lives must have been like, I have the impression of shooting quickly back in time. I am a young boy, dressed in animal skins, keeping watch. In my mind I hear the sound of voices in the nearby dwellings. I begin to think it is perhaps all in my imagination, when a pheasant calls loudly from a nearby enclosure in the farmer's field. The picture instantly fades and I am here as my present-day self, standing on the hill among the hidden stones and fields, with the distant sound of cars on the road below.

Honouring our Gentle Men

That evening, my hillwalking friend came over to where I was staying and we went together to visit one of the retired teachers from the Inverness school where we had both taught.

He had been the head of the technical department and a great friend of the head teacher of the art department, whom I regarded as my mentor. Both these men had been friendly in their early years of teaching with the Gaelic poet Sorley MacLean, who at that time was head teacher at Plockton High School, in Lochalsh, Wester Ross, on the north-west coast of Scotland. Nowadays the school has a great reputation as a centre for education in the Gaelic language and traditional music.*

As a young teacher, I had listened to the hilarious stories told in the art department's staffroom. These included descriptions of fishing trips the three men had made together in a leaky boat off the coast of Skye. I was unaware of the fame of Sorley MacLean at that time.

My hillwalking friend and I highly respected these two teachers from our school as did the pupils. Both men had charisma, a great sense of humour, excellent discipline and were always caring and compassionate. Their knowledge of their subjects, their creativity, craftsmanship and ability to inspire and motivate affected all who knew them.

Our retired teacher friend had recently made a fiddle and had become so interested in the music that he had started to learn to play it. Another of his friends, a notable fiddle player, was also there on the evening of our visit. My hillwalking friend had her instrument with her as well, so we ended up having an impromptu *ceilidh* (a traditional Scottish social gathering which includes music, dancing and storytelling). I watched intrigued at the way the professional player instructed the others. The house filled with music of the old tunes and I wanted to dance.

There was no time for the questions I had been burning to ask, but as we left, the old teacher caught me in a warm embrace and mentioned again that he would be happy to take me to the place of his ancestors in the hills above the upper Findhorn River, near Shenachie (Gaelic: *seanachaidh* - storyteller, tradition bearer).* He added that it would need to be in late spring or summer when the nights were long, as there were many miles to walk. "But hurry back, lassie," he added, "as I haven't got long now."

I later regretted that I had not been quicker to go with him into the hills to learn more about the lives of the people of past generations and their connection with the land and its spirit. He passed away the next month, with his family round him. His friend the art teacher died the following year.

I have a sense that we who are now the older generation must seek to follow, with hope in our hearts, the example of such people of my parents' generation, who stood up for the values of kindness, respect for the land and its children, and who met their life's challenges with great dignity and humour.

The Healing Power of our Native Trees

The day after our evening ceilidh, I made one more visit to Immortelle's pools. This time it took me longer than usual to get there.

I decided to take a detour to the top of the small craggy hill that had featured in the background of the paintings I had made in the 1980s. The hill has since been cloaked in a large plantation of spruce trees, but recently some of this area has been felled. I hoped to find evidence of old dwellings amongst the fallen trees but everything was a morass of mud, sawn off tree trunks and fallen logs and branches which stretched for miles.

The only feature I found was an incredibly large rock, an 'erratic' that had probably been dumped there millennia ago at the end of the last ice age. In the Nairn valley, some of these boulders are marked on maps and in the past formed places where people gathered or worshipped, such as 'Beltane Stones' or the famous Cumberland Stone at the site of the Culloden battlefield.

From the top of the hill, the views were stunning. It felt like a place that had been frequented in the past. Returning by an old path back to the road, I was soon in the forestry plantation and had to resort to following a firebreak - a gap between the rows of trees - crossing a bog and climbing fences in order to get back to the road.

Descending over the rough ground back to the road I was aware of the sound of many birds singing. The sound arose from a specific direction, from a small woodland further along the edge of the hill. In the distance the landscape spread out like a map. The path of the railway was clearly visible below me. Native trees line the river valley there, as well as the edges of the roads. These trees form natural corridors which have long been havens for wildlife, although the drivers of the vehicles that pass through may be unaware.

The colours of the natural trees were varied and extraordinary as compared to the dark green monoblock of the plantation. I could see that many new trees had been planted along the edges of the non-native trees. These were native species, young saplings, planted within slim plastic casings to prevent the deer eating them. I began to imagine how beautiful the place would become when they have grown up.

On reaching the road, I decided to go back up the hill as far as Immortelle's burn, but this time take a different route through the conifer plantation.

The track petered out in the dark of the trees so I instead followed a small stream flowing through a soaking wet bog. After some time, the stream took an abrupt turn and ran in a different direction through an impenetrable dark thicket. Realising that this was not Immortelle's burn after all, I headed through the thicket and, bent double, attempted to find my original direction. Meanwhile I tried to avoid the prickly twigs of the spruce trees from snagging my jacket or catching my eyes and hair.

The scent of the trees was strong and sickly. The smell of stagnant water under them caught the back of my throat. I aimed for a patch of light I could see through the trees, but didn't understand where I was and could see nothing of Immortelle's burn. The slope of the ground was in a different direction to the one I'd expected. I began to wonder if I would be able to retrace my steps and questioned why I hadn't left markers each time I changed direction. The trees were impenetrable, and I could see very little.

An hour later I finally emerged from the trees into a marsh at the edge of the plantation, from where I could make out a field and a line of fence posts some distance away. Up ahead, the familiar landmark of the pylon line indicated that I was close to where it crossed over the road. I squelched through the wet marsh at the field edge, climbed over a couple of barbed wire fences and was eventually back on the road where I'd left my car. Coming out of those trees, and the silence beneath them, I could now hear birdsong again. From there, and with a great sense of relief at being back on familiar tracks, I made my way once again to Immortelle's burn by my usual route.

We Need You All to Stay Strong

Whenever I reach the gate to the moor, I always have this feeling of reverence, as if I'm at a sacred shrine, cathedral, or art exhibition to which I've made a pilgrimage.

The small knoll is still visible among the young pine trees which now grow there. The rock which had marked the best place from which I painted the view in the 1980s is of course unchanged.

As I approach the pools I'm relieved to see that the trees are still here, as the deva had said. All is unchanged apart from the felled birch and logs lying as before.

I climb down to a mossy ledge some six feet above the lower pool and make a small seat for myself and a place to secure my rucksack in the rocky cleft. I listen to the water for a while. My thoughts fade out and the sound of the waterfall entering the upper pool above becomes dominant. Below is the sound of shallow water passing over the lip of the edge of the lower pool.

I let my mind relax and lose track of time completely. But it's impossible to stay here for long because my rucksack, with all my belongings, notebooks, flask and sandwich, is slipping towards the rocky edge and is about to fall into the water. I need to secure it by rearranging its contents onto a small rocky shelf where the ground is dry. Soon the sun comes out again and shines on my page. It's time to connect.

Immortelle - are you here with me?

> *Yes, forever at your service. I was with you earlier, when you walked by the main river - at the bend with the fishing pool and old mill. Many devas and water beings are there, they've heard your prayer. They won't harm you. You've been called here. You can write your message there. I, Immortelle, will be with you there as I am here. The whole of the river and the hill is my domain. We love you.*
>
> *The felled tree... it's of no consequence. Yes, it has been a part of our domain and now it has given its life to Earth again, but the elementals are not affected as they've moved to other trees. Don't grieve for the tree. Others are growing. Your vibration must stay high for us to impart our messages to you - so don't grieve, dear child. We need you all to stay strong and be in tune with us. Raise yourself up now. You deserve all that is given and more. Your visit here today has been arranged. You are meant to be here and we thank you for heeding our call.*

Below the curved shelf of the pool the water is clear and transparent. Light catches the rockslide and illuminates the upper waterfall and the tunnel of light-filled water shooting down from the upper pool.

Dear Immortelle, I am so happy to have this chance to be here again. Is there anything you wish to say?

> *You have all the information you need. We'll give you the words. Don't look at others' words or books. Write... write... write... our haven is protected. Don't worry about us, our trees, our rocks. All is well. We are working with you to bring this into being in right timing. We protect you here and at the pools of the Nairn. Don't stray further. We are happy with your researches. Be at peace, star child.*

You have returned and we are happy you're here. All is well.
The power of God is over all now. Darkness loses its grip. You are protected. Now go forward with this...the elves are with you in your writing. They belong to the trees. They sing with the birds in the woods. You heard them. Glory! Glory - the elves are masters of song. We are happy you humans can hear beauty and see beauty for there we are! Be at peace, star child.
Immortelle gives you these words, under Ariel.

Thank you, Immortelle. Thank you, Ariel.

20th March 2015

Humankind Still Watches the Moon

I am due to leave this morning and there is a solar eclipse visible in this area of the world. I glimpse it through the roof light of my accommodation. For a few moments all goes quiet and everything falls into the moon's shadow.

It is a magical moment and I am happy that I have the chance to experience it. Without looking directly, at one point I catch a tantalising glimpse as the crescent of the sun appears just visible moving through the sky behind the clouds.

After the eclipse the darkness disperses and light returns. From my room with the view of Cantray woods and over the Nairn valley, I see the sun shining again over the hill of the devas.

I wonder about the people who once lived around Clava and this river valley and who aligned the stones to mark the position of the sun, phases of the moons and paths of the planets. I think about all the people watching round the world, and how the continuation of natural patterns is so crucial for our survival.

There is a row of pylons close by, marching across the fields. I had meant to ask Immortelle about them, but instead became engrossed in watching the eclipse. I am worried that I have spent too much time on this trip walking miles over the land and not writing enough. During these spring days I've had an opportunity to explore the area of the river. Several large new houses are being built on the moor as many areas of natural woodland are sold off. The sounds of the building work and the beeping of vehicles as they back up with their loads of supplies, echo through the clear spring air.

Yet there are also enclaves of woodland clinging to the riverbanks, railway banks and roadsides. I've also noticed that young trees have been planted along the forestry edges where mass fellings of non-native species have taken place. Everything in the area is criss-crossed by old and new pylon lines.

I open the skylight, sit on the bed and find a new page in my notebook:

Dear Immortelle, what do you say about the pylon lines that march through your district? Does the energy disturb the natural flow?

She is there immediately:

> The devas and elementals cannot operate within these 'corridors'. We must protect ourselves if we must cross the lines.
> Child, go and pack. You will not connect if you feel distracted! Go and enjoy. We will speak further. You have not wasted time! All is well. We will speak of the pylons before you go.

With Immortelle's affirmation that she would speak about the pylons later, I pack up my belongings and am ready to leave. But then I decide to walk out to the River Nairn once again as I am finding it hard to drag myself away from this place. I sit down in the sun on a sandy bank at the edge of the water by one of the river's many fishing pools. I pull out my notebook and I write down my question.

I call on my angels. I call on Ariel. I ask for connection with the deva of Clava and Immortelle. After my friend and I had sent Light at Dalwhinnie and north towards Fort Augustus, I wondered if we had failed the devas by not praying hard enough. I am afraid that I didn't actively 'send Light' every day as I think they had wished me to. Could our prayers have stopped the destruction that was caused?

> We have heard your prayers from the heart and even if you had prayed every day you would not have stopped it.

You said in An Angels' Guide *that the prayers of one person can change the world, so why couldn't my friend and I manage to help save the wild areas from being disturbed and destroyed?*

> Alas there are not enough devas to withstand the abuse and there are not enough of you. You and your friend alone could not have stood against Scottish Parliament!

I think it might only have been a very few votes that won the decision to go ahead, despite the opposition. They wanted 'green energy' and that vote ticked the boxes for politicians despite the environmental damage.

> Alas, the way of the heart is a hard path to follow. It requires courage. It requires that people step out of line and be counted. Dear child, all is not lost. We call you to write for the devas. Write this book.

Thank you, angels. Thank you, Immortelle.

Chapter 20

Seeing An Elf Child

May 2015

I have arranged to go up north for a whole week to connect with the devas and write this book, and in the evenings type up the script from my notebooks. It feels like a daunting task. I need to buy a tablet in case I can type outdoors, that is if I can get myself comfortably seated at the edge of the pool.

This time I come with two friends. As we leave Stirling the sun is glorious and the skies cloudless, but further north it clouds over. We take an evening walk to a stone circle on cultivated land at Daviot, a mile or two from the main stones at Clava. We keep to the edges of the fields as we go, avoiding bogs and mud. The weathered remnants of the stone circle seem timeless. Generations of farmers have ploughed round them. Some stones have sunk into the ground or are smothered by field grass. The main megalith stands erect, pointing to the sky, the only unchanging part of the scene.

The smell of the earth is like a balm to the senses. The scent of gorse on the breeze transports me back to memories of wandering on the moor in the past. Orange bracken on the slopes smells like tobacco and there are white wind flowers showing through, and violets like purple gems. Shady banks are full of new bluebells, wafts of gorse flower sickly sweet, perfume of bluebell, mingling with earth's dead leaves.

I feel my energy sink down and I'm held by Earth. My tired head and sore heart settle into peace. We walk back along the switchback single-track road breathing scent of bluebell and gorse. My ego melts away and I've become the child again with total appreciation for my life as it is now, in this moment.

Rain has fallen overnight and I make my way back to the moor the next morning on my own. For the first time, as I encounter heavy showers, I'm not sure whether to turn back. But I call on Archangel Gabriel to cleanse my aura of all negativity, and on Archangel Michael and the Violet Flame for protection, as I know not all devas and nature spirits are in Light. My role here is too important for me not to be vigilant. I ask that my own negativity be transmuted so I may not bring any negativity with me or disturb the nature spirits or devas here.

Climbing down to the pools, I see that the water is slower than ever. Despite all the rain, the rocky edges of the basin are exposed, and the exit from the pool reveals a small staircase and waterslide. The place where the water drops down is deep and black, filled with bubbles churning up from an invisible source below. The water sprays into this small cauldron, swirling. So many patterns of spirals, and I can easily imagine the spirits of the pool playing there endlessly.

> *Yes, Immortelle is here! Yes, we remind you that each small pool, each bend in the burn, each drop from one level to the next has its water sprites, as each leaf and each petal of the flower has its fairy governing it. These ones you consider are of the water, and very joyous they are!*

I think I sense this, Immortelle - even though it's a rather dark, showery day and cold for the time of year. I sense the life and joy here by the water's edge.

Sunlight now pours over the page as I write and lights the waterfall which enters the main lower pool with its own thundering sound. In my left ear I hear the lower vibration of the bubbling water as it slides into the miniature cauldron below the pool's edge and sprays up flumes of water.

We welcome you here in our domain, star child. We greet you! The spirits here love you as you love them, though you do not yet see them!

Do they see me?

Yes, of course!

Will I one day see them or see you?

You have the ability and you may one day see us again.

Again? When did I see you before?

As a young child you saw us in the garden.

The deva shows me a picture in my mind of the garden at Nairnside. She shows me an image of myself as a toddler wearing a red duffle coat, sitting in my pushchair with legs tucked under a travel rug, watching the tarmac of the road go by under the wheels. I'm watching the sun and shadows of the trees pass under the wheels as my mother pushes me. I'm humming so as to hear the vibration of my voice as we go over the bumps.

Many of us were around you then. And now. We're here again because you've lost your pride and entered humility and grace.

My mind drifts. It is difficult to stay focused on hearing Immortelle, with the sound of the water, and watching the flumes and bubbles, the dark of the pool and deep green reflections of moss and white light, bubbles sliding over the surface.

I feel as if I'm being watched. Looking up at the sentinel birch tree and heathery bank on the opposite side, I sense a small child-like creature with a large head and skinny body. In my imagination I can clearly see its nut-brown face and slanted dark eyes, big, big eyes. The hair seems to be curly and dark, tucked under a pointed cap made of bark or birch leaves. The face is both ugly and beautiful at the same time. Its dull grey-green clothes are like shorts and T-shirt, and the limbs poke out, terribly thin and scrawny like birch twigs. However, when I stare at the heathery patch between the birch trees I see that there is nothing there.

Yet I feel it and can see the details in my imagination. Is this wishful thinking? I look away, then look back. I look towards other areas of the bank and close my eyes. Nothing is there! Not even in my imagination.

Yet I feel there is *something* on the bank between the two trees. Yes, there it is again in my imagination. If I look elsewhere, it disappears. If I look back at this particular spot, it appears again. When I look away to focus on the page to write all this down, I can feel it coming closer. It seems intrigued by me! The face is wise, but perhaps too old to be that of a child?

Yes child, do not doubt your heart. You perceive an elf. It belongs to the trees here, particularly to the sentinel as you call it. They belong here and are linked with the pool.

It looks and feels like a shy child. Does it have family? Is it boy or girl? Do elves have babies? If immortal, why do they need children?

You are thinking too literally! It is not clear-cut. We can shapeshift, remember? We can be male or female. Usually we remain in the same mode for the lifetime of the human to which we connect. We appear as thought projections although we are truly here and we are of God and of the Light. Therefore, I am Immortelle, your deva of the mountain and the River Nairn, revealing my presence to you as female... as you are yourself balanced towards, very much towards the female aspect.
The elf child shows itself to you as male, though they do not differentiate greatly. On the subject of children - yes fairies, elves, gnomes, dwarves and all your classifications of nature spirits do copulate and have children - when necessary. However, all are immortal.

Wouldn't your population explode?

Touché! Children are produced on rare occasions. It's not an everyday thing. When Nature is abused, the nature spirits have to leave Earth and exit elsewhere, even become extinct. Therefore, children are important to us at this time. You have seen an elf child of the New Times to come. It is a rare privilege.

Well, couldn't I just sit here, getting dreamy with the sound of the water, and imagine all kinds of things... all kinds of water spirits, fairies, dwarves, elves... creating fictitious ones and writing about them as if they were real?

No! You cannot and do not! Try it! When you looked at another part of the bank and then you closed your eyes, you could no longer remember him.

After some time in silence I ask Immortelle:

I feel like walking upstream, up the hill but I'm wondering if I should stay here to write more?

The hill is right!

Thank you.

Since seeing the elf child, it has not felt right to continue recording. I need time to take in the experience and be on my own for a while, so I walk uphill by the water. How strange that I feel as light as a feather, and easily stride over the heather and jump the patches of bog to a place a little further upstream.

As I sit munching oatcakes and cheese with the rain lightly spitting down, I feel out of place as a human being having this experience of meeting devas and elves. As I ponder why on earth I've come to this rather desolate barren moor, the sun comes out again, flooding the enclosure of birches and pool, turning the water above the rock shelf to pure amber, lighting the ripples and waterfalls to liquid light.

For that is what they are! Immortelle cries in delight. *Pure Essence - before the pollution happens.*

May I ask? As water is recycled, never the same, is it polluted before it flows through the pools, through the ground and into the earth? At what point is it cleansed? Does the rock filter it? Does the churning and bubbling aerate it? Does the junk collect and fall to the bottom or is it carried to the sea?

Yes, in a physical sense, this is what happens - at the level of your understanding of physics. However, this is the true reality: Listen! Listen!
The elementals cleanse the water. The undines and spirits of the pool are in charge of this.

Dear Immortelle, you speak of undines. I understand this is the generic term used for water spirits.
   I'm tired today. Should I persevere?

I had to stop there because the rain was dissolving the ink on the page.

You have a pencil, n'est-ce pas?

Yes! I didn't think of that!

We require you to keep going. Your own resistance is causing this. Please push through.

The feeling of sleepiness is overwhelming me and I'm uncomfortable in damp clothes. But Immortelle presses on with more to say.

We work with the Light from God, from Source. We purify and cleanse the water, air and earth. In the same way you were clearing your aura on the way here, calling on Gabriel, we also cleanse and have the ability to change forms from polluted water to the radiant crystal forms. We dissolve dark matter, transmuting it to Light. We are working on the layer beyond the physical layer you see, feel and experience as sound, wet, discomfort, warmth, beauty and so forth.
The connection between the layers is the Divine Light and love. This you experience in your heart and you feel

its heaviness, lightness or emotion. Your heart is a powerhouse affecting all your physical body. When happy you can dance, jump, run. Yes, run at your age!
And pure love heals you, makes you young again and radiates out to others the sense of your glowingness. And they receive wellbeing also unless they are in darkness of fear or jealousy!
Our raison d'etre as we said before is joy. The sprites that play in the small pool at your feet, the miniature cauldron as you call it, are resonant with the joy of being.
That is what transforms the water to clarity from a polluted state. Their joy is the alchemy that creates the transformation.
Yet what you see with your physical eyes is the turbulent spiralling of water, the fountain of bubbles and spray, the glissando of water over the rockslide charging full tilt into the cauldron. Water sprites continue the process of clarifying the water as it exits from the cauldron up over the lip and down again to the next pool.
You see the physical effect but it is happening on an unseen level. That is the astral level. Some of you may see us here.
Earlier you perceived the elf child. He's not in the physical you see; he's also at the next level, the astral. He is not on the same wavelength as the tree but yet he's linked to the tree.
In the same way you are not very aware of your astral body which we clearly see, but you could not exist without it.
Before, we have explained to you that the devas, fairies, elves, dwarves, undines, sylphs, salamanders - and all elementals - exist at the next level. So when people do see them they are seeing them as thought projections. This does not mean that they are completely imagined, but that they have connected with your consciousness at

this time and place, and show themselves to you because your awareness is open enough to accept them.

This is why when you stared at the heather bank on the opposite side of the pool hoping to see the elf more clearly, it dissolved. You were focusing too hard with your physical sight. It is an inner thing. You need to focus on your heart to see them, and let go of all pretence and ego. Then they decide if they shall allow themselves to be seen.

Dear Immortelle, I need to ask you. What is the difference between me conjuring up my imagination to see one of you, an elf or undine for example, and actually having the awareness of one, as happened unexpectedly while I was writing?

You cannot conjure up a deva or elemental by your imagination. Your imagination is to help you envision your life to create the things in your life and experiences in your life that will come to you. By making up pictures in your mind with your imagination, say, beautiful fairy maidens, ugly witches, gnomes, you may be in serious danger of calling forth the elementals or forces of negativity that masquerade with these outer images.

However, we do not do what humans want. We do not come when you call us forth. We operate under God's Light, some under Pan, who is also of God, and alongside your angels. However, unlike your angels, we have free will.

I thought none of you angelic beings had free will. I thought that you had to serve God!

Your angels, the angels of humans have no free will. They must carry out God's will. If you stray off the path of your own free will they cannot force you to go back or inter-

vene. They must wait patiently for you to ask for help. Then they can help you back or guide you by a different route - always to Light.

And we need to reassure you that there is never any blame or punishment for going through your free will or choice, only that blame which you place on your self. In this, human beliefs are corrupted. The belief in a God of punishment is an outrage to us.

We devas and elementals have free will.

However, we are of the Light of God and will never stray off that path of Light for it is our divine nature.

As we said before, we have the ability to snuff you out if we were to leave our blueprint and follow our free will.

Many devas and elementals have morphed into the most dark and debased versions of themselves. They've left the Light and now seek to destroy humans also. We cannot call them devas and elementals as they have changed form.

This is why you need your angels and our protection to come here and write for us. You are greatly protected and need not fear. You've been put to the test and have come through. You've been through many lives to come to this one at this point to tell our story now. Humankind is ready. And if not, its people shall perish with the false gods.

I start to think of the Biblical story of Adam and Eve being expelled from the Garden of Eden after eating the fruit of the Tree of Knowledge. There are stories of angels that had free will and how one angel was likened to a prince of Light and then fell from Grace.

It is correct: once the angels of humans had free will, but some fell under Satan. Yes, we do not wish to speak of this but we can say it is the same story to which we refer.

What is the same story? Do you mean that devas that change form are like the humans that were banned from the Garden of Eden, or like angels that fell from Grace?

> We devas were not included in that story for we are older than angels connected with human beings.

I sense that the deva does not wish to speak more on the subject. She belongs in Light and cannot speak of the dark. I feel uncomfortable and do not understand the Biblical references or know what to ask, so I change the subject.

I wanted to ask you about the harp music I once heard here. You told me this had happened so that I would come here again years later and that this was the elven harp. Suddenly I feel excited at the idea it might have been from these elves, the same ones who are making their presences known to me now, through the elf child?

> Yes, it is exactly the case. He, like you, had been prepared to come forward at this time to meet you. It is an important encounter for him as well as for you. He stumbled on you and can see you.
> Many elf children - also many fully grown elves - do not see humans. They cannot come close to your vibration you see. They cannot bear it. Humans are too poisonous to elves apart from those who truly love Nature and trees, and you cleared your aura today with Gabriel.
> The elf child is spiritually evolved. He's here to help his kin move into the New Times when humans shall co-operate with Nature and the elements.
> You have raised your children well, with awareness of their spiritual natures and gifts. They shall also work for the New Times when peace shall come to Earth.
> This is to happen at the eleventh hour. There's much more destruction to happen but then great Light is coming.

The time of healing is upon us all now - Nature and humanity. No time for karma to be played out. It's time to go forward, quickly release all negative karma, and not to create more.
We need your energies for the Light not to be wasted. Keep moving forward. We are helping you.
Always at your service!

Thank you, Immortelle!

Suddenly the connection is gone again. I'm aware of my cold hands and cramped legs and wonder what the time is.

Part Four

Creating our Future Together With Nature's Guardians

Your material world has taken control away from the true nature of Earth, and humans' greed separated us. Your angels were kept in the churches, though as you are aware, they are pure manifestations of God and God is everywhere. This belief was held throughout Celtic Christianity and survives in many countries of the world that have not been invaded or despoiled. The beliefs in the spiritual life of Nature are coming again as people grow wary of the abuses of power, war, greed and materialism.

The true power is within. You connect with it. Those of a pure heart hold the keys to the door, to the spiritual realms that govern your planet.

Do not lose hope. Do not lose heart. All is well. Many of us are here to help you. Our love for you is beyond your imagination and expectation. We connect with you because this is God's will. It is our joy to work with you to bring this message to Earth.
(Chapter 21: Pages 204 & 208)

For we are of the Essence and we guide you all. You are living through the changes. Fear not that you cannot change your world for you are all changing your world, every minute.
(Chapter 27: Pages 254 & 255)

Chapter 21

The Wee Folk and the Fairy Realms

June 2015

Oh Immortelle, your pool is so beautiful! I cannot take my eyes off the liquid amber where the sun shines through as the water of the lower pool exits over the lumpy rock, the rockslide and down to the small cauldron with its fountain of bubbles where the water sprites are playing. I hope and trust they'll live here in peace forever.

As I write, the fountain rises as if by magic. The sound of the fall to my right is eternal. In my mind's eye I see the moor of Clava, the heather giving way to scraps of birch woodland that cloak the edges of the burns flowing down to the River Nairn. The area is filled with birdsong. I can visualise the fields and railway swinging through the grand curve over the viaduct and the Nairn flowing through.

    The river is peaty brown and light-filled, full of the sound of a thousand voices. The beech woods are springing into leaf. Beyond the fields, woods and stone circles, the new houses gleam in the sun. Beyond the blue firth and the Black Isle, Ben Wyvis floats above, like a mirage with the sun lighting its flanks. I can see the hills beyond Beauly and Loch Ness.

Somewhere, this landscape connects to another in a parallel world that is inhabited by devas and nature spirits. Where the veil is thin, the mirror images of these landscapes connect.

All through these writings the devas have advised me that this physical landscape where we live everyday is so essential that, if we should destroy it, the spiritual counterpart would also be destroyed along with all the landscapes related to it. If that happened, the angels and nature spirits would either have to leave or cease to exist.

> *Those who perceive the beauty of the landscape see through a portal to the divine beauty which emanates from its etheric counterpart.*
>
> *We explain this by using the metaphor of a mirror in which you would look to see a most beautiful and perfect reflection. This you realise is reflecting back the beauty on your side of the mirror.*
>
> *So you understand that there is the spark of the Divine in your physical world around you, which is powered from Source. You glimpse an image of Source in that perfect picture through the mirror. Those who see only the mirror or the flaws in the mirror need to awaken and open their eyes.*
>
> *If you are blind, then you can sense the Divine through the sounds, the many layered voices, expressing the beauty of the world.*
>
> *Some of you feel the Divine through touch, as the mother's hands heal the scrape on the child's knee or as the grandmother holds the baby, or the father lifts his child and carries him on his shoulders.*
>
> *For you are all of Divine Source and to heal yourselves and heal Earth, you must come to your senses!*
>
> *Artists, musicians, orators, poets and scientists will show the way if they work through their hearts.*

We love you. We are delighted you're here. This book is three quarters through.

Dear Immortelle, are there many elves connected to this spot? Are they here regularly? Can you tell me about the other elementals - the undines and sylphs, fire and air spirits, the dwarves - and are they all local to these particular pools and this watercourse, or do they move about?

> They are linked to areas. Some can move about more than others.
> Immortelle, your deva, covers the greatest territory. This includes all of the waters that feed the River Nairn and as far as the sea and mountain where the streams emanate. The River Findhorn, which is also sacred and originates from the same hills, has other devas overseeing it.
> The mountain itself has its own deva, separate from us mountain/river devas. This one lives underground, deep in the core of the rock structure. It's not friendly to humans, yet it is of the Light and under God who made all things.

The fracking, quarrying, extraction of oil and building of tracks to service the wind farms and pylons - does this affect the mountain devas?

> Yes, it angers them. It's abuse to them, but they are so deep, it cannot but tickle the surface. It cannot deeply affect them, not as much as the water and air quality, and the plant life on the surface.
> The watercourses have their pools, each with a governing spirit. These are more male than female in their aspect, should they manifest in a form you can understand. They cannot leave their pools. When watercourses are dammed

for hydro-electricity, these nature spirits cease to abide on the Earth plane and lose their link with Earth altogether.

The waterfalls have their sprites. These play continually, though their function is also to give life to the water, aerate and de-pollute it through their joy (joie de vivre).

They are having a hard time because of acid rain and chemicals sprayed on land and in the air which end up in the water table. Some sprites have mutated and become deformed and gone to the dark. The water becomes poisonous to humans.

The water here is good though you must not drink it. Deer and sheep faeces are carried in the waters of Scottish mountains as you know. The deer and sheep population is out of balance.

The water cannot be cleared. The addition of chemicals exacerbates the pollution and spreads to plants that the watercourse feeds. Thus the land is polluted and this affects the Earth dwellers.

The dwarves (as you call them) are very angry. Do not attempt to communicate with them unless through Ariel and Immortelle, who is speaking to you.

The sylphs are between water and air, playing in the spray of the waterfalls. The undines govern the waterfalls. They are much in Light and wish for connection with humans to work together.

The sea kelpies are undines of the sea in the form of horses. They can be malevolent or helpful! They are of the Light but do not readily connect with humans.

The fairies belong to your trees, plants and particularly the flowers of all plants. They work tirelessly bringing the Light to make all plants grow and evolve. You cannot live without them. They manifest as the small flying Light forms. You humans see them as human forms or children with wings, similar to the way you perceive angels.

After angels, fairies are the closest to humans. It's why

you have many representations of them.

When I channelled the Angels' book, I didn't know of many other books about angels apart from a small number of mainstream angel authors in Britain, Ireland and America. There were also books I came across written in the 1930s and 1950s. By the time I had finished my book and allowed myself to read of others' experiences, other angel authors were coming into recognition from Scotland, Ireland and England. My local bookshop manager had told me there was no demand for spiritual or angel books. He later changed this view.

At this time of writing there seems to be a huge demand for all things to do with fairies. Garden centres and gift shops are full of their representations. I even saw a miniature garden, with a plastic house, toadstools and fairies, that could be planted with grass seed as a toy for small children. I remember being brought up with the Flower Fairies books and also reading fairy tales as I grew up.

> Yes, angels have come back to your consciousness, not for the first time. We are in fashion again. Many people are having angel encounters and raising their awareness. Now, because of the need to respect Earth, love of fairies and recognition of their role in your life brings our image to your consciousness. People are manifesting images of us by their focus on us.
>
> However, as we said before, it is a two-way thing. You cannot have true encounters with us unless they come from real love and respect for us, and your destiny brings us together.
>
> We do not come to meet you by your will alone. We do wish to meet some humans, and then we meet.

Our histories tell us we once lived in closer communication with you?

Yes, many were more respectful of Earth and its kingdoms, because of the dependency on Earth for food and spiritual well-being.

Your material world has taken control away from the true nature of Earth, and humans' greed separated us. Your angels were kept in the churches though as you are aware, they are pure manifestations of God and God is everywhere. This belief was held throughout Celtic Christianity and survives in many countries of the world that have not been invaded or despoiled.

The beliefs in the spiritual life of Nature are coming again as people grow wary of the abuses of power, war, greed and materialism.

The true power is within. You connect with it. Those of a pure heart hold the keys to the door, to the spiritual realms that govern your planet.

Dear Immortelle, though many fairy stories tell of fairies helping humans, making their wishes come true, there are also stories of fairies being malevolent, causing havoc with crops, stealing babies, kidnapping mortals and taking them to fairyland - as in the story of True Thomas, famous in the UK. There are the stories of the little people, also known as fairies in Scottish folklore. I have heard of recent sightings of them, and I'm confused because they are described as small people two to three feet high, often wearing jackets and red caps as in the poem, The Fairies, by William Alligham.

> We daren't go a-hunting
> For fear of little men;
> Wee folk, good folk,
> Trooping all together;
> Green jacket, red cap,
> And white owl's feather!*

At the Findhorn community, through the books of Dorothy Maclean and other founders of that spiritual community, the understanding of the key role of fairies is, as you've described to me, as being the spiritual guardians involved in the growth and wellbeing of plants and flowers. Are the 'little people' also fairies that govern the growth of plants, or are they different?

> The fairies are huge powers although the thought projections of humans and artists through the ages depict them as miniature beings that work directly with plants and flowers, and have wings that flash with light. The 'little people' are also fairies. Yes, this is correct. They manifest in a form which is closer to human in appearance.
> They show themselves to humans in two aspects, the sweet creature with wings or the humanlike form, clothed, gathering or marching like an army, tramping the woodlands, fighting with bow and arrow on occasion. This manifestation is a lower vibration than the one that works with plants. This form is closest to human. However, they will not hurt you if you truly love and respect them. So do not be afraid.

Is the fairy of the plants like the 'higher self' of the humanlike form of the 'wee folk'?

> No.

I am stuck, Immortelle. I need to go and digest this information. It's not making sense to me yet. I can see how the 'wee folk' are as described in the fairy tales and encounters with humans, but I do not see how they are also fairies that regulate the growth of flowers.

> We'll help you.

Thank you, Immortelle, and fairies.

Thank you.

I take a short break and then come back to my questions.

I'm sorry. I'm still confused. I need to be true to your words for this writing, but my mind can't make sense of this. You say the 'wee folk' are fairies. You say that the shining beings that over-light every petal and leaf are fairies and these ones, that over-light the plants, are huge powers, no less than angels of us humans. The 'wee folk' are a lower manifestation, closer to humankind, but are they also called fairies?

> Yes, generically they are all called fairies. We are all immortal, unlike men and women. We shape shift.
> The 'wee folk' can perform magic and transform themselves to animals, or play tricks on people. They, like humans, are closely bound to Earth... the body of Earth. And they are of the mountains and hills. Some dwell by the sea.

Are there any here?

> Yes, they have been seen by people here. Some stay in the hills where you walked yesterday. Many of these 'wee folk' have left because of the forestry plantations and wind farms.

Where do they go?

> Like the plant fairies, they move to a parallel world. We must emphasise that if humans destroy Earth, this parallel world cannot continue to exist. Their plight is as serious as yours.

Are they in the Light of God? Do they work with their hearts? Do they feel emotions like physical humans?

> Pain is unknown in our realms, only the pain of destruction and pollution of Earth. We are all guardians of Earth, including the 'wee folk'. They have their world within this world. They do not tamper with God's creation. They show themselves to you. If you respect them, no harm can come to you.

Why do they show themselves to humans? Would it not be better for them to remain invisible to us?

> Some encounters, as we have said, are not purely your will. You cannot, by your imagination, force a fairy to manifest itself to your physical eyes.
> The same applies to us. We have no power to make you see us at our beckoning, though sometimes we call you. Humans see fairies at those moments where the veil is thin and when they have tuned out from their mind and into their hearts, or have simply lost normal awareness through tiredness, drunkenness, drugs or through being in a meditative state of higher consciousness. You'd never see us because you willed it to happen.
> It's why children see us, and lose the ability in later life. Besides, we do not want them talking about their sightings to adults and revealing our sacred places.

I am unable to complete the message at this point. It may be because of my own fear of speaking about the 'wee folk' and what people might think of me.

We have a terrible history of the treatment of witches here in Scotland, and I believe that the association of witches and fairies go together. As the true nature of fairies as part of the divine realm has not been recognised, people have unsurprisingly been afraid to speak of them even to this day. Perhaps I am one of these people fearing openness. The problem of fear when taking the deva's message is that it lowers my vibration and then I can no longer hear her words.

Immortelle responds to my concern about becoming caught in fear and then losing our connection.

Do not lose hope. Do not lose heart. All is well. Many of us are here to help you. Our love for you is beyond your imagination and expectation. We connect with you because this is God's will. It is our joy to work with you to bring this message to Earth.

We are of the water, wind, fire and rock, of flower, tree and mountain. We exist to praise the name of God. We're sent from cherubim.

We connect with those who love Earth, have compassion for their fellow beings, animals and plants. We hear your prayer of supplication. Earth is to rise again. We love you, Earth child. We salute you. Come here again!

Thank you, angels. Thank you, Immortelle.

And in your dreams you may connect with us. The spirit of the pools shines here. All is well.

Thank you.

Chapter 22

The Spirit of the Rock Speaks to You

July 2015

I return to the moor in late July, tired of the cold grey Scottish weather and weary of paperwork and working online. The journey up the A9 is slow and by the time I reach Clava it feels like a different world, a different layer of time.

On my way up to the moor the owner of the nearby cottage smiles and waves and we exchange a few words about the weather. I'm thankful that she never asks me what I'm doing or where I'm going. In my mind, she's the person who's always there, gardening or walking her dogs. To her, perhaps I appear as a tall stranger in walking gear always heading for the moor.

Her cottage is perched on a hidden hill, its views over the Moray Firth and Black Isle unchanging year on year. The verges are abundant in pink grasses bleached with summer wind and rain. The yellow flowers of broom and gorse have gone, replaced by the frothy white of cow parsley and meadowsweet, pink clover, lady's bedstraw, purple vetch and blue harebells climbing the fences.

The conifers of the plantation are thickly scented, shaded and mysterious.

Approaching the gate, I see through to a world of colour - tangy yellow-green of deer grass and soft green pines. Clusters of bell heather and cross-leaved heath bring stunning purples amid green browns of ling heather. Bog asphodel and white bedstraw carpet the bogs. White lichen, ochre lichen, red and black lichen - the moor has become a kaleidoscope of colour, more glorious even than its flowery mantle of early summer.

I climb up to the rock that featured in the foreground of a large painting of the moor I had painted while in college. Today, the distant mountains are clearly in view. They appear as a ring of blue beyond the firth, layered below with green of fields dotted with white sheep and deep greens of the plantation. The flowery dome of the moor surrounds me.

I sit down with my back to the rock and begin a dialogue with my angels. I share my concerns about how to write this book, how to make the time, how to get it right for the devas. But the peace of the moor, the birdsong, the sound of flies droning, the soft breeze in my ears, dissolve my thoughts.

Dear Earth and all devas, nature spirits and angels, we cannot live without you! We need you. People cannot live by bread alone, I realise.

I hear a response but it isn't Immortelle.

We are happy with what you have written, we are happy with your description of the moor. It is necessary for the book. Do not delete this. By your description you bring the vibration of the moor to your page in the same way you brought the energy to your paper when you painted here as a child.

I believe the spirit of the rock is speaking to me. The memory of painting here is so clear that I feel as though I'm in a time warp. I had a plastic ice cream box with me and in it, nine mustard jars filled with paint, as much as could fit in my bicycle basket: lemon, ochre, cadmium and crimson red, cerulean and ultramarine, white, black and… cadmium yellow, says the voice. It seems very unreal hearing the rock spirit speak about artists' paints.

I wonder what you think of our poor efforts to reproduce pictures of Nature. I always longed to paint the watery-ness of water, the shining light. No paint is bright enough for the petals of bog asphodel or tormentil!

All painting, as you have come to understand, is a memory - a reminder.

The reaction of the rock spirit confirms something that I've always thought about as an artist.

You try to describe the essence of the subject matter. Some of you make a good interpretation. Some artists can match the vibration of their subject using orchestration of shapes and colour. This impacts on the person who is observing the painting and transports them by changing their vibration also.

So art uplifts people?

Yes, some art achieves this. Some merely reflects the lower energies of the person who created it. However, art can only be memory as it is fixed in time, a still snapshot. Live music is pure vibration, capable of raising or lowering the vibration and transcending.

Which has more impact?

Music.

As I listen, I start to draw the outline of the hills on the horizon across the page.

This is because you are vibration and must respond to the vibration of the sounds you hear, as the surface of the pool must change its pattern when a stone is flung in. Unless you stop your ears you cannot avoid the effect music has on your vibration.
With art, there is choice. You may connect with the subject matter, you may be influenced by the resonance of the colours, you may pick up on the vibration of the spirit of the soul who painted it, or all these things, or you may choose simply to close your eyes and look away.

What do you and other nature spirits know of human beings, art and paints? I had assumed your knowledge would be confined to the subject of plant growth, soil, water, air.

We, the nature spirits that overlight the plants, soil and rock (and it is the rock spirit that speaks to you now) are intelligent beings.

More so than human beings?

We would not offend you with our answer.

Thank you.

This interchange with the spirit of the rock has startled me. I am humbled to think it is likely to be far more aware and intelligent than I am, unless I am not channelling these messages correctly and have gone off on some curious train of thought.

The rock is not large. It's beautiful, but it's like any other rock on the hillside that has been here for centuries until it gradually wears away to sand, or is used as rubble to build roads or walls. How can the spirit of the rock be intelligent?

> We need to remind you that the rock itself is dense matter - denser than you - made of granite, quartz, mica. This matter vibrates. The vibration holds memory. Its spirit is not the rock but resides in companionship and harmony with the rock. In the same way your spirit is not your body, but is with you as long as your body lives, as long as you eat and breathe.
> Then your spirit transcends, creates a new reality, to match the vibration that it has reached.
> Old bodies house beautiful souls ready to transcend and continue on their path.
> The spirit of the rock stays until the rock is ground to pieces, too small to be cohesive together, then it moves deeper into Earth.

So, may I ask, does the sand and gravel under all our roads and building sites still carry the vibration of the original rocks that they were quarried from?

> We answer by saying that within each grain of sand is an infinite world, but each rock or grain of sand resonates differently. Millions of grains of sand and small rocks beneath roads and building sites create dissonance as they are not vibrating cohesively.
> The stones of one house resonate together as larger blocks built for one purpose. A stone wall also resonates as one.

What about a concrete block or road? Say one road built for one purpose, like the A9 I drove up today? What about the new tracks you can see from the A9 to make access roads for new corridors of power lines?

We answer you thus: Within each grain of sand lies a beauty of infinity. However, as the sand and rubble for roads and building sites have been transported from their original source and are no longer cohesive, the particles do not vibrate or resonate as one. There is dissonance. This is not in accord with Nature. The spirits of those original rocks have moved away or stayed in the original source - the beach or quarry. There is no soul there in the road rubble, in the extraction of minerals, yet each grain vibrates true to form - even glass, which has been made from silica, has a vibration. Concrete creates dissonance. Plastic has negative energy because it is made by abuse to natural matter.

A house is in one place and frequented by humans so it takes on a vibration and even has an angel connected to it. An old house may be full of the spirits of people. And because a road becomes a familiar route through places, then the road takes on a vibration from these places - such as the A9 as it passes through Dunkeld or Scrabster! These parts of the A9 have different vibrations because of the surrounding landscape.

Your association with roads is also highly emotive and charged with energy. Therefore there are guardians and angels overlighting roads, houses and cities. They are attracted to them because of the vibration of human activity and thought.

Rock spirit, I thank you for this message.

After the interchange with the rock spirit I make my way back from the moor to the car. I stop at the nearest pub for a lime and soda, unable to decide whether I should drive home or find somewhere to stay the night. I am desperately thirsty after being on the open moor in sunshine.

This pub is near the Culloden Battlefield and Visitor Centre and stands at a crossroads at the top of the road leading down to the village of Balloch where I had lived with my family. On New Year's Day, in the early hours of morning, I remember hearing the revellers walking down the steep brae past our house on their way home. Otherwise it was a quiet village.

Now the pub has been upgraded though it's still simple in style. My schoolfriend remembers how it used to be called the Heatherlea Tea Rooms when he was a child in the 1960s. The bar is empty apart from the barman and his mate who stare at me unashamedly. My face is burning from being in the sun, and I am unsure whether I might still have a sprig of heather caught in my hair. I know they are sizing me up whilst they continue to comment about the weather turning showery.

I listen to their Invernessian accents, which I miss, though one thing I always like about Stirling accents is the way people laugh, which sounds warm and infectious. I leave the men guessing. I finish my drink, walk out to my car, then drive on and stop again in a layby where I now continue my writing. It is hard to drag myself away from this corner of the moor. I have parked by the side of my favourite road. I am watching the long clouds forming over a vast cobalt sky and the swallows flying low over the ground. The verges are full of ferns and grasses, bejewelled with flowers: clover, yarrow, lady's mantle, and purple vetch. White briar roses tumble over old walls.

Suddenly, I realise that the adjacent field to where I am parked is the very place where I had made a large painting of a barley field as a young art student. I have a black and white photograph from that day. Barley isn't grown in these fields any more, but I recognise the field because of a footbridge over the railway visible on the horizon.

These arches and bridges throughout the railway line network were built by the Highland Railway Company in the late 19th century, to enable farmers to move their livestock from one field to another, across the line. Though small by comparison, they are built with the same attention to detail as the magnificent Clava Viaduct, which spans the River Nairn nearby. The viaduct is a huge structure of old red sandstone, gracefully curved, the arches being different sizes to fit into the landscape. It stands near the ancient Clava Stones.

As I sit here in my car I realise that the next time I visit will be different. Just as the water changes, so one day is never the same as the next. Yet beneath the surface there is something that seems eternal about this place. I feel as if I am in a love affair that never grows old, though I myself am older each year. Generations of swallows have visited these farms and barns for centuries, and now the oldest of these buildings are collapsing into the earth from which they were made.

I turn the key to start the engine and drive back south.

Chapter 23

Enchantment of Sounds and Places

September 2015

It has been a while since my last visit to Clava to write the devas' book, as I have been involved with my art classes and the spiritual workshops I am now facilitating. These programmes are based on the concepts elucidated in *An Angels' Guide* and support people who want to connect to their divine inner guidance with the help of their angels.

However, I have begun to have recurring thoughts of Immortelle's pools and a heartfelt desire to connect with Dorothy Maclean. She was one of the original founders of the Findhorn Community on the Moray coast of Scotland in the 1960s.

In our family photograph albums there are small black and white photos from that time, of family outings to Findhorn Bay. They show our beloved grandparents sitting with my sister on a tartan travel rug on the beach, with the boats of the bay beyond. There's one of me, with bucket and spade, engrossed in building a sand castle.

In my teenage years the Quaker Meeting we attended was sometimes held in the Findhorn Community library, so that people from towns to the east of Inverness could more easily attend without having to travel into Inverness.

I remember seeing the main Universal Hall being built. There were wooden planks used as walkways across the mud for the builders' access. A girl from my school had lived at the Community and gave a talk about it in our English class. People tended to laugh about the giant vegetables that were said to flourish in the sandy soil of the Findhorn caravan park area. In those days, people didn't always understand what the Community represented with their experiments in working together with Nature.

People have come to Findhorn from all over the world. Eileen and Peter Caddy and Dorothy Maclean, the original founders, wrote many books and travelled abroad to give lectures. Findhorn became a place of cutting-edge environmental renown. More recently they experimented with some of the first wind turbines to create electricity locally for both the Community and Findhorn village, and there is a sewerage system using a 'whole systems' approach to biological technology.*

In 2012, when I had been at Findhorn Park to leave a consignment of my books at the shop, I saw Dorothy Maclean out walking along the paths under the trees. I didn't want to approach her out of respect and knowing that, by then in her nineties, she had long been retired and would probably not appreciate people asking questions about her past work.

Now, in 2015, I'm not sure if she still lives there. I search online. Intuitively I feel that I must meet her and ask about the devas, and possibly show her my book script. I have no idea how this might be arranged.

My intuition pulls me like a magnet. I decide to follow it and head north to do some writing, although I am so busy at home. My Stirling friend has offered to accompany me, share the petrol costs, and find us accommodation overnight. Her support makes the journey much easier. I'm grateful for having true friends.

For some unknown reason, there are no bed and breakfast places available in Inverness this weekend. Following her inner guidance, my friend chooses a list of accommodation from Findhorn Park, a place she knows well. Starting from the bottom, she selects the first phone number and immediately secures a place for us to stay at nearby Forres.

Forres used to be at the northern end of the main railway line from Granton-on-Spey in the North Cairngorms. The line was dismantled in the 1960s due to the Beeching cuts and plans to increase the efficiency of the nationalised railway system in Britain. The link from Aviemore in the Cairngorm area to Inverness was built later and became part of the main rail route north. The A9 trunk road runs parallel. Forres is on the east-west railway line between Inverness and Aberdeen. It's a beautiful town but I feel a little disappointed we haven't been able to find somewhere to stay in the nearby Findhorn Park.

I am grateful for the companionship of my friend, who is always happy to wait at our favourite place at Daviot and never rushes me. We agree to meet again later that afternoon and then drive the twenty miles to our accommodation in Forres. I set off for the track to the hill and Immortelle's pool. On reaching the pools I climb down the steep bank and pick my way across the rocky side.

I'm now sitting on the narrow ledge beneath the overhanging birch tree, with just enough room to avoid being in danger of falling into the water. This is my favourite place to write but is only possible when the water level is low. The ledge is usually submerged or covered in green moss. Today, the exposed surface is warm in the sun but damp and patterned with a few yellow-ochre birch leaves. The rock of the pool is composed of old red sandstone, which is prevalent around this area of the Moray Firth.

Many old buildings in towns such as Inverness are characterised by the warm rose colour of this stone. The beach and fossil bearing cliffs at Eathie, by Rosemarkie on the Black Isle, north of here, are remarkable for the orangey-pink colour. Here at the edge of the pool there are pieces of white quartz and nuggets, shards and specs of mica gleaming within the sandstone and catching the light. I used to collect flakes of mica in a tin as a child, thinking they were precious silver, not knowing their real worth.

Part of the pool's basin and steep banks here are made up of conglomerate stone, which looks like a giant Christmas pudding with its mixtures of larger coloured pebbles cemented together in the softer stone.

Scotland's rocks are ancient. The prehistoric stone circles contain white quartzite. I have seen huge pieces in some of the large monoliths. None are as old as the Lewisian gneiss rocks of Calanais on the Isle of Lewis, which are thought to be some of the oldest rocks in Europe, at least 2.7 billion years old. I feel humbled to be sitting directly in contact with rock that is by comparison only 359 million years old, weathered over centuries by glaciers and the flow of water.

My trainers are already damp as the water seeps up. The lip of the lower pool - its curved shelf with the water above - glows like amber and is patterned with waves of brightness. Mica and quartz sparkle like jewels. The water then spills over the edge to the bubbling cauldron below, which is gentle and quiet today.

The sun falls at my feet, warm on wet rock, as it reaches across the rippled surface of Immortelle's pool, bright against deep dark with sparkling points like stars.

The waterfall enters the pool opposite me. I half expect Immortelle to emerge from here. I am tired after a late night clearing my emails to make space to come here today.

In my left ear is the sound of the waterfall entering the pool: water on water like the sound of a bath filling but multi-layered, gurgling and spraying. In my right ear I hear the chattering of water over rock, spilling down.

There are elves present, says Immortelle. I ask in my mind why the elves stay here at this place and, as usual, the answer comes back telepathically by thought transference.

Enchantment… they bring enchantment… they bring life by their music.

At first I doubt the words I write, then suddenly awareness comes. *En chant*. I'd never noticed that before! The deva has always mentioned music and elves as being inseparable. Immortelle picks up on my thoughts.

The music humans hear, sing, play, create is an expression of the Divine. When you sing, the angels sing with you, when you dance, we dance with you. It is all vibration. When you tune in you attune to Earth and we resonate with you.

Dear Immortelle, is it true of all music? What about rock, heavy metal, acid house? What of discord and hard beat?

It is all expression, and urgently we require you humans to express yourselves creatively and get in tune.

Is one form higher vibrationally than another?

> Yes, it is so. However, we say to you that any attempt by humans to arrange sound is a form of expression that can change a person's vibration from one level to another: from fear to love or love to fear - to action, to peace, to excitement. The movement is of life. All the universe is sound.
> Much of human noise pollution is dead noise, disharmonious and disruptive. It breaks the flow. It stagnates matter like the water of the pool with no exit, no life - full of rotting vegetation. Yet in the rotting there is change and the water dies to live again.
> When humans attune to Nature, they hear the harmony of the spheres and beautiful music ensues.

Dear Immortelle, I am thinking of one day when I was here on the moor and could hear the beeping of a truck backing up. It must have been far away but the sound carried right up the moor and disturbed the peace. I expect the person who was driving the truck had no idea how far the sound had carried.

> Alas, human noise pollution creates heavy energy that is as destructive to us as the blasting away of rock and hill by industrial exploits.

What about the sound of the wind turbines or electrical appliances?

> It is not music. It is opposite. As we have said, it's destructive. Many of you are deaf, many are blind, many have lost your ability to feel the beauty and love, to hear the song of the hills, the laughter of water. The stars in the sky are put out by your harsh lights to light your roads, buildings and machinery. Your young ones are attuned to their gadgets and feast their eyes on manmade fantasy. They come to live in that world. They do not see, hear or sense the real world.

> We speak of the real world as that which is accessed by our gateways. The hills, oceans, trees and rocks are gateways; they are manifestations of the world which are all from Source and all linked to the real world.
> To sense the real world, children need love, the freedom to play on the sand and under the trees, to practise sport, and not feast their eyes and brains on false gods.

This sounds harsh, Immortelle. Many of the children I met during art teaching were desperate to know more about Nature, to make models of birds, know the names of trees, and help animals.

> Yes, this is because children are naturally attuned in a corrupted world.

Is this is an old-fashioned view of things? Is there a possibility that children can evolve with the technology in a healthy way?

> Yes, and no. Yes, children can evolve in a technological age if that technology is not based on abuse and disrespect of Nature. No, children cannot evolve healthily and happily in an environment that abuses Nature, that corrupts goodness, and blocks out the sun.

Do you mean, Immortelle, that people are living in such a material world that they build houses or bunkers underground, and all must be lit by electricity? Of course, there are already people planning to live in such places in the event of nuclear war or natural disaster.

> We laugh. Natural disaster is all created by human evil: the refusal to live naturally.

What has caused this, Immortelle?

> Greed caused this.

What is the opposite motivation that could correct the need for greed?

> The realisation that your world is unlimited abundance, creates the belief that there is no need to take more than your fair share.
> The realisation that you are all connected creates the true feeling, motivates compassion: compassion for each other, for your Earth, and all that lives thereon. The lion shall lie down with the lamb.
> Then, humans may co-create with Nature and your children shall thrive. Do not despair. This time is coming. You witness the mass migration of peoples from slavery and from their war-torn lands. They vote with their feet. They walk to freedom. They walk with their families and children.
> Their vibration is too high for them to exist any more in their homeland. Their homeland is corrupted and torn apart by fear. Its vibration is altered and its people cannot exist there.

Dear Immortelle, isn't it simply the case that if these people stay they will be killed or have no food or be sold to slavery? Therefore, they have to risk their lives to find a place to survive?

> We answer you: on a superficial level and to outer appearances this is true. On a vibrational level, they move to the place where they now resonate - where they do not feel fear. The people in the hosting countries have raised their compassion and are now able to welcome them.
> Child, there have always been movements of people over Earth. There have always been refugees, pilgrims, travellers, nomads.
> Some of these movements of people are enforced, as you see today in your world. Others are caused because

people like to wander and explore. They resonate differently in different places. They explore the vibrational frequencies of the places that attract them.

Am I one of these people too? I have always been drawn to the idea of a gypsy style caravan or modern camper van, but they use precious fuel and so it seems rather a luxury.

Your vibration matches the places you love. It's why you're attracted there. Your vibration also matches people you love. It's why you can't leave them. It's not to do with your lifestyle. It's to do with the vibration. Vibrational matching comes first, then lifestyle.

Thank you for this information.

When I come down from the hill to meet my friend, I don't feel very keen to drive all the way to Forres. It isn't Findhorn after all, and the possibility of meeting anyone who may know about Dorothy seems like a vain hope.

We arrive at the doorstep of our accommodation. There is a small statue of a Buddha and some white gravel paths carefully laid between the plants. A set of bells chime and an elderly woman comes to the door. She is beautiful and poised and it is hard to guess her exact age. She welcomes us inside and it is like stepping over a magic circle. Surrounding us all round the hall are artefacts, photographs of nature, weavings, and crystals. A large notice board displays posters of events happening at Findhorn Park.

After only a few minutes, she mentions that she is a sound healer, and I tell her of my writing about the subject of sound this very day, up on the hill at Clava. My friend and I have hardly had time to set our bags down before she leads us upstairs to a large spacious room. It is clear and light, full of the most enormous crystals imaginable, a complete set of crystal bowls arranged side by side on a shelf in ascending size, musical instruments from all over the world and a very large Japanese style gong.

"You must come and do an angel workshop here! *Everyone* who comes here, is here for a purpose," she says.

She leads us into the garden where she shows us the sound chamber she's had built. My friend and I follow as if sleep walking. We are tired after the journey from Stirling, the long day and the further drive to Forres. It is September and I am chilled from sitting outdoors, yet also amazed at this synchronicity of having arrived at what feels like a hub of Findhorn on the edge of the town of Forres.

We are invited to eat our sandwiches in the kitchen, where we sit at the table surrounded by an array of teas and health foods of every kind.

A young woman enters, her arms laden with green vegetables gathered fresh from the garden. They are some of the most *alive* vegetables I've ever seen, apart from those grown by my parents, who are wonderful organic gardeners in their eighties. I immediately notice her vitality and her face full of life, with twinkly eyes, just as I'd imagine a gardener in a fairy tale book.

I try to be discreet as I pull out a limp lettuce from our picnic bag to eat with our sandwiches. The young gardener looks on in shock.

"Don't eat that!" She exclaims. "Eat this!"

She refers to her vegetables. They are practically jumping out of her arms. It almost seems murderous to eat them but we do and they taste heavenly!

October 2015

A month later we are back for my first angel workshop in

the sound healer's studio. At the evening talk preceding the workshop day, the room is full of people, sitting on cushions, on the floor, and on extra chairs that are brought in as more arrive. I feel welcomed into the heart of a community of people who respect and value the spiritual aspect of Earth and have no problem with the word, angel.

The following day, a gentle smiling lady arrives early to the workshop.

"You must speak to Dorothy!"

She seems to know Dorothy well and is keen to arrange for me to meet her on my next visit. I don't even have to ask.

Chapter 24

Meeting New Findhorn Friends

14th February 2016, Valentine's Day

My opportunity to meet Dorothy Maclean was to come five months after first meeting the Findhorn friends in Forres. I write our conversation from memory as accurately as I can.

"Don't treat her like a celebrity; she doesn't like fuss. Just be yourself," I had been advised. The room is filled with flowers, so the bunch I have brought crowds the table. I wish I had been able to bring wild flowers from the moor, but at this time of year, the moor is covered in snow.

We start to talk generally. I say something about not wanting to be an upstart. She laughs and says, "Aren't we all afraid of that?" She clearly likes some banter.

She asks me to pull out from the bookshelf a folio of her drawings from her art college years. I become engrossed in looking through them as they are exceptionally wonderful drawings.

One shows a toddler with hands on the floor in front of him, head down and peeping through his legs, as if about to do a somersault, seen from a ground level view from behind. I know from experience this is anatomically difficult to draw, and requires much technical skill. To get the angle right you practically have to lie on the floor to draw, and besides, toddlers tend to move about. Yet she has caught that movement in the drawing. There are drawings of buildings, people, birds and flowers, portrayed in great detail and sensitively observed.

I can see that she is immensely enjoying my attention to her artwork, not because of pride, but rather a common understanding and appreciation between us. I take my time to look at each drawing and become increasingly absorbed, almost forgetting my list of questions about the devas.

That is why I have come. I want to talk about the devas with her, and when that moment comes, I can't really think of anything to say!

Then she refers to my writings, as part of my script is laid out on the coffee table beside us. She asks me a question so pertinent that in this moment I know that she has understood everything perfectly.

"How do you believe the information you receive?"

I say, "I feel its truth in my heart."

"Good. Do you have a guardian with you when you connect with the devas and nature spirits?" she questions me.

"Yes, always. I ask my angels to be there to protect me."

She seems satisfied with that and changes the subject.

Reflecting afterwards, I knew that she had answered what was most important in that two-sentence conversation. I wondered if she could see nature spirits everywhere outside. If she did, she would not speak of them. When we have a true understanding of them, there is no need.

We sat in companionship for over an hour. I remember her very blue eyes looking out through the window, as she enjoyed watching the birds in view on the feeder. It was a beautiful February day: Valentine's Day, 2016.

I had been told not to concern her with speaking of her fame or all the books she had written. This was easy when I was there. I was told she really loved the book script excerpts I had sent. Her caregiver had read them to her. As I left, my feeling was that the devas had connected us.

Chapter 25

Temples to the Planets

Late September 2015

Back at the moor, it's getting late in the day.

Soon the light leaves the grassy spur and the pool moves into shadow apart from the rocky shelf. Watching the flow of water in the light is entrancing. I've crossed the burn to find a warm place in the sun on the other bank above the sentinel birch trees. This is more or less where I perceived the elf child standing on the bank a few months ago.

From where I'm sitting by these birch trees above the lower pool, I see down to the small cauldron below the lower pool and the flumes it throws up. That part of the burn seems to have a life of its own, a miniature fountain, full of power and light. I cannot believe the force of the water, though the burn is one of the smallest that flows from the hill.

The white-barked tree exudes peace as its leaves turn gold. Cushions of green-ochre moss light up on its trunk.

Behind it the white stream of the fall pours over the rockslide. The tree that leans over the bank is by contrast covered in hanging pom-poms of pale green lichen.

Dear Immortelle, are you here?

> We laugh that you ask.

Dear Immortelle, why is one tree free from lichen and the next one covered in it?

> The elementals that guard the tree have chosen that one.

I observe two types of lichen, the crinkled flat-growing kind with curled edges and the more yellow-green beard-like growths that hang down, and then there's the cushion-like moss at the base of the trunk. The branch overhanging the pool is broken, cracked near the trunk and hanging down vertically, yet is full of buds and covered in lichen beards.

> Lichen is important as an air purifier; it only grows where the air is pure. It maintains the purity. See it as a barometer of air condition.

It seems strange that only that one tree has the lichen even though the others around are growing in similar conditions? How do the elementals connected with the tree decide which tree harbours lichen?

> The spirit of that particular tree takes on that service for the area of the pool. The tree hosts the other life forms, such as the lichen that grows on it… a symbiotic relationship.

The block of Forestry Commission Scots pines is very close by here.

I wonder if the trees that have been planted as a crop are also in service to God? Do they purify the air?

> Yes, they function as filters and give of their bark, but they do not carry the life in the way that natural trees do. There are few devas and nature spirits there. The trees' auras are retracted. They don't support other lives, apart from the insects that burrow, and the birds that nest in them.
> The earth beneath them is full of dwarves of the kind that have become malformed and debased, as are the trees! They don't like their branches touching! They prefer space. They need light. The natural burn that flows through the conifers gives respite, though its domain is infringed upon.

In contrast, the edges of the natural burn are filled with life and birdsong. Birch, rowans, ash trees, some holly, cherry, bird elder and juniper grow in abundance, clinging to the banks as they do here. Once when I walked by the burn as it ran through the plantation I came to a small glade. Two rowans grew close together beside a pile of boulders that may once have been a human dwelling. There was a very magical atmosphere at that point and I felt the fairies were around. I was only a few metres away from this place by the pools, where I usually do my writing, though hidden in the thickets of the plantation. The Forestry Commission has completely obscured a layer of living and natural plants that was there before.

At this point it begins to rain and waking from my reflections I head back to the road.

Back at the pools later that month:

Dear Immortelle, I'm sorry. I've been in the vicinity but didn't come here. I got as far as the wood, but it felt disquieting and forbidding. I wanted to pay you a surprise visit, but I realised that you are bound to know when I am approaching your sacred place as you are a greater power than human. There is no possibility of surprising you, is there?

I felt as if your presence was there with me though, warning me to turn and go back. Then I heard rifle fire. I could hear the sound of bullets ricocheting and ripping through the air as if they were close. I didn't want to be mistaken for a deer, especially if my head was sticking up above the edge of the bank of the gorge as I sat by your pool. I turned back and then drove over to the harbour at Nairn to see where your river goes into the sea. I realise that is your domain as much as this place, though you say you hang around here. After being at Nairn harbour for a while, I drove to meet my friend at Burghead. Now I'm here again but I don't have long before I need to get back home.

We are happy you came today. It's safe to be here. Don't fear. All is well. Earth ascends. Many are praying for us. Many are praying. We love you. We join forces. The one God is overall and we rejoice. We are helping you.

Several questions enter my mind and I am concerned whether I am truly connecting with Immortelle and hearing her divine words. The problem with thinking of questions to ask is that it requires the logical analytical brain, whereas hearing the devas requires a letting go of the mind and fast writing without thoughts getting in the way.

I move across the rocky perch in the bowl of rock beneath the sentinel birch tree so the sunlight is pouring directly down the lower fall and across the pool towards me. The air is filled with dampness of moss and scent of leaves and earth, but here it's clear of ticks and midges.

I record a visualisation on my laptop as I perch rather

precariously on the rocky edge. My rucksack becomes damp, so I need to fold the laptop in scarves, waterproof jacket and polythene bag and hold it on my knees. I place my notepad on top and write by hand.

The sun skims the heathery horizon. I cannot visualise a world where people will respect Earth so much as to leave wilderness alone, and allow the natural balance to redress. Yet I know so many people love Nature, trees and water, and feed the birds and care for their animals.

Do you have any words to say to me, Immortelle? Can you advise me today?

> You are here in perfect timing and we reassure you that this book from the devas is of utmost importance and to be widely read. You fear that it is too personal and your descriptions of your homeland will not resonate with those from other places and countries or city dwellers. This is far from being the case.
> Humans are highly attuned to the vibration of water. Most have their favorite pool, lagoon, river, waterfall or sea. Even in the towns, the fountains in the square are an oasis in summer particularly, a place to recharge. The fountains of the great cities represent, of course, the great fountain of life.
> Water is life force. You are composed of water. When you breathe, the vapour of your breath goes into the atmosphere. You can even breathe out toxins; you breathe out negative energies to be recycled and transmuted to Light. Your trees recycle your atmosphere.
> Many of you breathe out love and gratitude and we devas can measure this vibration in its energetic form. That is why we say to you that we connect. We feel your love for us.
> Many humans treat Earth with respect and work tireless-

ly and committedly to help by recycling, by gardening without chemicals, by looking after plants and animals and teaching their children to do the same. It was thus and ever shall be so. For all else will perish and those who work with the Light shall remain.

Earth cannot any longer sustain its low vibration, nor support evil intention and abuse by humans. We require people's co-operation, respect and understanding.

Immortelle of the waterfall speaks to you. Immortelle, the deva of this place, this waterfall, this burn, that runs to the river and the sea of dolphins. Immortelle, your deva from the angelic realms, upholding the vibration of this particular kingdom forever and ever.

We greet you, star child, and we thank you for coming here. You are safe with us and we will not allow you to be harmed by our kin.

We entrust you with this work. We trust you with our words. We are angels of Heaven. We are your angels. You must not fear lack. See how abundant is your world. You are free to sit in the sun and write. Your friends support you. We need you to write this work. Do not denigrate yourself or your descriptions of our moor and watercourse. This book is a revelation.

I wonder about the book's title. Earth's Voices? Messages for Our Times from Nature's Guardians?

Yes, it's perfect.

Immortelle, why is Scotland a heartland?

The rocks are ancient. People came here and practised connection with the Divine through Nature. The practice of speaking to fairies is integral to the old religion and common to many countries within Scandinavia and also

> Europe. Many times, people were persecuted for practising their art from the time of...

The message tails off. I cannot hear the words giving the time when the practice was banned, though I really wanted to know. The deva continues without waiting.

> Religion became human-made and parts were outlawed. Now it is time that the truth held in the rocks and stones of the ancient temples be revealed again.

What are the temples you speak of?

> Those that are aligned with the power of Nature, for the devas are the architects of all things of God. We are the architects and when humans work with us, not against us, we can achieve world peace and a time of plenitude.

Will many people die in order for this to come about? Our population is exploding.

> Your population shall come back to balance when man respects woman and woman respects man. Your indigenous societies practised birth control without cruelty. They knew the herbs to use and how to administer them. They could not afford to let their population explode or there would not be enough food.

Are we in this situation now?

> You're past it, and yes, some will die. However, the wars and poverty cannot continue into these new times and ways are found to feed many without practising crude and intensive farming methods, which further poison the land and abuse animals.

We must pray for this, Immortelle.

I am too tired to argue with the deva about intensive farming of which I know so little, and yet I feel her words are true. Just as I am feeling uncomfortable and damp, I glimpse elves standing in a row on the opposite bank, staring over at me. I think of my mortality and how this burn and waterfalls shall be here long after I'm gone.

> *We are happy with all the questions. You're on target. You've done well. Type up what you have. There's only one part left. Yes. It's about Clava.*
> *We sing! Glory to God. We help you with the writing now, whether you're here or at home. You have been faithful. Your abundance is dependent on your dreaming and asking. All is well. We're helping you. Thank you, star child.*

Thank you. I don't want to go but I'm uncomfortable!

As I begin to pack up my notebook and belongings, I am excited to think that Immortelle will reveal more about Clava and our human connection with these sacred places, and the star systems and planets to which they are linked.

I think back to a few evenings I spent with old maps of ancient Britain spread on the kitchen table and star charts up on my computer screen, attempting to find connections between the position of the stones within one area, their link with the stars above and also between one stone circle site and another.

I began to realise that from the perspective of the ground, the plans to site stones as a mirror image of a star system mean that the pattern is reversed.

Sometimes I thought I was getting somewhere, and then I would think it was wishful thinking on my part, or some star didn't seem to quite fit the pattern. I have also tried to link different strategic sites from one ancient location to the next using thread and sticky tack. As I looked at the emerging pattern on the map, there seemed to be crossing points and many patterns of stars. Often the summits of Scottish mountains were in alignment with the stone circles. However, I didn't feel I had enough knowledge of either the stars or the structures on the ground in order to decipher the underlying patterns.

I have looked up the notes I made from this summer's visit with a friend to Avebury, the great stone circle in Wiltshire, England, which is the largest megalithic stone circle in the world. I overheard a guide talking about how artefacts had been found there that originated from the Orkney Islands off the north-east coast of Scotland, which meant that people must have made pilgrimages between these sites in ancient times.

I had taken down this message:

Each stone has a guardian sent from Venus. The people who built the circle channelled energy from Venus - bringing love and Light for the well-being of their people whom they believed were from Venus also. Other groups of people of those same times were affiliated to different planets.

During that visit to Avebury I also became fascinated by photographs of the patterns of the *crop circles* that occurred in the fields around this site and I had asked my angels if there was anything they wished to communicate that was relevant to this book. This is what they told me.

Yes, people did travel throughout the land and many were displaced. Some were pilgrims. Others were traders or itinerant labourers on the land.
The crop circle patterns... Yes, they are linked with the

stones, of course. The people who built the stone circles were making temples to the planets. Humans showed awareness of Heaven by the mathematical alignments within their stone buildings. The crop circles also show the planets, and reveal your awareness of the links between Earth and Heaven.

We angels show our acknowledgement of human understanding. We can only work in the places where people have connected with us previously, at the portals, which have been kept active. The stones anchor the energy to the Earth. The energy resonates. We see the patterns.

Is beauty a portal for art and music, and to show us where the divine connection lies?

Yes, if you like to explain it this way - the art patterns and circle patterns show the symbols that are building blocks for structures of life.

Orion the gateway has opened. You are a way-shower for many.

The people who built the stone circles knew they were from the stars and they were also linked telepathically with other groups.

Why do the crop circles show us the patterns in this way?

The aim is to gradually come into human consciousness and acceptance. We are bound by God's laws and have no will. All angelic beings that are working in the Light are not allowed to exert their will or to impose their knowledge on humans. Therefore they are allowed to create the crop circle patterns without damaging plant material. It is left to your free will to choose how to understand the patterns.

Why are the architects of the crop circles drawing themselves and these designs to our attention?

> We must show that humans cannot be allowed to destroy this planet, and that there is more in the universe than this small world... as some people see it. Humans are in danger of losing their free will if they don't comply with their promise to be caretakers.

Did we ever promise that we would look after Earth?

> Yes, humans were given Earth to look after. They disobeyed.

Who did we humans make a promise to?

> Gaia.

Who is Gaia?

> Mother Earth.

Thank you, angels.

I wondered if there was anywhere in the Christian Bible that said that humans made a promise to be caretakers for Earth and whether this was a promise to God. I discussed the message with my hillwalking friend who had been a teacher of religious studies. She found several references that confirmed this was indeed the case. (For further information, please see the *Appendices* section.)*

Chapter 26

Fracking Nature and the Sound of OM

17th March 2016

Catching sight of the lower waterfall from over the heathery rise, it forms a stream of pure white light cascading down over the rockslide from the dark basin of the upper pool.

Leaning over the edge by the sentinel tree, I see the foaming water plunge into a swirl of white bubbles that splash upwards creating a mist of rainbows. The water then streams towards the centre of the heart-shaped pool. Here it slows up and forms bubbles that chase each other across to the curved rock shelf. Then the water slides down to the small basin where it shoots up flumes like a jacuzzi, then continues down over the next pool of liquid amber.

I clamber down to sit in the sun on the grassy spur facing the point above the shelf. Here is where the face of the spirit of the pool has shown itself before. I wonder if he will show himself this time?

I no longer introduce myself here. For the nature spirits, time is immaterial.

It feels warm and safe here. I sit, bathed in sunlight, and enjoying the warmth, watching the bubbles and rainbows, white and green gleaming water which slides over deep green moss. The sound of the waterfall roars in my left ear while flumes spray and gurgle below.

Dear Immortelle, I am happy to be here. But after seeing the visual impact of the pylon lines and wind farms at Farr, at Duntelchaig and Errogie, and knowing that this development is not there to serve the people locally but for profit elsewhere, I am feeling too depressed to be able to connect with you. I struggle with the feeling that the wild in-between places are designated, not as sites of beauty or national parkland, but as resources to be used. Is there any true wilderness left in Scotland?

I believe wilderness to be a concept that includes visual impact. I've read the reactions of hill walkers in particular. I know I'm not alone in perceiving the negative effect of seeing these changes to the wilderness. Today, instead of enjoying the beauty, fresh air and views to distant snow-peaked mountains, the openness of moors and lochs glittering in sunlight, all is spoiled like a beautiful face or body with ugly scars across it. I feel shocked. Instead of being raised up by the scenery I am totally depressed. Some might say it's a luxury to be able to enjoy scenery and not everyone can afford it. But I believe that even knowing it is there gives a sense of well-being, while knowing it is not there is distressing. Some people may travel abroad for scenery if they can't experience it here but where is wilderness safe anywhere in the world? What can we do?

I experience the pain as a huge weight upon viewing the changing scenery. I sense I may not hear Immortelle today because my vibration is low and in order to hear her it's necessary to raise it.

> We thank you for your commitment to us. We are, as always, happy you are here. We wish you enjoy our healing power and pass this, and our words, to others through your descriptions, through your words. This knowledge is important. And this is your task now.

Despite the deva's words to me, I feel as if I can't connect with the fairy realms today. My heart is so heavy after seeing the degradation of the beautiful wilderness in the hills above Farr and Loch Duntelchaig. What had been a joyous place to cycle and wander in is now criss-crossed with pylon wires, substations, wind farms and forestry operations. I have heard other people comment that this area has become an industrialised wilderness. At the time, hearing this description completely burst my bubble of elation at being back in a place I had loved to explore as a young woman.

I try not to see these hills as an industrialised wilderness, but how can you *unsee* something that is right in front of your eyes. I feel grief in my heart for the mess and destruction. I have no idea how I will be able to channel, as I know that the devas cannot reach us when our vibration carries low thought forms.

I'd like to ask you about the destruction of the land round here to build the pylon lines, wind farms and the infrastructure for the roads that service them and housing developments. How does this affect the devas and natural life force?

It seems as if any remote beautiful place is under threat of development. I have heard that the wind farms planned to service the pylon line through the Highlands to Central Scotland are to be sited on what is known as the 'Sacred Mountain', the Sleeping Beauty near Calanais, on the Isle of Lewis. Tourists come from all over the world to see Calanais but do they know that the focus of their pilgrimage is about to be defaced by wind farms which generate power to supply other regions far from here, and create profit for the power companies? It feels as if the small campaign groups are powerless against the multinationals.

(Reader's Note: Approaching the time of publication: A huge windfarm of 33 turbines and 184 megawatt capacity nacelles to supply electricity to 230,000 homes and provide over 200 jobs was given the go-ahead in 2021. The giant turbines will be visible across the Isles of Lewis and Harris and from the Calanais Stones, with widespread diverse effects due to the intimate scale and richly diverse character of the landscape around Stornoway. The site is on the breeding grounds of recently established hen harriers, vulnerable rare birds.*

At the time of writing in March 2016, I did not know about another small community wind farm, Beinn Ghrideag, built on the common grazing lands in the Point and Sandwick area of the Isle of Lewis, installed in May 2015. It is the biggest community wind farm in the United Kingdom, a small 3 turbine system, with 9 megawatt capacity nacelles producing profit for the local Western Isles community once capital costs have been repaid. It is expected to generate 2 million pounds a year.)*

The pylons marching over Strathnairn across your domain have now been built but are yet to be switched on. I understand that they are waiting for the wind farms to be built and have been ordered in advance. There's a push for Scottish energy to be in the forefront. In the last few years so many wind farms and pylon lines have been built on sites all over Scotland and can be seen from most of the mountains.

Now fracking is proposed for some areas and being promoted as the oil runs out. It's said to be clean and that oil bubbles in the earth are viewed as surplus to Earth's requirement, a natural abundance for us to solve our energy crisis. Nuclear energy is also seen as clean, but all is expensive in some way or other.

> The visual mess you see, the destruction of beauty in the name of clean energy is an abuse to us nature spirits. We cannot continue to live here where Earth is disturbed in this way. We see this as a mismanagement of resources.

So much of our world is dependent on oil, not only to run cars but to make plastics and clothing. It would be hard for us to give this up. People will not want to give up their cars and lifestyles.

Cars do not have to run on petrol. Plastic is an unneces-

sary evil to us. It is possible to live without oil. Humans have the ability to use non-expendable materials for everything, without going back to a primitive way of being.

The use of resources in the way that is currently being promoted is driving the planet to extinction and dependency on materialism. Country after country is plundered. Earth is raped and the same pattern is everywhere. Communities must take responsibility and become self-sufficient using local non-expendable resources, not stealing off each other, not selling their assets.

Humans must respect Earth now for their survival. The extraction of oil, and fracking, run counter to this. It kills the Earth spirits and throws the world into chaos. The earthquakes, volcanoes and floods are happening because of the imbalance created by such exploitation.

It seems to happen most often in areas where people are poor but are not necessarily themselves abusers of Earth's resources.

Abuse by disrespect towards people or Earth's resources, always causes poverty. In the same way that women and children are the victims of war, in the same way Earth Mother is depleted of resources. This path of greed leads to war and ultimately to extinction of your species and ours. The practice of greed - the taking of more than is necessary to live, of wasting and squandering - leads to more greed.

There are many children now on Earth who've come with gifts and abilities to turn your world around. They carry compassion in their hearts and do not walk the path of violence. They hold the true power. This power is in their hearts.

Some of them have unique gifts and abilities. They are scientists, engineers, mathematicians, physicists, alche-

mists, magicians, artists, musicians, dancers and athletes. They show the world how to be, and they manifest magic. They are gifted beyond anything yet witnessed or recorded on Earth. They come to reverse the destruction and show the world how to live in abundance. They do not need war, greed and poverty.

Yes, it's true. We are witnessing the coming of these children.

Some that live in war zones are being killed. Some came to die as heroes; they show the way! They teach people compassion. You are seeing this everywhere. These children have the capacity to bring many people to Light and their Light can never be put out. Although they die, there are so many of them, so many come to influence the world.

So are we to wait to be saved by these miracle-manifesting children who will know what to do?

We laugh. No, it's not what you would call a quick fix. Many are leading the way and are way-showers. You are all connected. The time has been prophesied.

    I crawl down the bank to reach the water a little way upstream from the pools and waterfalls, and climb onto a large boulder that sits in the middle of the burn. From here I can see the water flow down the rock channel and hurtle over the edge into the higher waterfall. I sit astride the rock, half afraid I will fall in. My hands are frozen but I hold on. I sit on the rock for a time, experiencing the grief of seeing my favourite places spoilt, and then I begin to cry like a child for the enormity of the destruction.
    I know that no-one can see or hear me, so I let go and weep and wail for the mess that we have caused to the

wilderness, to the devas, nature spirits and elementals. My voice blends into the water. Now I can hear myself howling with rage, remorse and grief as if I am apart from myself.

In no time it seems, the sound of the water carries away my thoughts and feelings and I find myself singing. As the sound I make joins together with the water, I start to sing one note over and over. It is relieving and comforting. My voice echoes in the water and the water sings in response. The song is filled with life and I cling to the rock as the water flows past me on both sides. There is great power as the water rushes through the gorge and carries away all my fear. Then I hear Immortelle:

Dear star child, we hear you! Go ahead and tell our story. This is what you can do. This is your contribution. Leave the politics. It's of no consequence. Politics come and go like the leaves of the tree. The wind farms are already outmoded, the power lines will crumble in time, and the roads that serve them will grow over. They burn us, cut us and scar us. It pricks the surface. The power of the devas is greater. We who work deep beneath the Earth continue forever.

Dear Immortelle, you said before that you needed humans' help and prayers, so I am not sure I understand you when you say that you continue. Can Earth continue without life on it?

We say that when the turbines are superseded there will be no purpose for the power lines. It is the disrespect of humans that we cannot tolerate.

How quickly I move from weeping and wailing to singing. One note pervades and I hold onto the rock and sing loudly the same note again and again together with the water. Long notes blend with the voices of the water. Joy fills my heart and for a time I sit on the rock singing and singing in a way I have not sung since I was a child or in the school choir. I sing in a voice from deep within my heart.

All is well. Blessed be. Blessed be.

Immortelle's words affect me profoundly. Now in a calmer state, I wander upstream to find a level place along the bank in the sun where I can listen to the voices of the water. The weather is exceptional for the time of year and it's hot in the sun. I have the idea of recording visualisations for my angel workshops with the true sounds of Nature in the background. The voices of the water are hypnotic.

I pull off my jersey and tie the sleeves round my head in a turban with the back hanging down over my neck and shoulders, acting as a shield against the intense light. I take my laptop from my rucksack and place it in the grass beside me with a stone to stop it sliding down to the water. I find some favourite music by Scottish and Scottish/American/Canadian fiddlers.

At first the music sounds tinny compared to the full, thunderous voice of the burn, but then the sound begins to naturally ebb and flow with the water like a heartbeat. It accurately describes the course of the clear burn as it breaks over the rocks, rounds the bend under the banks of heather and over the green moss, then disappears down the rock chute towards the upper pool. A soft breeze wafts, bringing the tobacco-like scent of last year's dead bracken and damp moss. The music blends with the water.

Are the nature spirits enhancing the sound? It is different. It is alive! Is fiddle music from Scotland different from that of another country? How can this describe the landscape of any other place on Earth? It calls, it dances, it pulls at the heart strings, it calls me home. I remember the harp music I heard downstream from here at the lower pool nearly forty years ago. The makers of that music are still here.

I know it! The immortal ones that guard this watercourse are here forever, long after my bones have decayed into Earth and my soul returns here to this land that I love. In this moment, nothing else matters.

I lie on my back and listen to how the music merges with the water in a way that seems perfect - as if the composers and the musicians have channelled the spirit of hill and moor. As the melodies of water and music continue wafting on the air, I fall into a doze among the grass and flowers of tormentil and bell heather.

Get up! Get up!

My angel calls suddenly, loudly in my right ear.

On awakening, I clamber back up the bank, pass through the bog and leave the moor. I make my way through the plantation and return to the place where I am staying. At night I sit writing by lamplight, recording the events of this day. Later, as I drift off to sleep, the stars are shining through the skylight.

Chapter 27

The Coming of the Children of Light

18th March 2016

Immortelle, I wanted to pick up from yesterday's conversation. I was feeling too low in spirits to connect properly with you after seeing the pylons criss-crossing the wild landscape of the moors above Farr, Dunlichity and Errogie. The beauty is still there but I feel shocked to see what's been done. I don't think I can go there any more. I wish I had recorded the place in photographs in the years before the pylons, though I do still have some old photos. Is my view of the place nostalgic, sentimental or unrealistic? I feel I'm always looking back at my past, feeling it was better than now... like an old person! Is it simply a fact of ageing that we see our environment change?

It must have been a shock to people when the first pylons were erected or when the first forestry blocks were planted. But that was in response to war and deforestation and was regarded as a new supply bank, so perhaps it was reassuring for people to see those changes. When my parents came to live here the pylons were newly erected. Maps of this area only show the pylons from the 1950s revised version, but patches of wind farm symbols are now beginning to appear on newer maps which include access roads to the large-scale wind turbines.

It's impossible for their presence not to affect me. The area in which I was brought up is near the point where the pylon line from Beauly to Denny begins. Cutting through scenery well known to me, the line ends up at Denny near Stirling, where I've been living and teaching for many years. Even from my living room I can see the new line of pylons erected this year, shining silver behind the Wallace Monument at the edge of Dumyat as it crosses to Fallin and Plean by Denny. The area for the base of a pylon has wiped out most of a field and two old trees, a favourite place where I used to take my children in summer. So, whether here in the Highlands or at home, their presence is high profile on the skyline. Should we feel reassured when we see what is being done to secure our green energy future?

Dear Immortelle, what would you wish to say? What does a deva of this mountain area and waterfalls wish to say?

> We say this: All is temporary. The wind farms are outmoded before they're built. You humans do have the means to create the technology you need to provide light, heat and electricity, for your cities, your transport and computers, without disrupting the environment.
> The wastage and resources the system needs to run is greater than the energy it can provide. It bankrupts itself, whilst some rely on bankrupting the nation for their wealth. Their profit is another's loss. Humans see Nature as a source to plunder. Greed demands greed. One wins, another loses. Earth is seen as a commodity to own or steal from one another.

Dear Immortelle, investments in wind farms and solar power are sold to people, but they require destruction of landscape for their building and operation. It's big business, big politics and Scotland is seen by some as being at the forefront of this modern-day gold rush.

> We laugh at humans' shortsightedness. We devas renew all things on Earth; we aerate, we re-oxygenate, we repair. We require humans' co-operation. The technology to provide you with renewable sources of energy is clearly here. Natural kinetic energy does not destroy life forms. The information is here. All that is required is for humans to manifest it.

> It's necessary for people to change their understanding of the concept of ownership of land. Humans are only custodians here. It's necessary for those people in the Light who have wealth, to buy land and preserve and care for it, by allowing the devas to work there.
> There are bees natural to Scotland, and every bee has its own land. Keep them in Scotland and every bee to its own land. The bees are your life blood. It's necessary to keep the rivers clear from toxins, to allow the wild places to flourish around the water, to fence off natural areas, not as a commodity to own or steal from another, not as playgrounds for the rich but for their preservation and as amenity for all.
> These places need caretakers, not necessarily environmentalists, but people who know the names of the plants and trees and understand how they grow. These are herbalists, homeopaths and others who work with the essence and vibration of the plants for healing.
> No one shall own land other than to care for it with respect for the devas, and there shall be cars that run off fossil-free fuel, houses with no wastage, gardens that grow food, communal gardens. Leave the wild places. Do not garden them!

Dear Immortelle, there are communities even in Scotland where people already uphold such a dream. Dorothy Maclean of the Findhorn Community upheld the work of the founders by her presence there. Many still hold the Light and wish to work with you devas and nature spirits.

> There are communities which shall rise into prominence where all is self-sufficient, where a new biodegradable form of plastic is discovered that does not abuse resources in its making. This is used for polytunnels. Geothermals and local wind turbines that belong to small communities

generate the power, and cars are developed that do not run on fossil fuels, but with wind funnels.

There are children amongst you that have come here with knowledge of the technology required to create these systems. They are attuned to Nature and protected by their angels. They shall not seek profit or destroy Earth. You are aware of some of them. Some of you are already parents of these children.

Some of them suffer depression because their gifts are suited to the future and not the present. However, they shall live through these times and rise to full glory. We have spoken of them before. Some are dying in the regions where war rages. They shall always return in future. They are artists, musicians, inventors, mathematicians, sportsmen and women.

Dear Immortelle, in this world of the future where children and adults use their gifts to create peace and abundance, where does computer technology feature? So many children seem to spend hours of time on their tablets as to be in danger of suffering from lack of sleep, lack of natural light, air, darkness, loss of social and communication skills and have no time to experience Nature as their world is seen through the interface of the screen. When teaching art I have noticed that some are incredibly talented and sensitive, technologically skilled, yet others of the same age group struggle with basic skills of handling pencils, scissors. Some find it extremely difficult to focus on any subject for the length of time that's necessary to produce a piece of work.

I don't know whether to stay here - or move further up the burn?

Stay here for a while. We have more to give you on this subject. The children of Light know their purpose, their task. They are sent here to physical Earth in perfect timing to people and places where they can fine-tune their skills.

They are guarded and guided by angels. They are already amongst you.

There is a new time coming now. Anything based on greed cannot proliferate further, though at times it seems to you that the opposite is true.

We have told you that the wind farms and pylons are outmoded as they are erected. The technology to create electricity without destruction of the Earth is already here, as yet untapped. This shall be discovered. It is not something that can be explained by words.

It's important not to imagine the destruction or despair, but to envision the future peaceful. Visualise the trees growing!

The children bring in the new ways to create clean energy. They hold the knowledge. They watch what is happening and in right timing they bring in the knowledge. It is not brought in by one soul, one personality, but by many. They can neither be identified nor stopped.

No one can know who they are or where they are, and when the technology arrives it spreads so fast that no one shall know who holds the power. It is not a secret to be discovered, but a happening. Many hands hold this power. It's the true power and does not rely on destroying Earth, but caretaking Earth.

Dear Immortelle, is this wishful thinking? It would be easy to write this book if I base it on hopes and dreams.

We ask you this: Do you feel that our words are true - or not? And we ask all those who read these words to close the book and not read further if these words do not ring true for you too!

For we are of the Essence and we guide you all. You are living through the changes. Fear not that you cannot change your world for you are all changing your world,

every minute.
Hold the Light. Send the Light out - to your friends and those with whom you do not feel connection, to places you love and more so, to places you don't like, and to animals and Nature.
We hold the eternal vibration. We hold the Light.
You, who are of the stars, we see you shine. So do not deny yourselves or denigrate yourselves any longer.

Thank you.

Chapter 28

Remembering the Ancestors

18th March 2016, in the evening

After leaving Immortelle I make my way back over the moor through the wood and drive to the place where I am staying overnight. It is a beautifully restored 19th century dairy, with original courtyard surrounded on three sides by cottages where the farm workers would have been housed.

Although it has been wonderful sunny weather earlier in the day, it is still only March and the night is dark and windy. My companion from Stirling has gone home early and I am now alone. I've been told that I'm the only person staying in the building tonight. As I sit at the table poring over my notebooks of the deva's messages, I can see out through the window, the shadows moving across the cobbled courtyard in the lamp light. I can hear the wind and the owls calling in the trees. I wonder if there are any ghosts around the old building and feel very glad to be in the cosy luxury of the cottage.

The Inverness friend who had first introduced me to the place on the moor where I have been taking down Immortelle's messages lived here when he was very young. At that time, during the 1960s, the building was still a farm. The courtyard was filled with tractors and cows kept in barns below the workers' accommodation.

I thought of the people who had lived in this very building at the time when it was a prosperous dairy. I've seen some photos on display, where the people looked well dressed and happy with life, though they must have been involved in hard, physical work.

I wonder whether tomorrow I might leave the vicinity of Immortelle's burn and explore further up Strathnairn, the valley of the River Nairn, and possibly stop at Loch Duntelchaig. Perhaps I might then explore further over the moor, visit the great stone circle at Gask and then drive down to Scaniport and Dores at the head of Loch Ness.

The high Essich Moor is bounded on its western side by Glen Mor, or the Great Glen, where Loch Ness lies. The River Ness and the canal flow north to Inverness. On its eastern side lies the River Nairn, which also flows north-east to the sea in parallel with the rivers Findhorn and Spey. All of these rivers emanate from the Monadhliath mountains.

My thoughts turn to this beautiful area of upper Strathnairn as it remains in my memory, the hill and moor area not far from here. I remember how the last time I cycled there it was a beautiful summer evening, my final visit before I left to live in Stirling.

I'd once met an old lady who lived at Brin in the days before motor cars. Brin is famous for an extraordinary outcrop of rock that is popular now with climbers. The whole area is strewn with stone circles and carved rocks, many submerged under dense Forestry Commission plantations. When walking above Loch Duntelchaig you can pass through a corridor of native woodland with blocks of non-native spruce trees on either side. An old route used to pass through there between forts and chambered cairns and down to the loch. The path itself has not been planted over, although the old stone circles and dwellings are now lost in the trees.

I met the lady who had lived at Brin by chance when I was in my final year of school. Sixth year as it was called, was a time when we could take extra exams and prepare for university. We were also required to take part in some community service for a few hours a week in addition to studies.

I was assigned to help at a local nursing home in the old Hilton Hospital, which was within walking distance of my school. The nurses were relieved to have any extra hands and gave me easy tasks like making cups of tea and talking to the women in the ward to try and engage them. This was easier said than done as most were asleep and there wasn't much I could do to help them.

But there was one lady, Jeannie, whom I have always remembered. She sat in the corner tall and straight with a woollen shawl around her shoulders. She was beautiful for her age, though I had no idea how old she was. Her white hair was drawn up in a huge bun, carefully arranged.

"Please read to Jeannie," the nurse said. "She likes to have her Bible read every day."

At first I was in awe of her, but I was willing to read to her and opened the Bible near the back on purpose to get to the Psalms. I began to read as well as I could, slightly under my breath, as I didn't want the whole ward to hear me. At one point I remember looking up. A most calm and reverent expression had come over the old lady's face. Her eyes were closed and her lips moved as she mouthed the words... for clearly she knew every word! I would have loved to have drawn her portrait.

I tried to test her then by jumping to different passages, but she seemed to know them all by heart. After a while she came out of her concentration. She looked at me directly. "Lassie!" she said, "Do you know Brin? Brin stables? Near Flichity? My father was the head coachman. Oh! We had beautiful horses! Do you know it? You cross a stream by the bridge and go up over the hill."

"I confess I have passed the place," I said. "I think I know where the stables are, Jeannie."

I didn't tell her that I'd recently cycled past a large old sandstone building by the side of the road. I had noticed the *Brin Stables* inscription in the stone. This must have been Jeannie's stables! It was amazing to think that she was there as a child and young woman. I wanted to ask her so much about what life was like then, before there were cars on the roads.

I began to enjoy my visits to the home after that and tried to get round the teas in double quick time so as to have chance to hear Jeannie speak of her childhood in her traditional old Highland accent.

"Awww, lassie with your bonnie auburn hair. You're back!" she'd exclaim with delight when she saw me.

We would get through a few Bible passages and then onto the next chapter of the *Flight of the Heron* by D.K. Broster, a book she seemed to love. Then I'd go round the ward and come back to her again to hear her talk of all the horses her father had looked after and the workers on the estate. She spoke about the people of the big house with much detail of daily things that I cannot now remember. I tried to follow her story.

None of it was there any more. I never learned what happened to her once she'd grown up as she usually recalled summers at Brin when she was a child, maybe up to the age of eleven. Perhaps she'd been sent to work in one of the big houses, as my own grandmother had been sent to work in town after completing junior level schooling. Despite her intelligence and ability to recite huge volumes of poetry and classics from memory, my grandmother and women of her generation did not have the opportunity for further education.

"Jeannie, did you get married? Did you have children?"

Something passed across her face. I couldn't gauge her expression. "I don't remember if I married," she said.

Her face brightened again. "Do you know Brin?"

I knew then that this would be the last time I would see her. I don't know why I felt such a connection with her. I was around seventeen years old, and she could have been ninety, but clearly she had a love of the place where she grew up as I did.

"I have to go, Jeannie."

"When will you be back, lassie?"

"I'll see you again, Jeannie."

She reached out and stroked my hair and cheek lightly, then clasped my hands in hers. "God bless you, my dear!"

Ten years later, in 1988, I was married and living in Stirling. I was in a new life and had a new teaching job. I didn't think back very much to the places I had loved near Inverness, but a series of dreams came to me at that time that shook me to the core with their vivid detail and the precise feeling of being in specific places.

Among these dreams was the most startling and significant I've ever had, such that I wondered if it might even have been a vision.

Part Five

Now You Are Listening!

I had read through some of the testimonies of the native peoples, and the protesters' words reflected the great teachers of their past, such as Chief Sitting Bull, Lame Deer or Crazy Horse - names that had been familiar to me since childhood from my father's book shelves.

Their messages also closely reflect those that Immortelle has imparted: that we are caretakers for our home ground, our planet, and that our survival is dependent upon saving Nature. We are Nature.

(Chapter 33: Page 310)

Humankind is taking a quantum leap of faith and the world can be saved.

(Chapter 33: Page 316)

Chapter 29

Dream Vision of the Eagle, the Owl and the Wolf

The dream-vision which I had during my late twenties while living in Stirling has remained with me as extraordinary in all its detail. I can't define it as a dream, but it must have occurred during sleep. It stands out in my mind as something more real than here, than now - the present I am living in. It is more compelling than any other dream or waking experience I have ever had.

This dream-vision took place at a specific spot on the road through a place called Scaniport, near Inverness, on the road to Dores by Loch Ness. It was a place I knew very well. The local Quaker Meeting met there in an old mission hut.

As a teenager I used to sit in Meeting for part of the hour, and as there were no other young people my age, I used to creep out towards the end. With a great sense of freedom, I roamed the countryside nearby - through the wild glen to look for deer and down to the River Ness, the fastest, cleanest, most beautiful river I knew at the time. Sometimes, if there were visiting children at the Meeting, I would take them with me and introduce them to my friends, the plants and trees, as if that was a natural thing to do!

After university and college, I returned to Inverness for my first teaching job and attended the Quaker Meeting regularly, cycling to Scaniport from the town as I didn't drive at that time. Just before I left Inverness to move to Stirling, I revisited all my favourite places, leaving my bike by the Scaniport road and running down to the river in time to see an otter coasting along on its back with its white tummy showing.

In my dream a few years later, I was back on the Scaniport road walking northwards. It was an unusually hot day towards the end of June and the tar was forming bubbles on the road. I suddenly stopped. There was a shadowy figure on my left, about my height, which also stopped when I did.

Everything had so much detail that I could tell you within an inch exactly where I was standing on the road in the dream. I could see every strand in each blade of grass, and hear and see the crickets in the grass verge. The wind formed music as it blew through the pine needles of the trees on my left.

Then all was still. I looked upwards, instinctively, into the sky that seemed so clear and infinite, and saw a tiny, moving speck. Closer and closer it came, and I could see that it was wheeling and circling. As it came yet closer I recognised with absolute certainty that it was an Eagle. I knew this as I had sometimes seen them on mountain walks with my father. The Eagle kept approaching. In fact, I couldn't believe how near it was to me.

Then I had a feeling of being struck by a thunderbolt, completely filled with awe and the certainty that this Eagle was coming to me personally with a communication. The part of me that couldn't believe this was struck dumb, and my body felt as if paralysed and numb. I was only aware of my eyes watching as the Eagle swooped down to within six or ten feet of my head.

As it did, it transformed itself into an unimaginably beautiful Owl, with its six-foot wingspan stretched over my head. Its huge orange eyes were as large as dinner plates pinning my gaze, only about a foot away from my own eyes. I had no time for fear. Fear seemed irrelevant beside this magnificent creature.

For what seemed a long time, I took in every detail of every feather of the speckled belly of the Owl, and the depth of its orange eyes with their huge black centres. I will never be able to adequately describe the detail I saw and the reality I felt.

Everything was magnified and I was tiny and insignificant in comparison. I felt that the Owl was there to convey a message. But I couldn't understand it and was filled with a huge sense of wonder and humility.

Then, suddenly and unexpectedly, the Owl dived to the ground on my right, giving me a tremendous shock. For a moment its massive wingspan was splayed out as it paused, half on the road by my foot, and half on the grass verge, with a mouse it had caught in its beak. Now I could see each fibre and colour of the feathers on the back of its wings.

After a moment, it shot up into the air again and made a complete somersault right in front of my face. As the Owl spiralled and tumbled in the air in front of me, I was alarmed to then see it turning into a Wolf. This was the most magnificent silver-white/she-wolf I could imagine, about four or five feet at the shoulder. It sprang lightly over the stone wall by the edge of the road and bounded away over the fields.

There was a small wooden hut in the middle of one of the fields, and a man with a brimmed hat came out of it. He was followed by his two dogs which looked like cartoon creatures compared to the Wolf. I watched in horror as the man pulled out a gun and shot at the Wolf. But the man looked puny and the gun like a matchstick, and it was clear that the gun was nothing to the Wolf because the Wolf was a magic creature and was real.

I began to come to my senses as I watched the Wolf darting further and further into the distance until it disappeared. Then I saw a speck in the sky, circling upwards. The transformation cycle was complete and Wolf had become Eagle once more.

For the next few days in my waking life, I was completely stunned by the magic of this dream-vision. At the same time I had a feeling of terrible loss. Nothing seemed real any more, and I longed for the Owl to return and for her message to be revealed.

My father had always been a keen supporter of indigenous peoples and had many books about the lives of Native North Americans. I sensed that there must be a connection here. When I was a young child, my father had spoken of an incredible dream he had of a snowy owl, which was the size of a human. I have never asked him more about it.

As I type this at 11.30p.m. I hear an owl outside. This is uncanny!

I've had another dream in recent years, which took place further along the same road as in the Owl dream-vision. I was back on the Stratherrick road from Inverness that leads up onto the moor. Beyond a high wall running alongside the road was a woodland of old beech trees whose rich green hue was as deep as the color of stained glass.

In the dream, I was transported over the wall and into the wood on the other side to a place I had always wondered about when cycling past as I couldn't see over the wall.

I had an overwhelming sense of homecoming as the trees all recognised me and made a tremendous fuss. The trees stood back, forming an aisle for me to walk down, laughing and bowing and saluting me and flinging huge glowing golden and green leaves onto me, like confetti. I walked along this aisle on a beautiful carpet of leaves, weeping with joy at being home. I was welcomed like a queen amongst them. I didn't know why or where I was being led... and then I woke up.

Other dreams have been of tree spirits: kings and queens of the forest coming to me, begging for help, as described in the Prologue. I have felt powerless to help them. I have never understood these dreams, but in the context of recent developments, I think I am beginning to understand now.

Chapter 30

Children as Caretakers of Our Planet

19th March 2016

After thinking back yesterday to the dream-vision, I feel all the more excited to go and find the exact place where it had occurred.

I only have two more days to stay at Daviot to take down the messages of Immortelle and the nature spirits. Yesterday's March sunshine has disappeared and it is now misty and damp. I don't like the idea of sitting at the pools on the moor with the midges, so I decide to follow my plan to explore towards Loch Duntelchaig and drive further up Strathnairn on the other side of the A9 trunk road. The thought crosses my mind that I might go by Flichity and Brin to look for any sign of the old stables… then round by Loch Duntelchaig to find a sheltered place and see if I can connect with the nature spirits there. I could then drive over the Essich Moor to where the road drops steeply down to Loch Ness.

I can hardly wait to go back to Scaniport to try to find the place of my dream-vision of the Eagle, Owl and Wolf. I am also anxious to keep writing for Immortelle, as my time here is short. It might be a month or two before I can return.

On setting out I find it too misty to explore. I can't see very far ahead on the small winding roads so I make my way straight to Loch Duntelchaig and find a quiet place by the water to sit and write. I have always loved this place and now realise that my connection with the River Nairn is probably the reason, as this loch (which is also the water supply for Inverness) is near to the source of the Nairn. I have read that the name Duntelchaig (*Dun Seilcheig*, or an older form of Gaelic, *Dun -tseilcheig*) means Fort of the Snail.* As viewed from Abriachan on the other side of Loch Ness, the shape of the hill above Loch Duntelchaig looks exactly like a large snail. Even though the sun isn't shining, the lichen-filled trees by the roadside seem full of fairy spirit. By the shoreline, the air is astonishingly clear.

I am here with my angels and guardian, Ariel. I come in peace with love in my heart for all devas and nature spirits here. If you have any message for me to take back to humankind, please let me know. Please speak.

I watch the water rise to meet the mist, the air so soft there is hardly a distinction where the water meets the sky. I remember being in this spot as a student, drawing the rocky hills and water in many layered colours with my chalk pastels.

As I think of this, the deva of the water speaks:

> A time of transformation is upon you, upon us. It's a time of miracles.
> We inhabit the spaces in between your consciousness and the Great Spirit - in the portal called Nature. We stand at the door between this world and your world. Your greatest tool is your mind, yet it has been used for deception. Humans must turn their hearts and minds to the Truth. They must live by Truth. We speak of the gap between manifestation and reality. This is the connection point.
> You ask in your head how kinetic energy can be harnessed without destroying our places. It is necessary to go to the connection point and work through your heart to receive the inspiration. The inspiration comes from the Divine. This is the energy that drives everything. By the power of your mind you can create miracles of technology, of healing, but you must work with us devas. We are of God and hold the power, but we do not will anything on to you. Humans use their will and abuse power for gain. Go within and visualise. This brings about the necessary changes.
> The means of harnessing the power to heat your homes and for your transport comes from visualisation and mind power. The technology is here. It is so simple.
> The ancients knew of that power of visualisation and used it to build their temples, but then the focus of worship changed onto the material world. As the focus of worship changed, the power of visualisation was abused and no longer understood. Many have been exterminated and the true power was lost.
> The vision is here. The will of the human mind is giving up its pursuit of satisfying ego and greed and shall turn to Light.

Sound technology is the way forward. It's been used before to erect the great stone circles. It was not done by labour but by prayer.

Who is speaking? Is it the deva who overlights this region of the upper reaches of the rivers, Nairn, Dulnain and Ness?

Loch Duntelchaig is connected. Many devas are here.

Can you tell me more about the sound technology and how it was used to make things move and for healing? Can you also tell me more about the gap between our human mind and manifestations of ideas or dreams to reality?

Metatron's cube shows the pattern that creates form from consciousness. We cannot give you the answer in one word because it's a process you are going through to reach a state of awareness high enough to be able to manifest. Some people already practise the art of manifestation, teleportation, levitation. They're a chosen few.

Dear deva of Loch Duntelchaig, what are those people supposed to do with their gifts in this lifetime?

They come to demonstrate magic in your reality and show the possibilities. At present it is demonstrated as entertainment, in the manner of wizards. However, their magic is older and their knowledge shall become wider.

I can hardy imagine this yet, though I've seen some young talented magicians who have totally dumbfounded their audiences by their power to appear to teleport, telepathise, and manifest reality.
    In time, will we manifest heat in our homes and food on our tables without burning fossil fuels or using any form of energy at all? And will the food be of real plants and animals once

they've manifested? I mean ones that have evolved to maturity on physical Earth. Or are you talking about some parallel universe where everything is manifesting to look like reality but isn't real?

> We speak of manifesting food in your physical world: real food… plants and animals that have developed within the food chain and that you can eat. For you are also part of the food chain, part of the animal kingdom but with higher consciousness than some.
> Do not mock us! We do not speak of a vibrational world such as you see on your computer videos and games. We speak of the physical, biological world made manifest by God and created by humans by the power of their minds. As we have said before, without the physical trees and rocks, without the pure water, we devas cannot stay linked with Earth. Without us Earth dies. Without Earth, there is nowhere else to go. You can transcend to spirit but cannot come back here in future generations.

I leave Duntelchaig and go back to sit in my car parked at the roadside, as some youths have come down to the shore nearby. I feel uneasy here with others around. I am also perplexed, as I have heard of the possibility of many worlds, universes within universes, worlds within worlds. I thought that some of them were dream-like visions with no physical substance. But the deva's words have suggested that without the physical part of Earth, those other worlds could not continue. Perhaps this is what the angels referred to when they said:

> Earth is a tiny fragment, but of the utmost importance.

I sit for a while, reflecting on the information the deva of the loch had relayed to me, watching the beads of mist condense on the car windscreen. Eventually, I start the engine and drive slowly along the narrow roads, up over the moor past the pylon substations and water board complex, then down again by way of the steep road on the Loch Ness side.

Very soon I arrive at Scaniport, which is quite changed and seems smaller than I remember, with only a few traditional houses. There are several newly built houses too, and I immediately see the old mission hall that our Quaker Meeting hired for gatherings in the 1980s. The old building looks tiny and its windows are boarded up. The plot on which the building stands is for sale; clearly new houses are to be built here. I drive on a little way, park in a bay and set off walking along the road.

I only have to walk a few yards to find the exact place. In the dream-vision it was June time. Its colours and light were much brighter and sharper than my current reality, where all is subdued. The stand of old Caledonian Scots pine trees by the roadside on my left is exactly as I remember it in the dream, but now I can't hear any wind in their branches. I remember that there had been a campsite nearby and standing at this spot on the road, I realise that it had been right here in the field by these trees. The old toilet and shower block building is now derelict and closed.

To my right, I can see over the low wall and up towards the horizon of the moor, exactly as in the dream. I want to take it all in and compare remembered past and remembered dream with present-day reality. I am trying to stand in the road discreetly as there are new houses nearby and neighbours around. I need to keep still and focus my mind, but this is impossible. The road where I am standing is a main route from the south of Loch Ness, through Foyers to Inverness.

Without warning, a line of cars sweep along the road, showering spray from the puddles and causing me to jump into a ditch. As the last car slows up, the passenger window rolls down and an American woman asks me for directions to Urquhart Castle. It is years since I lived in Inverness and there have been many changes, but I direct her to the town centre as best I can and from there to the road which runs towards

Fort Augustus and links to the west from Invermoriston on the other side of the river and Loch Ness.

More cars follow. It is impossible to find any peace to reflect upon the past or my dream, so I leave the road by a small gateway through the fence into a birch wood. I am now inspired to re-discover the walk to the River Ness, which I had taken with the children of the Quaker Meeting all those years ago.

My route takes me through fields and prickly gorse bushes, and eventually to a muddy path by a beautiful stretch of the river where there are small islands. I return to the road by a circuitous route into a large beech wood on a steep bank with a gorge. The trees feel very alive and rather forbidding, yet are filled with mystery and magic, just as I remember them. I am amazed at the tenacity of the children and myself to have done such a walk in so short a space of time. I am quite exhausted as I finally come out at the road by the old campsite and the stand of pine trees that had featured in my dream.

The next day, I am eager to get back to the pools on the moor above Clava to seek Immortelle's help. The mist has lifted and the sun is out again, warming the earth and turning the sky to pale cobalt. The distant mountains glow on the horizon, a sprinkling of snow on their summits. Nearby, the birch trees' twigs are purple with the rising sap and new leaves soon to burst forth. Immortelle's pool is deep blue on the surface, though the rock shelf reflects amber.

Immortelle, I feel really stuck now in writing this book, because in seeing what is happening it looks as if very few people believe in the divine connection powering everything, every leaf, every blade of grass, every insect or grain of sand. Nature is seen as something to battle with, to tame, to develop in concrete and metal. All the roads are so busy with cars. Even the country roads here are busy with commuters driving to or from their new homes built in the housing developments which encroach here on the moor. Traffic has increased on the minor roads while service vans, grit lorries, and vans to service the electricity, forestry, and water board greatly increase the traffic from that of local farmers. Turbines and pylon development seem to be everywhere.

Yesterday after writing by Loch Duntelchaig, I went to Dores and Scaniport to reconnect with the devas there. I had to keep jumping in the ditch to let the cars go by. I couldn't connect at the point where I had experienced the dream-vision of the Eagle and Owl and Wolf. When I did have a quiet moment to find the exact place of my dream, a car pulled up with tourists asking me the way to Urquhart Castle. They were on the wrong side of the river. I redirected them but it crossed my mind that by purely focusing on castles they would miss some dramatic scenery on this particular side of the Ness by Dores and Foyers Bay. However, that is probably not their interest or guidance.

At the Culloden Visitor Centre, the focus is on the history of the Battle of Culloden with excellent, well researched information and a powerfully emotive 360-degree battle immersion theatre. There is a café and shop selling books, Scottish whisky, tartans, artefacts, and confectionery. The older history of the area is out of sight, hidden in time.

The many stone circles are ploughed round, covered in gorse bushes or forestry. It's necessary to go over rough ground and bogs, and to skirt fields of sheep and barbed wire fences to reach them. So it seems that the farmers are in a way the protectors of these forgotten stones.

It seems that tourists are coming here because of a respect for beauty and the history of clans and castles. Meanwhile some of the richness of the history of ordinary people who lived here is harder to find. The ghosts of Culloden remain here because of the focus on them, but the spirit of the people who lived and farmed the area has gone into the ground.

I feel it though, Immortelle! When I was exploring the hut circles in the hills above Cantraydoune and by the river near Clava Cairns, I had an insight about the people there. I had been standing in a hollow of the hill by one of the hut circles and I felt I heard people near me, as if I'd slipped into a past life. I felt I was a young boy and was keeping watch over the firth below.

The hut circles are numerous there, but hidden in a fold of the hills, in the same way that some other stone circles near the main Clava Cairns are also hidden in the folds of hills, though the views from them are quite extensive.

When you speak of humans co-operating with Nature, I'm not sure what you mean. I don't know how it can be done from the stage we've arrived at now?

I'm often asked to do a workshop on devas or communication with devas. What do you wish to say?

Immortelle responded:

> We urgently need you to teach about the real connection with Nature. It always comes from within and from the heart connection. It's not about categorising and naming different kinds of nature spirits.
>
> When people come to understand the divine flow and how they can synchronise with this flow and manifest magic in their lives, then they naturally respect and love Nature, clean up their diet, work for good in every area of their lives, for it would be impossible otherwise to manifest these positive things.

So, are you saying that people can't manifest who have a bad intention or want to hurt or destroy another person?

> They may appear to manifest - but it is based on stealing others' Light so they may appear to manifest whilst another is losing out or dying.

Can I ask this: if someone manifests wealth based on greed, such as taking over a country for its land or resources by eradicating its population or Nature, and creates what people term obscene wealth, no-one would dispute that these people have succeeded in manifesting wealth for themselves?

> Yes, this is what we mean by saying they are stealing.
> People who manifest from the heart, by the power of their imagination, may create something for themselves that they wanted or believed they needed; however, it is a situation where everyone benefits.
> We explain to you that by their disbelief of God-in-all-things, humans have created negativity.

I wish to ask about the so-called industrialised wilderness. It's all done in the name of green energy and renewable energy that harnesses and stores and converts kinetic energy. We witness how this creates damage to the environment and destroys beauty. Sometimes the profit is only for a few people who live far away as compared to the people who actually live in these places.

> Yes this is so. Power and ego have created this.

As a country, should Scotland allow wind energy, whisky, fishing, forestry, beauty spots, islands, glens and so on to be owned, developed, and commercialised by other institutions abroad, or the land to be sold or rented to institutions that are not local?
Would it be a spiritual development for people in each and every country to look after and care for their own land?

> Yes, this is so and it shall come to pass!

Does it mean that we will go back to living as we did one hundred plus years ago, and walking to work?

No. As we have said, cars may run on other means than electricity. However, people shall respect their land and not sell it for profit.
It's necessary to teach the children so they are caretakers, custodians and learn how to work in the Spirit, in communities that act from the Spirit. Yes, your children shall learn the true way of manifestation, which benefits all. It's based on truth, honesty and joy. Joy begets joy. You were not meant to live in hardship and struggle.

Dear Immortelle, if people learn to manifest a good life where their needs are met, wouldn't everyone get bored and begin to manifest bad things for fun, or go into their egos again?

It is not possible to live in Light and Truth and manifest anything that would disrespect another person.

Earlier you spoke of the children who have come here with special gifts. We spoke of the young magicians who dumbfound their audiences. Is this because they are acting in Truth, that they are able to alter reality? Is it because people believe in magic or believe in tricks of the camera if the trick is televised or recorded on video? Either way they accept it, and it seems that most people are happy to think that magic exists.

Yes, the ones who are most powerfully working with manifesting reality are in the Light and cannot hurt another. Their art has been relegated to magic and entertainment.

What would be the difference between magic to entertain, which is acceptable, and witchcraft?

The difference is in the perception of the one who witnesses or observes. At the time of the witch burnings in Scotland, any woman close to Nature, practising healing

> with herbs or talking to angels or nature spirits could be falsely believed to be an agent for the devil, often by those who were not in the Light of God, themselves seeking the dark and turning from the Light and manifesting bad things.
> The magicians who worked purely to entertain people could be exempt because people believed they were using tricks.

As they do now?

> Yes. However, the boundaries are being pushed by the magicians to show people the power of manifestation.

I feel nonplussed. It's hard to take down your words because I just cannot see this happening. So much of the way things work here is based on profit for the few.

And yet, outdoor learning is being implemented in schools now, although the outcomes of the new learning are prescribed by the teachers, rather than being left to discovery by the child. The programmes are not necessarily written by herbalists, arborists, conservationists, gardeners or environmentalists specific to each region. However, it's a big step towards putting children in touch with the Earth and giving experience of the outdoors. Having often taught about Nature through art, it's good to see this subject on the general curriculum now.

> There is nothing you can do to stop the movement forward to Light. Do not despair about the wars and destruction, but hold the Light and send Light out from wherever you are. The Light always benefits all people and places.
> We ask that you pray for the devas as you know our function is in purifying the water and air and to grow the plants and trees. We ask that you pray for the bees without which you cannot live. They need clean air and

natural plants.
It's not only necessary to take care of your local environment but to encourage the natural vegetation, not introduce plants from other areas. The natural vegetation proliferates in its local areas for a purpose.
The oak, ash, rowan, birch, aspen, willow, dwarf birch, dwarf willow and scots pine, the bushes of hazel, broom, gorse, myrtle, cowberry and bearberry are most natural here. There are one thousand species of flowers among the heathers that bring their perfume to the insects and on the air.

Immortelle, I am so grateful to be kneeling on a carpet of heathers, with scent of birch bark, juniper and moss filling my senses. I am so grateful that my father taught me the names of trees and how to navigate the hills in all weathers. I'm grateful for the wild flower books I cherished as a child and collected as a teenager. Now I am in a world of magic and flowers and all is real! This is where I feel my home is.

Chapter 31

The Great Grey Man ~ Am Fear Liath Mòr

July 2016

I have been staying in the Cairngorms for a week, setting aside some days to drive the thirty miles north to Clava Moor to work on this book. I had hoped to go up Ben MacDui (*Beinn Mhic Dhuibh*) to connect with the Great Grey Man to see if he has a message for the book. The weather hasn't been good enough to hang about on the summit and I also feel that to try and do this could be dangerous to say the least. I did attempt it on one of the days, but there were too many people there that day. Even when I hid amongst the rocks walkers came by asking for directions.

As the weather wasn't good I was afraid to stay on the mountain once everyone had left, in case I became too cold. Even in July summits can be below freezing level, temperatures can plummet and mist can obscure visibility completely, causing disorientation. The summit of Ben MacDui is scattered with cairns and shelters made of piled rocks, all within a short distance of the top. This is due to people not knowing where the top is in bad weather conditions, or needing immediate shelter. A line of cairns leads north towards Cairngorm, the mountain that gives its name to the group. This line of cairns on the path between Ben MacDui and Cairngorm has often been a welcome sight looming out of the mist to guide the way.

I have often thought about staying the night on the summit of Ben MacDui at midsummer. However, in the last few years it has been wet and cloudy at the end of June and I haven't attempted more than a late evening walk on the mountain. In Scotland at mid-summer, it is light until 11pm or later, so the conditions for a long day's walking in the hills can be very favourable.

The Dream

Now writing retrospectively, I was disappointed at not being able to attempt communications with the Great Grey Man in July whilst in the Cairngorms. However, after completing the book manuscript I had a very vivid dream.

In the dream I was on the rocky summit of Ben MacDui with my father and my hillwalking friend who has often accompanied me on my long Cairngorm treks. I was planning to pitch my tent right at the summit. In reality this would have been impossible as the boulders of the summit are huge and there is nowhere to hammer in any pegs. The tent in the dream was not my normal tent, an old A-frame, but a more modern green dome-shaped tent, big enough for one person.

Next to the summit cairn and triangulation point, on the eastern side of the mountain, a clear fountain of water in a single jet came gushing from the rocks. It emanated from a smooth slab of stone with a triangular-shaped and beautifully carved aperture. This was not a natural feature in the rock but had been made centuries ago by skilled human hands. The triangular-shaped slot was as perfect as if it had been measured exactly, and its corners were rounded, again perfectly formed.

Its depth was perhaps thirty centimetres. Out of this aperture came the water.

In my dream I planned to pitch my tent directly over the fountain by the summit cairn. My hillwalking friend was unsure if it would be right to do this, so I asked my father whether permission was needed. His answer was something on the lines of "Of course not!" but in stronger language.

My father was lying on his stomach on the ground to keep out of the wind. It was a familiar characteristic that in the days when we did the long walks together, such as Dundonnell to Poolewe, he would like to be the first to reach the end of the walk and then find a sheltered place to light his primus stove and make tea for everyone. I have a strong memory of the joy at hearing the whistle of the kettle as the water boiled, having been completely parched after a long walk.

In the dream, he was on the mountain in his dark green anorak and old bobble hat, telling me it was alright to pitch my tent. I began to be afraid. The others would leave, and I would then be on my own all night. What if the Great Grey Man wasn't happy about me being there?

I walked away from the summit cairn a little, towards the north. In the distance I could see a town on the horizon. In reality, Aviemore can be seen in that direction, but in my dream I was seeing a different settlement there. I could also see Ben Ledi, as I do from my home in Stirling. Ben Ledi is in fact a hundred miles to the south of Ben MacDui, not to the north.

I suddenly noticed a huge gorge with slippery wet rocks dropping into a deep cleft, rather like the clefts in the rocks of the descent from Ben MacDui down its east side to remote Loch Avon. This cleft was filled with large yellow flowers, globe flowers. These flowers were profuse, despite growing amongst the rocks. I have seen them before in steep corries, such as at Coire Raibert on Ben MacDui's eastern side. There is also another Lochan Uaine, a green lochan on that side of the mountain.

The others had left now and I was preparing to go into my tent for the night, when some young men appeared, having run up the hill. They were dressed in modern gear and lycra clothing, rather like cyclists. They carried water bottles, and I invited them to fill their bottles from the clear fountain pouring from the rock inside my tent before they went on their way.

The dream ended there. When I woke I was shocked at its reality, the visual details of the rocks and the feeling of being on that unique mountain. But I had no understanding of why this dream came to me nor clear memory of any direct conversation with the Great Grey Man.

I searched for answers in the following days and finally contacted Gelda MacGregor, a healer practiced in helping clients understand the significance of dreams, whom I'd met within the wider Findhorn community.

We had an online session together during which she encouraged me to go back to the mountain in a meditative inner journey. She offered to guide me back there in a visualisation so that I could ask permission to meet the Great Grey Man.

I knew that I had been sent the dream for a purpose and had wondered if it had any connection with my book. I knew nothing about the identity of the Great Grey Man or how he related to the angelic realms, except that he was of the Earth and the guardian of that mountain, which the angels had said was situated at a heart chakra point for Earth. I could not pass up the opportunity to hear what he would say, though I needed to be courageous to dare to approach him via a shift in my consciousness.

In my living room is a small collection of crystalline rocks that I have picked up over the years. During the visualisation I held a piece of white quartz in my hand that I had found on the summit of Ben MacDui years ago.

The dream therapist led me safely up the mountain of

Ben MacDui and I sought permission to speak to the Great Grey Man whilst she scribed for me. This is what she wrote.

~ Laura's Dream Dialogue
with the Great Grey Man of MacDui ~

Laura calls on the support of her guardian angel, also Archangels Gabriel and Ariel. She requests that her human companions, her friend and her father, are present as well as the deva of the River Nairn, Immortelle.

Laura approaches the summit of Ben MacDui and asks permission to speak to the Great Grey Man. She comes here with great reverence, love and respect for Earth. He approaches and shows her the word: BODHISATTVA.

We know you, we have been enjoying you here. We see your whole life, and we know you very well. We know you respect us, and always have.

Laura is shown a picture of herself as a wee girl, dancing amongst the rocks.

The mountains must be left in peace. We are sacred. We are the eyes of God.
We have no desire but to BE, be what we are, and hold the sacred channels open.
We have come up from the deep centre at this time to ensure that the connection is kept sacred.
We have no respect for humankind, apart from those that love us. Our patience is wearing thin.
There is a margin of time wherein humans can make peace with us. That time is short.
You must come here again.

You have been on my mountain fifty times because I have called you. Now you are listening. The dream was sent by your angels, who urgently require you to include our voices.

You are privileged with this important task. But we can tell you fear is inappropriate. Let it go.

The Great Grey Man ended by giving thanks to the dream therapist for encouraging me to return to the mountain.

After our session, Gelda commented that the word for love and affection in Gaelic is *Gràidh* or *Gràdh*, which is often pronounced *grey* or *greye* whereas 'grey' in Gaelic is *liath* (quite a different sound). Could *Gràidh* have evolved into the name The Grey Man? Great love would be *gràidh mhòr*. The Gaelic word for man is *fear*, and this English word may have led to him being experienced as fearful, rather than loved and respected? *Am Fear Liath Mòr*.

Our ponderings also led us to think that the size of the Grey Man may indicate a huge etheric body as he is enlightened. Allegedly, there is an ashram of enlightened Tibetan masters who commune at the summit of Ben MacDui.*

Chapter 32

The Secret of Clava

Late July 2016

Dear Immortelle? Are you here today?

> You've been called today. You're in the right frame of mind to hear us. We're here, at this pool, in this tributary of the Nairn all the time. It's you who comes and goes. You come and go in your journeying here by car, but also in your thoughts, you come and go.
> You must let go the worrying about completing this! In many ways you have already completed this book. In other ways you feel there are questions still untapped and unanswered.
> Each of you must unveil your own truth. You see what you need to see in this lifetime and you glimpse beyond the veil. We, your angels and guardians, cannot let you go too far beyond your energy field. That is your soul's work for when you die in your current physical form, and move on to the greater dimension, then that is your soul's journey. It's always a journey to life and love, and for revelation of the greater significance. However, the journey cannot all be done within one time frame, one life. We cannot allow you to see the whole, but through your microcosm you see the greater pattern.

The deva shows me a picture of Metatron's Cube, the Flower of Life, expanding outwards. I am at one point of the flower from which the pattern continues. I see a huge red light and the Angel Metatron sitting behind the pattern. He appears to hold the cube in his hands. He's smiling and the patterns burst forth from the cube in harmony. The patterns sound as music whilst light emerges like flames from every crossover point of the lines. As he speaks, he says that he is God's representative. God is too great to represent directly.

> Beyond your darkness, child, there is Light. You're called to write for the devas and us angels.

Who is speaking, please?

> Metatron.

Who designed your cube?

> YAHWEH (ELOHIM)
> WAKAN TANKA
> There are a thousand names for the one who cannot be named.
> To name is to limit.
> God is over all.

As the angel speaks, the names for God from many world religions flash through my mind. I ask: *Is God to be feared as one would understandably believe, given our violent histories, wars and religions?*

> True religion is represented within all your religions. The manner of worship causes war.

The vision of the angel then fades out and Immortelle's voice becomes recognisable again.

You must look to Nature now for your salvation, for you

are dependent on it and us, your devas. We work with Metatron. We are the architects of the star patterns, water patterns, rock and fire patterns.
You cannot go against Nature for this produces toxins and death. Nature gives life.

When terrible things happen where is God? Where are the angels?

We are here, but we cannot act without your permission. We cannot go against human free will.

If someone is being killed, it's not their free will that put them in the situation!

I cannot write more. Although I have only settled down and made a start, I feel uncomfortable. The damp from sphagnum moss penetrates the back of my jacket and midges are biting my arms and neck. In spraying the midge repellant, some leaked from the bottle onto my new waterproof jacket and I had to take water from my thermos to clean the greasy mark. I am distracted from writing and have lost the connection again. I feel as though I've been asking the same questions that had been answered in *An Angels' Guide*, and the effort of hearing Metatron has shaken me. To be sitting here dabbing midge repellent off my jacket after encountering Metatron seems incongruous. Channelling becomes difficult for me when I become self-conscious.

I pack up and find a place to cross the burn near the fairy cauldron, which is bubbling quietly. I scramble through the prickly juniper bushes, up the heather bank and over to the rock where the birch tree had been felled last year. The rock is warm in the sunshine and inviting as a seat. I perch on it for a few minutes to admire the bell heather and cross-leaved heath, chewing on *blaeberries* (occur throughout Scotland especially in the Highlands). This place is too close to the overhead power lines for comfort, so I wander up through banks of purple heather to the next white lichen-covered rock overlooking the glade of birches where I had perceived the wee folk.

The route down to the water is impenetrable with bracken. There is no point in even trying. Whilst wondering whether I should try recording the gurgling water from above I notice a tick crawling over my hand. This seems like a warning that I should not go farther in that direction today. I apologise to Immortelle explaining that I don't think I am connecting. I am too uncomfortable.

I hear her say,

We thank you for coming despite your irritation with the midges. You're welcome here always. The sprites of the pool like your company. They know you appreciate them. For sure you're connecting. Go to Clava.

The water sounds like a voice repeating "*Clava, Clava*". So, I pack up and wander through the sultry heat, over the bog without looking back, through the gate and then down the road to my car. It's only a short drive to the Clava Cairns, where I am now writing.

It seems ironic to be sitting here at this picnic bench writing, while watching the tourist coaches pull in and offload groups of people carrying cameras. The noise of mowers and strimmers obliterates everything as the men from the council tidy up the verges of the car park and picnic area. I feel protected here, almost invisible, as everyone heads in the direction of the main enclave and cairns. No-one appears to be interested in the western and outlying stones in the surrounding fields, isolated from the main group. The smell of cut grass pervades and the sun comes out. Summer is in its full glory.

I've walked the banks of the Nairn here and also where the hut circles are further east. The Nairn is a field away to my right, but it's difficult walking there as it is so full of cattle, mud and barbed wire fences.

The people from the first coach are already heading back after a fifteen-minute tour round the three main cairns and megaliths. This is hardly any time, but for sure the impact of the place will have made its mark.

The area of the picnic tables is surrounded by grassy mounds and scatterings of ancient stones. They extend beyond the road, which cuts through what was once a much greater complex, now dispersed. Ploughed up stones can still be seen in the surrounding fields, and smaller circles follow the line of the Nairn valley.

Immortelle, are you still here? How big was Clava Cairns? How important was it? Why do you speak of this place within the Nairn valley, which is far less well known than Stonehenge in Wiltshire, England, but is so well known to tourists and travellers in the Highlands?

> Clava is central. It is the pivotal point of the star maps of Britain. It represents the pole star. The key is in its name: Balnuarin of Clava. The outlying stone circles follow ley lines through the Nairn valley and point outwards to the Four Directions.

Immortelle's voice fades out.

I used to have a recurring dream. In the dream I am cycling from the village of Balloch, where I lived, and which is also the name given to lesser-known stone circles in the adjacent fields that lie alongside the Moray Firth.

I have a great feeling of expectancy and excitement, like the feeling of a homecoming. It's always Easter time in the dream. I'm free-wheeling on my bike down the narrow single-track road along the bank of the Nairn overhung with hazel catkins, and down to the bridge by the fishing pool where we used to swim in the hot summer days of the late 1970s. There the dream ends.

I am now only a few yards from the place of my dream, within sight of the Nairn Viaduct and a few metres from that same winding road along which the tourist coaches now navigate their way as they bring the next group of people. The mowers and strimmers have stopped and the men have packed up for the day. The birdsong and sound of lowing cattle come back once the noise has abated. Beyond is the sound of the river.

I sit here for a long time, waiting for Immortelle to speak. Her words come back unexpectedly just when I feel as though I'm miles away in my thoughts.

> Your dream represents the place where you return... here at Clava. It's why you're here now! You have caught up with your dream.

Am I in effect living my dream now?

> We laugh! You've come here again to unveil a mystery. It's your life purpose.

Is my life purpose this book? Once I complete this book, is my life purpose over then?

> There is more to be revealed.

Another book?

> Most importantly it's time for you to paint again, and to help others connect with their angels.
> You fear you'll die? No, it's possible to enjoy life to the full.

So, now that I'm back at this point on the planet, at Clava Cairns, as you say, the heart of the star map of Britain, what do you devas wish to say?

We ask that you listen to the stones.

As she finishes speaking I pack my bag again and wander through the cairns with my hillwalking compass in one hand held out in front of me. It's not so easy listening to the stones as the deva requests. I feel rather indignant that after all this channelling over the years that the deva has requested that I listen to the stones! How on earth am I expected to unveil any mysteries of civilisation by a mere visit to an ancient monument 4000 years after it was first built?

The wooden gate constantly slams as people enter the enclosure. Cars are parking or leaving every few minutes and voices can be heard. A tourist exclaims loudly, "I think it's a wolf!" at the sound of a farm dog howling from over the hill.

One voice rises above the rest, talking about history. I quickly tune in hoping to pick up some useful information about the Cairns. However, the guide is not talking about the stones but the Battle of Culloden, and although this is a fascinating history connected with this place, I can't take it in when focusing on other layers of time.

I photograph the stones with the star maps on them again, then walk down the road past the outlying northern megalith standing on its own in the adjacent field. I pass the grounds of the Victorian Lodge where swallows swoop around the eaves of the building, and walk on to the bridge over the Nairn. It's hard to focus. The air is so summery with the heady scent of meadowsweet that fills the river banks.

I hear the distant rumble of the river as it flows through the fields in the moments between the cars driving past or the occasional aircraft overhead. Such layers of noise give way to the softer sounds of bleating sheep, the twittering of the swallows and house martins, and voices of people amongst the stones in the distance.

Dear Immortelle, I feel that I am disconnected from you. All this seems far from the deeper meaning of the stones or their placement here in northern Britain. I don't understand why you devas that overlight the nature spirits of water, rocks, and trees talk so much about these human-made cairns!

> The Clava Cairns are one of the greatest star observatories in Europe.
> You are also from a star system. It's why you're back. We have told you where you're from, and why you came back. Your planet is linked to Earth. It's necessary for Earth to survive, for the whole of your galaxy. Many star children are here again to help bring the good news of the angels to Earth.
> You have the ability to help people connect. This is undeniable. You've come back to the observatory of the stars.

Oh Immortelle! What you say triggers the memory of another dream where I was hiding with other people inside a chamber housing a giant telescope. I was given the key to the telescope and told to keep it safe. The great doors were on the point of closing and we were inside, but out of compassion I let someone else into our hiding place. He proceeded to smash the giant glass plate of the telescope. It fell into smithereens. I heard a great crashing sound. I don't know what happened after that because I woke up in fear and shock. I felt I had betrayed my task for the angels.

> The mystery of Clava is being revealed. It cannot be done too quickly as the true secret must be preserved.

I find it hard to believe! Yet on another level it all makes sense. Are we in time?

Yes, the timing is perfect. There is much chaos to come, but the devas are returning in their full glory.

The people who built Clava... the first cairn... who were they? Where were they from?

Andromeda, Pegasus and Pleiades.

Why did the people who built the cairns make such a magnificent structure, one that has now lasted for over 4000 years, if they wanted to track the moon and stars? Could they not have made it easier for themselves and carved the patterns on stone or clay tablets?

You have separated your knowledge from its source. Your society sees mathematics, science and the arts as separate subjects. The link with Nature is absent. The people who built Clava related the patterns of the stars to Earth and Earth to the stars. Each part of the landscape had its significance. This site was chosen because of a crossing of networks of what you call 'ley lines'. These correspond to the patterns below the Earth and also to the matrix that surrounds Earth. This matrix of energy lines around Earth is being rediscovered.
The Cairns are protected by an invisible force. They have a counterpart in the ether. This happens at a particular point. It's all for a reason.
The builders of the Cairns knew what they were doing. It was all measured. They were in touch with the devas and with the angels. The Cairns were a place of worship as well as an observatory of the skies. They were in touch with other communities and in contact with inhabitants of other star systems. People have been called here.

It's hard to imagine what was going on here nearly

4000 years ago. Today it is peaceful, in between the slamming of car doors when people arrive or leave. I hear the roar of the Nairn in the distance, bleating of sheep, rustle of leaves on the summer trees, calling of birds, cars in the distance on the single-track roads and voices nearby.

Beyond the level area of the river the land rises to the horizon. Past the distant fields I see the edge of the forestry plantation beyond which Immortelle's burn lies.

A van draws up in the car park at this point, throwing up dust from the road. Sun lights up stones. All around, the verges are resplendent with rosebay willowherb, vetch and cow parsley, yellow hawkbit, red and white clover, lady's bedstraw and meadowsweet.

I try and imagine how it might have been - a warmer climate at that time with wolves and wild boar in the pine forests and people living in hut circles here by the river and further up in the folds of the hill overlooking the firth. I've heard that the largest Pictish graveyard has been discovered while building a local supermarket and industrial area east of Inverness. But even this belonged to a time after the people who built Clava. Were they enlightened mathematicians and astronomers who understood the precise movements of the stars? Did they commune with angels? Were they in touch with similar communities in Britain and beyond?

I fear my book may not reveal more. I have come to the end of my ability to channel and perhaps this information is not supposed to be available to us now. But we must rediscover it. Every time I go to the Cairns I feel that its mystery is locked in. Perhaps the force field of protection surrounding the stones that Immortelle described is keeping its secret safe. I was keen that the messages about Clava would round off this work of channelling, based on my visits here over the last four years.

I'm very interested to hear more about the people who built them and how they were in touch with their angels and devas. But now I'm only receiving fragments from Immortelle, and the interesting bits only come in when I am too sleepy or packing up. It's as if my mind focuses on this information and then it slips away again. Sometimes the messages stop abruptly and I feel that my angels are protecting me from receiving more than I need.

When I feel truly happy the messages are easier to hear but staying happy and relaxed enough to hear them requires much clearing of my aura and letting go of worrisome or distracting thoughts. Attuning in a state of intoxication would not work, nor would being in fear. It's a shame that we humans are so heavy in our energy fields. If we were better able to lift ourselves up without losing our sanity, tuning in would be easy and perhaps then much more would be revealed.

Immortelle, I can't tune in any more here at Clava Cairns. It is so busy. Can you and the devas and nature spirits of the Cairns stay here with people around?

No, we stay by the river. People don't go there.

I don't know whether to drive towards the source of the Nairn today at Duntelchaig. It might be quieter there than here at Clava, but I don't want to go home yet. I miss you when I'm not here, yet when I'm here I'm distracted and can hardly channel your words. I don't know what to do.

I am unable to do any more channelling as I have come to the end of my time here this summer. I have driven to Immortelle's area every day to work on the book whilst staying in the Cairngorms. It isn't so far as driving from Stirling, but at this point it is time for me to go home.

September 2016

I have made one more day visit this year driving from Stirling, hoping to complete the questions I have for Immortelle regarding the secret of Clava.

Back at the pools:

Dear Immortelle, I'm here. I hope that I've connected?

A white birch leaf floats on a carpet of sphagnum moss. The sound of the water today is euphoric, if a sound can be that! Myriad shades of amber gleam from the rock shelf and bubbles float, bob and burst as they veer across the surface to the fairies' waterfall, below which the miniature cauldron explodes upwards in a fountain of jewel-like foam crystals. Below this, only revealing itself today, is a rocky step. As the water pours over, it forms a wave right in the middle of the third pool. I'm reminded of the shape of the wave of a *Hokusai* Japanese print in miniature.

In the lower pool the green of moss is reflected. It is a shade that could never be described in terms of artists' pigments, but is more of a combination between lime and sienna.

Breathing in, I sense a great peace and joy of being. Here and now I am alive and safe and I cannot think about the wider world because I am here, not there.

Immortelle?

Soon I realise that I am hearing the voices of the elementals of the water.

> We join you here. We delight in your presence. Fear not. We are of God. We make all things flow and the flowers to flower. We're in the trees, the grass and the wind, the rock and the pool, the river and sea, in the sun and moon

and fire, and as sylphs we play in the air.

Immortelle responds:

The sylphs are in trouble through human poisoning, and through the deforestation which affects them greatly. Send Light for the sylphs! Without the sylphs to aerate the water, people cannot live here.

Humans cannot make a better environment than that which God has created. They have separated God from Gaia. Gaia is God's heart chakra.

Men must respect women and women respect men, and all must respect their children, their lifeblood, their environment. When this happens, all war shall cease.

Dear child, things in your material world look bleak now, but we reassure you that the new dimension is here at last.

Earth has raised its vibration and humans must raise theirs or cease to live here. We need your co-operation, then all is restored and the healing happens. We rejoice.

Dear Immortelle, when I read the news it can seem that good and innocent people are the ones who are dying and the abusers and perpetrators of evil and greed seem to get away with it. There's so much pain and suffering everywhere. Even within my small circle of friends and acquaintances it can seem pretty random as to who is taken from life. Often it seems unfair and unjust.

I pause after my question to listen to the waterfall behind me, and the small fall that exits the pool in front of me. The sounds are so alive and multi-dimensional, and I can feel their vibrations through my boots and through my whole body. The sunlight catches the grass and surface of the water. Before I take down the words I already know Immortelle's answer.

All is not lost, she whispers. *No thing is random. Only people through their attempt to control Nature and others believe in randomness. Random only happens when humankind is out of synch with the connection to Source.*

The bubbles gather and pop. They sometimes merge to form larger dome shapes, complete with reflections of the birch tree and myself with my notepad as I sit on the bank. I try to capture one in vain, just as I did all those years ago when I heard the harp music playing here. That day I caught one of the larger bubbles on camera. Years later I found the photograph as I was scanning through film-strips of negatives, complete with its perfect reflection of a tree on the bank.

Immortelle, you don't give me the bigger picture. I realise that now! I don't know whether to ask you the question: Will humankind survive here on Earth? Am I allowed to ask?

We laugh. We thought you'd never ask! Suffice to say, as long as we are hearing humans' prayers for Earth, so long as we hear your heartfelt thoughts of gratitude, then there is a beautiful future.

World peace?

> As we said before, this could be achieved in a short space of time, in the blink of an eye, if people would turn their thoughts from fear to love. And we rejoice. It is happening!
> You don't see it. We see it. We feel the vibration of your cities, your populations. Many are praying for peace, for their children. The dark forces can no longer compete.

I wish I could feel that too, Immortelle, but I see greed operating everywhere, even within political and societal structures.

Regarding the destruction of nature, even in this small part of Scotland I see destruction of beauty. Today I was sad to see the scale of the road widening on the A9 completely taking out some rocky outcrops, old trees, and dells. Areas have been levelled and it looks like any old motorway now as it passes Kincraig. I know it's to save lives, but it must be making a huge impact on the devas and nature spirits of those old woodlands and wiping out local history. Every time I come here to Drummossie Moor there are more small areas of woodland being cut down for house plots.

> As we have said before, there are many who will not survive. In the future the human population will rebalance in sync with its environment.

I become engrossed in taking photographs and videos of the pool, trying to capture the bubbles, the nature spirit's face, the fairy fountain, the colours. Layers of sound arise from the water. To my ear, the superficial surface of the water sounds shallow and tinny, whilst below the water reverberates in all its intensity with a thunderous roar. Once the sun has moved away from the rim of the pool I climb up the bank to the moor again and trace a path through the heather, skirting the precipitous edge of the upper pool and waterfall. Further upstream I once perceived a troop of wee folk, but the bracken, now dead and orange, is virtually impassable, so I cut back up the hill to my painting rock.

The moor reflects intense light; the deer grass is green, russet, with bright orange stalks of bog asphodel growing through. The wind makes my eyes water and it's hard to see the pages I'm writing on as I've left my sunglasses in the car.

The young pines that now ring the edge of the bog and scatter across the lower slopes of the hill are fully lit by the low sun. Beyond them the fields stretch out to the Moray Firth, while further in the distance are the Kessock Bridge and the hills beyond the Beauly Firth, just as in the painting I once did. I listen to the sound of the wind for some time. All is peaceful in between the passing aircraft from Dalcross, now Inverness airport.

Immortelle, you have spoken of Clava, of the people who built the Cairns. You've said they knew about the stars. The structure was, as you said, a giant compass/observatory to track the sun and moon. So not a burial place then? Am I allowed to know more? Why am I drawn here to write this book? Is it anything to do with Clava?

> It has everything to do with Clava! The Clava Stones' formation is set on this part of Earth, as we said, and forms part of a series of great circles that were once built as a giant star map. Clava marks the pole star and Andromeda. It is linked with all the outlying circles of that time in Scotland and beyond.

It beggars belief, Immortelle! How did people nearly 4000 years ago communicate with each other in order to synchronise their star map?

Some groups did travel by the stars and could chart their movements. Some information was channelled. They were close to their angels, and us devas.

Wouldn't the night sky from Clava look much the same as the night sky from the great stone circles of Calanais or Stonehenge?

No, the sun and moon set at different times in different places. This is what was being measured.

Why the huge trouble to be accurate in their measurements and in the building of these structures? Were they temples?

Yes.

Were sacrifices made there? Did they use slaves to build them?

No, not initially. Slaves were used later after the first phase of building.

Tell me more, Immortelle!

After the fall from grace, humans lost their ability to connect with the Divine. They lost their power. They lost their ability to divine.

When was the fall from grace? What do you mean?

Humans began to control the land and misuse power. They began to war, to take slaves, to own land and pay for land with blood.

When did this happen?

Between the first and second phase of the building of the

> Cairns at Clava.

2500 BC?

> Yes. Many atrocities happened then. Huge movements of people and starvation.

What caused this?

> Children came to Earth who were not of the stars. They came only for power.

Were the people such as the Romans part of this tribe?

> Child, go tell our story now. It's complete, as you shall soon see.

Thank you. Immortelle, one more thing. Will we humans become close to our angels and the devas again?

> The great cycle has begun again. It's time now for humans to come home to Earth, to come down to Earth.

Thank you, Immortelle. Thank you, angels.

I leave the moor as the light is waning and walk hurriedly back down the path through the plantation returning to my car. I drive along the road a short way and pull in at a layby where there is an old stone wall on one side and views towards the viaduct, fields and woods, and houses on the other side. Above this the edges of the distant hills to the north catch the last of the light.

The clouds are scurrying across the sky and it is getting dark fast. I can see the buttercups in the field over the wall on my right as if lit up and glowing. I feel as if my life is in pieces, like the layers of history of this region. Memories flash by and I feel the sadness of different times and people who've come and gone. I feel the happiness of different times and I sit and watch it all, my body heavy and relaxed. Sadness for the passing of time merges with gratitude at being here now. I want to sink down into the earth and sleep. I'd like to lie down in the field on soft grass but I need to drive back home. The wind is blowing the trees on the moor and rattling the grasses of the verges. The beauty of Nature is all around.

I pour myself a coffee from my flask, set it on the dashboard to cool, and sit gazing at the light over the moor through the back to front reflection in the car mirror. Finally I switch on the engine and drive past the favourite barley field, glowing like old gold in the light and edged with dark silhouettes of larch trees, then back down the road singing to myself. The words of a hymn come to mind…

Abide with me; fast falls the eventide
The darkness deepens; Lord with me abide.
When other helpers fail and comforts flee,
Help of the helpless, O abide with me.*

Thank you, Immortelle, for the gift of your words. Thank you, Ariel, for translating the deva's words to my consciousness.

Chapter 33

The Tide has Turned!

February 2017

I have come back to complete the typing up of my notebooks. On the second day I take a walk up to the moor and Immortelle's pools to seek her blessing on this book:

Dear Immortelle, I come with my angels and Ariel. I come in peace and I'm delighted to be here again and that the sun is shining. Is there anything I need to know? Is there anything more for the book - your book, your words?

> The time is favourable. It's time to bring our words to print. We have no more information except to say the same: that God is here in this dimension. We transmute energy to Light, form and growth. All is infinite. Blessed be.

Dear Immortelle, even as I write there's more destruction, continuing of wars, a morass of hate - new world leaders, abuses of freedom and human rights, animal rights and Nature's rights! We are not caretaking as a population.

> Speak not these words! Even as the forests come down the seeds of the new trees are growing. Many are coming to awareness of the need to live from the heart. The destruction shall stop. Nature bounces back.

I then speak to the deva again of the widening of the

A9 and how more old trees had been cut down, rocks quarried and excavated, the landscape ironed out, bulldozed, rammed through and changed beyond recognition, albeit for the purpose of saving lives - my life included - and long awaited by many who regularly use that road. The road should be safer. It will be much wider and faster.

> Not in your lifetime, however, when humankind stabilises in population the wild natural places shall grow again.

At present some areas have an ageing population whilst at the same time there is more immigration into the country. Will people put down roots and begin to care for Nature in their local vicinity, whichever country they're from? All over the world, even if people originally came as invaders, settlers or refugees, will their families put down roots?

> We have said before that you have a destiny and the place you are born is important. Therefore, the second generation born in a place forms an attachment.

With the land?

> Yes.

Some old Highlanders, such as the two teachers I knew and loved and who have both passed away in the last two years, had profound knowledge of their locality. They'd both been friends of Sorley MacLean, whose voice and poetry embodies the landscape of the Western Isles he knew and loved.
   How can someone from another culture take on all this history and meaning of their birthplace if they are second generation Scots for instance? I realise I am second generation too. My parents were originally from the English Midlands.

> They've been destined and attracted to the vibration of the place no matter where they originate from. They belong there if the vibration matches. If not, they must leave.
> We devas cannot change our vibration. We hold the vibration of Light. The devas and nature spirits hold the vibration of place. Humankind comes and goes.

Take the A9 situation at this time for instance - many devas and nature spirits have been disrupted, have they not? How can that place be the same when parts of it have been literally taken away?

> Yes, it's a problem for us. The nature spirits move away to other trees or neighbouring areas. The memories of the place as it was, are held by the trees and rocks and water that remains. However, some devas must move into the etheric, further away from human consciousness because of the destruction. It shall come to the point where there must be rebalance.

I cannot see how this can happen if our population continues to expand until the last scraps of wilderness and woodland are taken over.

> Humans had a choice: to respect us or self-destruct. The tide has turned, even at the last trump.

Are you speaking in parables?

> Yes, we always speak to you on different levels of meaning, dependent on who is reading.

I hope that in my old age there'll be some wilderness left as I have known it and not more beauty destroyed.

The time of the motor car, as you know it, is almost over. Do not despair. Humans find ways to live in harmony with Nature without going back to living in caves! Keep holding the Light for us - pray for the trees. Pray for your beloved places. Learn the names of the flowers. Be as the flowers. Flow with Light. Flow with song.

Thank you. Is it you, Immortelle?

Immortelle speaks. Ariel translates the messages for you.

Thank you. I am blessed to have received your words.

I have been staying at Daviot again. Apart from the walk up the hill into Immortelle's domain, I've spent every day of this particular visit continuing the task I started last November of typing up my hand-written notebooks including the messages of Immortelle. The messages began in 2012 and continued until she signed off at this point, telling me to go ahead and complete the book. I finished this on 13th February 2017.

The following day, I hear that there is to be a water healing ceremony in the main Universal Hall at the Findhorn Community thirty miles away. This will be followed by a walk to the shore to send prayers where the River Findhorn flows into the sea. It feels most appropriate for me to go along, although I rather wish that it was the River Nairn being celebrated. Within a few years, I would eventually achieve my dream of walking to the source of the Nairn. When I did arrive at the source, at that point in time, however, a wind farm had been constructed there.

Today, my main purpose at Findhorn will be to join with the group in their mission to dispense healing water and for me personally to celebrate the end of my journey with

Immortelle.

Someone has been up to the source of the River Findhorn in the Monadhliath mountains to collect water from the small lochan near the summit of Càrn Bàn that joins the tributaries flowing down to the river and sea. After a meditation, the water is duly dispensed in small quantities into the bottles that people have brought. Alas, a few of these are plastic, but I feel that it is only be a matter of time before many people become aware of the need to carry water in a way that is compatible with its vibration.

After the meeting in the Universal Hall, a small number of us walk in glorious February sunlight to Findhorn Bay to return some of the source water into the sea and sing in gratitude to the water. We have been advised to make the *AH* rather than *OM* sound on this occasion.

A dog belonging to some walkers races up to join us. He stands by the water's edge with his ball in his mouth, bemused but patient. I wonder if he or his owners might join us in our singing. The surge of the waves carries our voices out across the water and an echo comes back as if the water has heard our gratitude.

The next day after the water ceremony I have one remaining day at Daviot. As I type this script I am startled to realise that the words I have recorded from Immortelle seem to be aligning with three-dimensional reality, as stories of people communicating gratitude to Earth and stepping up as guardians are currently becoming headline news.

Coinciding with my previous visit here in November, the news of Standing Rock protests in the USA had come to a climax and were widely documented in British newspapers and online. The Dakota Access Pipeline was to run from the Bakkan oil fields in western North Dakota to southern Illinois, crossing beneath the Missouri and Mississippi Rivers, and under part of Lake Oahe near the Standing Rock Reservation. The pipeline installation and potential future oil spillage was seen as a threat to drinking water supplies, to farmlands, wildlife and ancient heritage sites belonging to the indigenous people.

I had read through some of the testimonies of the native peoples, and the protesters' words reflected the great teachers of their past, such as Chief Sitting Bull, Lame Deer or Crazy Horse - names that had been familiar to me since childhood from my father's book shelves.

Their messages also closely reflect those that Immortelle has imparted: that we are caretakers for our home ground, our planet, and that our survival is dependent upon saving Nature. We are Nature.

Footage was shown of people standing in protest and being forcibly removed from the land in front of our eyes, in what looked like a present-day re-enactment of a historical battle between the indigenous people and early settlers. This new battle is now the fight for Nature herself, with her guardians forming a human shield against the land being taken and exploited for use as a corridor for an oil pipeline. Violations of human rights and Nature's rights are happening in synchronicity.

There seems to be a great swell of recognition across the world, even in Scotland. A local newspaper carried a photograph of a handful of wind-blown demonstrators in their waterproof jackets standing on the shores of Loch Lomond in solidarity with the people of Standing Rock. At that point in time, such demonstrations about our Earth were unusual. People might have wondered what was the point was of standing beside Loch Lomond to make some kind of case for Nature in a different and distant land. We did not know then the scale of public protests that were to come.

People are now talking openly about their concerns of abusing or using up Earth's resources. Some of my friends are already making the decision to change to electric cars. I think that many of us have been concerned for years, as we have composted our waste and attempted to minimise strain on resources in awareness of the growing problem. We could not see how our modern lifestyles would be sustainable in the future, having remembered how things were in the past before single-use plastics and disposable culture.

On a holiday in 2014, whilst walking along the beaches of Dornoch and Embo in the north-east of Scotland, my son and I noticed the incredible amount of nylon rope, plastic fish boxes and other plastic litter that we had assumed was mostly due to the use of plastic in local industry, rather than being washed in from the greater ocean. I still remember as a child the wooden fish boxes washed up on beaches, and on family walks over the years I have observed the escalation of plastic waste littering the natural landscape.

My mother told a story of receiving her very first plastic household item when my parents moved to Inverness in the 1950s. My father had bought it for her in town and cycled home from work up the steep brae to Nairnside, carrying a red bucket alongside his briefcase. The treasured bucket, now badly faded, is still somewhere in my parents' garage having survived over sixty years of use.

When Immortelle stated that *'plastic is an unnecessary evil to us'*, I had felt the poignancy of her words. Until recently, some of my friends and I had naively thought that bottles collected by the local council would automatically be recycled locally. However, many of us have been made aware of the uncomfortable truth by watching TV documentaries and drone footage of scenes of plastic-filled oceans on Earth's surface. This kind of information has only recently become available due to the more widespread use of drones. This has also led to similar images being spread on the internet and viewed globally on mobile phones, tablets and other technology.

We hear about the prevalence of micro-plastic everywhere, on beaches, in the food we eat and the air we breathe. I have seen a video clip online of a man working on beaches near the vicinity of the Grangemouth petrochemicals and shale gas processing plant in Central Scotland. He was actually trying to hand sieve plastic granules from the sand, and through the internet such a herculean task was made visible to significant numbers of people.

The mudflats and salt marshes of the Forth Estuary at Grangemouth are an internationally important wintering site for birds travelling from as far afield as Scandinavia, Iceland and the Arctic, and a haven for rare wading birds. In summer, there are large gatherings of non-breeding mute swans.

The effluent from factories has always been a suspected pollutant but the truth, and information made accessible through availability of scientific data, is almost beyond our ability to take in. It also seems beyond our capability to reverse the damage; therein lies the unfolding of our worst nightmare. Wherever we live, everything is impacted. Everything is affected, from the air we breathe to our mental health and inner peace, as well as our capacity to be able to live both individually and in community.

Immortelle's words of hope are ringing in my ears, although there is still much I can't comprehend.

Humans find ways to live in harmony with Nature without going back to living in caves!

Regardless of government policies, many of us are already looking for ways to take responsibility for resources we personally use, in hope of Nature's and our own survival, and that of future generations.

I didn't understand Immortelle's reference to the *'coming of the children'* when writing the script.

I had been receiving messages about children leading the way ever since writing *An Angels' Guide*. "The great peace of God is present on Earth. We hold the Light as a way forward for the peoples of the Earth to reach that peace, whilst still in the physical realm. This has been done by the mystics of all faiths but will now be achieved by ordinary souls and children too. Some will lead the way. These are blessed times, which have been prophesied, but which continue beyond the prophecies. Now we know that there is a way through, and that Heaven and Earth can connect. For mankind can be lifted up as one heart connects with the next. And so it shall be."

I had heard about many highly gifted children and my brother had mentioned that the level of music performance had reached unprecedented levels. Many very young students were already virtuosos. At that time I was also unaware of the emergence of Greta Thunberg and the Planet Extinction Rebellion movement and how that would make complete sense of Immortelle's words regarding the children of our Earth.

I step outside in the February sunshine to sit in the cobbled courtyard of the old Daviot Dairy in a shaft of bright light where the frost hadn't reached.

In my hands are the collected notes from the channelling work that I did between 2007 and 2011. They refer to Gaia and the changes that are to come about on Earth. These messages had been communicated to me while channelling for others and are instrumental to the work I began with my healer friend when we first went into the hills to send Light to Earth. They mark the point where I was impelled to come to the hills to scribe the messages of the nature spirits. They have inspired me in my search to find the deva Immortelle.*

I remain confused as to why the Clava Cairns seem to be a central feature of the script in the context of the environment, and the devas' and our own human role in its guardianship. Immortelle spoke in parables at the end of her dialogue yesterday and I feel that there is nothing else to do now but to commit her words to print.

Suddenly, in the unexpected kind of way that the angels

bring their inspiration, it is revealed to me why this book ends at Clava and there is a sense of completion. The inspiration, though powerful, doesn't come in words at all; it is more a kind of inner knowing. I jump up, leave my writings on the table, grab my coat and scarf from the porch and hastily put on my walking boots.

As the sun is low on the horizon, I head out to the Cairns to see how the sun shines through the stones. I have a great sense of expectancy and my legs and my body seem to know exactly where to go as I stride towards the cairns. There is still snow on the ground in the Nairn valley. A tourist coach is parked up and a group of people leave the fenced enclosure as I wait to go in. A tall man in the group is wearing full kilt and sash in red tartan, totally dressed for the occasion. I wonder what they'd think if they knew that this tall woman wandering discreetly round the edges, compass in hand, is communicating with the devas and nature spirits of the area.

I walk amongst the stones and spend some time simply being drawn to different ones. There's always something new to see. Then, at the western cairns of the main set, I stop by a kerbstone on the outer wall and notice the cup marks although this side of the cairn is in deep shadow. The sun shines from the opposite side, falling into the chamber on that other side.

I can make out the pattern of the cup marks. It is very familiar. As I study it I can make out more... the constellation of the Plough? I lay my hand on the stone and feel for the marks. Something goes through me like a current. The pattern is deeply familiar. The cold stone with its indentations feels as alive as my hand. I sketch the pattern on a piece of paper to take back and check later against a star map, but I already know that constellation.

I leave the enclosure by the gate where the road cuts through and walk along to look at the stones of the westernmost group. Very few people visit this group as it requires a short walk along the road. How folded is the valley with the low sun sending its raking light over the fields. One of the cairns is hidden in a fold of fields over there and I've never seen it. It would require climbing over fences and through fields. From the hill above, anyone in the fields can easily be seen, unless they're hidden in one of the dips. From below, the place where the cairn is situated is completely hidden.

Next to the outlying westernmost stones, which are open to the public, is the ruin of what is thought to be a medieval church situated next to the megalith. It's been a common belief in Scotland that to build a Christian place of worship next to a pagan site would ward off any evil from the site. The site of ancient worship at the stone circle was probably chosen because of the underlying ley lines to be followed by the church construction centuries later at the same location. It seems incredible how the Cairns have survived as well preserved as they are now, given centuries of deliberate desecration, and the fact that roads, farms, houses and the local school, even a private house, are sitting virtually on top of the ancient site.

I walk back to the Clava Bridge past other old sites of stones now turned to rubble or buried under the ground, then back again to the main three cairns. Now there is only one other car in the carpark, and the sun is going down behind the hill. The Cairns take on a peaceful and magnetic aura.

I stop for a while to say a prayer that all Nature will be left in peace. I begin to whisper to myself, as if chanting a mantra the play of these words:

>   *Earth...h...hearth...heart*
>   *Earth...h... heart... hearth...*
>   *heartbeat...beauty...earthy...*
>   *ether...ethereal...ariel*

Ariel! Dear Ariel! I've just realised something! Am I stupid not to have noticed this before? It's so obvious and so simple: Earth... heart... hearth.

The stones circles - they are hearts and hearths, symbolic of fire, the central place of the home where people live and from where they look outwards at the sky and stars from whence they came!

> We laugh! Yes, life is so easy and straightforward. You are all called home and you live on Earth which is also your home. Home is where the heart is, and also where the hearth is.
> We weep that humans are destroying their home on the physical plane but now so many of you are waking up to the realisation that everyone is involved in the process together of bringing compassion to your view of the world, forgiving your brothers and sisters and all who have hurt you, and being compassionate towards those who are so misled and misaligned from Source that they seek to destroy their Mother Earth.

Oh angels, are we in time? As I write, so much destruction is taking place everywhere.

> Child, even as you write, so many acts of compassion, forgiveness and love bring about healing. Humankind is taking a quantum leap of faith and the world can be saved. We must remind you to write for the devas. Their story is in your hands. They need you!

Thank you, Ariel. I am so privileged to have been given this task to take down their words. Thank you.

I watch the last rays of the sun lighting the stones in a golden glow. I trust in Immortelle's prophecy that these stones, which have held their magic for four thousand years, will be a testament at last to a time of peace, where humans and Nature can co-exist in harmony and the angels' singing will be revealed on Earth.

Epilogue

During the course of writing this book I had another vivid dream. In the dream I had recently given birth and was holding the little child on my chest, cradled in my arms as I used to cradle my own sons when they were babies many years ago. I could feel the weight of the child as it rested there, its heart beating against mine. I held its head with my free hand. Its ear was resting against my face, pressed against my cheek. I could feel its warmth.

I lifted the child away from me a little so I could gaze in the way a mother gazes in wonder at her child, in the way I did when I had my own children, although this also seemed real. As I held up the child, I noticed that its head was too big for its body, and its ear, which had felt hot against my face… was different.

The child's ear suddenly came clearly into focus and my wonder then turned to great surprise… The ear was not human, but elfin. It was long and leaf-shaped with a sharp pointed tip. Once again, I held the child close to my heart which was thumping in my chest, and I wondered at this for a while.

In the dream the male presence of my partner was also in the room. I took a deep breath, and held the child out to the man, in complete trust that he would accept it.

I then placed the child standing on the ground, for it seemed to be growing fast, impossible for me to hold, and was turning into a toddler, now taller than the man's knee. I was still trying to work out whether the child was loved and accepted by its father, and could safely be handed over to him. I suddenly woke up with the feeling that the father and child symbolised emerging understanding, respect and compassion between the natural world and men, women and children. This also reflects Immortelle's message about our potential.

A few days after receiving this dream, I was with a friend from the far north of Scotland, who is also a psychic medium. Suddenly she looked at me with her very blue eyes and then said directly and emphatically:

"You're going to have a baby!"

I laughed in disbelief. *"It's not possible!"* I retorted.

"No!" she said. "You are *definitely* going to have a baby."

At first, I took her words literally and instinctively placed my hand on my abdomen, which felt normal. I almost believed her as she was so certain, whilst at the same time knowing that it was physically impossible. Then I paused for a while to consider her words and said: *"I recently had a dream that I'd given birth to a baby. In the dream the baby was a fairy child and appeared to me as elfin."*

"Your baby is a book! It's your book!" the lady cried. I marvelled at her ability to divine this. She couldn't have possibly known that I was writing a book.

In my mind I see the baby again. I lift it gently and wrap it in a soft blanket of Scottish tartan and offer my child, my book-baby - to you, the reader - and to the world. I offer it in the hope that this child will thrive along with all of its kind, and along with all of Nature's guardians in a peaceful world where humankind and Nature co-exist in harmony and mutual respect.

References

The channelled writings in this book are purely my own and I completely avoided reading any other material whilst collecting the messages from Immortelle, the nature spirits and my angel guides.

My background knowledge of trees and flowers has come from my personal experience and life-long interest in natural history, flora and fauna. I am grateful to the authors of the books that have inspired my interest in the wild flowers, trees and mountains of Scotland. I include references to my treasured collection of wild flower books from childhood and early adulthood.

I have resourced a few books that have inspired my love of the Cairngorms. These are from my existing collection rather than any new updated versions. They include *The Cairngorms* mountain guidebook, *Scottish Hill and Mountain Names*, and the *Big Grey Man of Ben MacDhui*.

I am grateful for the information that I received from friends about the landscape and the geology of the area of the Moray Firth basin.

A copy of the *Secret Commonwealth of Elves, Fauns and Fairies* arrived on my doorstep on the completion of the writing of this book. I thank my brother. This and the information in *The Gaelic Otherworld* was brought to my attention and I look forward to expanding my knowledge on this genre as recorded by our wonderful writers and authorities on the subject.

I acknowledge The Estate of Sorley MacLean for kind permission to quote the first verse of his poem, *Hallaig*.

My personal knowledge of Gaelic is meagre, limited to names on maps and consultations with my Gaelic-speaking friends, to whom I am grateful. I apologise for any omissions or errors in my interpretation of the hill and place names or fairy names.

My thanks are also due to several writers, sometimes anonymous. Their postings on the internet on the subject of hill names, history and place names of Inverness and surrounding areas of Strathnairn and Culloden Moor have provided me with background information and further reading to add to my personal knowledge of these areas.

The description within this book of recent developments in renewable energy plans and proposals is a snapshot in time and likely to be out of date by the time of printing. The latest information is generally available from current newspaper and online articles, the energy companies' public websites, local communities' websites and conservation and campaign groups online. Research and monitoring information on the impact of renewables is available on Scotland's Nature Agency website, which is a rich resource on many topics. I have included examples of website pages that are relevant to the areas described in this book.

There are now many local projects in our areas where people are adopting a caretaking role for the land, and planting trees. I have chosen one small garden project to highlight here.

I hope you may also enjoy further reading and inspiration.

In gratitude to all who have helped and inspired me to write this book.

Mountain Books

Preface: (Page III)
Adam Watson, *The Cairngorms, Mounth, Lochnagar - Scottish Mountaining Club District Guides* (Great Britain: The Scottish Mountaineering Trust, 1975), p. 103.

Chapter 1: (Pages 3-4)
Gerald Ponting, *Callanish & Other Megalithic Sites of The Outer Hebrides* (Glastonbury, Somerset: Wooden Books Ltd., 2007), p. 45.

Chapter 1: (Pages 10-11)
Peter Drummond, *Scottish Hill and Mountain Names: The origin and meaning of the names of Scotland's hills and mountains* (Great Britain: The Scottish Mountaineering Trust, 1991), pp. 6,10.

Chapter 31: (Page 285)
Affleck Gray, *The Big Grey Man of Ben Macdhui* (Edinburgh, Scotland: Birlinn Limited, 1994), p. 49.

Donald Bennet, Editor, *The Munros - Scottish Mountaineering Club Hillwalkers' Guide, Volume I* (Great Britain: The Scottish Mountaineering Trust, 1995).

A Selection from a Treasured Collection of Wild Flower Books

Preface: (Page VII)
W. Keble Martin, *The Concise British Flora in Colour* (London: George Rainbird Ltd., Ebury Press & Michael Joseph, 1974).

Derek Ratcliffe, *Highland Flora* (Edinburgh & London:

Highlands and Islands Development Board, Morrison & Gibb Ltd., 1977).

Preface: (Page VII)
Reference to a guide to the Mountain Flowers of Europe from the Pyrenees to the Julian Alps including the Scandinavian Alpines - Anthony Huxley, *Mountain Flowers* (London: Blandford Press Ltd., 1967).

Treasured Collection
(not specifically mentioned in book)

Richard Mabey, *Food For Free - A Guide to the Edible Wild Plants of Britain*, Illustrated by Marjorie Blamey (St. James' Place, London: William Collins Sons and Co. Ltd., 1974).

Roger Phillips, *Wild Flowers of Britain* (London: Pan Books Ltd., 1983).

Roger Phillips, *Grasses, Ferns, Mosses & Lichens of Great Britain and Ireland* (London: Pan Books Ltd., 1981).

Children's Books

Preface: (Page VII)
Cicely May Barker, Author & Illustrator, *Flower Fairies of the Wayside* (London & Glasgow, Blackie & Son, Ltd., Undated, probably 1950).

Flower Fairies of the Spring (London & Glasgow, Blackie & Son, Ltd., Undated, probably 1950).
Flower Fairies of the Summer (London & Glasgow, Blackie & Son, Ltd., Undated, probably 1950).

M.C. Carey, *Wild Flowers at a Glance*, Illustrated by Dorothy Fitchew, (Great Britain: J.M. Dent & Sons Ltd., 1971).

Brian Vesey-Fitzgerald, *Ladybird Book of Trees*, Illustrated by S.R. Badmin, (London: Wills and Hepworth, 1963).

On the Subject of Fairies

Chapter 1: (Page 12)
Robert Kirk, Introduction by Andrew Lang, *The Secret Commonwealth of Elves, Fauns and Fairies* (New York, USA: Dover Publications, Inc., 2020).

Chapter 1: (Page 25)
John Gregorson Campbell, Edited by Ronald Black, *The Gaelic Otherworld, John Gregorian Campbell's Superstitions of the Highlands and Islands of Scotland* and *Witchcraft and Second Sight in the Highlands and Islands* (Edinburgh, Scotland: Birlinn Limited, Ltd., 2019).

On the Subject of Devas

Chapter 2: (Page 20)
Channelled message quoted here with kind permission of the recipient.

Poems, Songs and Music

Poems

Chapter 1: (Page 7)
Sorley MacLean - *Hallaig*

First four lines quoted with kind permission of the Estate of Sorley MacLean - *http://www.sorleymaclean.org/english/*.

Chapter 1: (Page 8)
Lady Carolina Oliphant, Lady Nairne (1766 - 1845)
Rowan Tree - First 3 verses

Chapters 3 & 21 (Pages 28 & 204)
William Allingham, *The Fairies* - First verse

Song, Music & Hymn Titles

Chapters 5 & 18: (Pages 39 & 171)
The *Faery Song* was written by William Sharp (1855-1905) as Fiona Macleod and published 1919, with music by Rutland Boughton (1878-1960) as part of the opera *The Immortal Hour*.

Chapter 6: (Page 57)
Johann Sebastian Bach - *Sheep May Safely Graze*

Chapter 9: (Page 95)
Johann Joachim Quantz - *Flute Concerto in G major*

Chapter 9: (Page 99)
Beatles - *Here, There and Everywhere*

Chapter 15: (Page 148)
Pete Seeger - *Where Have All the Flowers Gone?*

Chapter 32: (Page 304)
Hymn, *Abide with Me*, (1847)
Words by Henry Francis Lyte -
Often sung to music of *Eventide* by William Henry Monk.

Websites - General

Sorley MacLean Official Website:
http://www.sorleymaclean.org/english/poetry.htm.

"Strathnairn - A Brief History", William A. Forbes, 23rd April, 2008, retrieved 23rd March, 2009,
https://www.strathnairnheritage.org.uk/.

Strathnairn Community,
https://www.strathnairn.org.uk/.

Scotland's Nature Agency - Buidheann Nàdair na h-Alba, retrieved 31st December, 2021,
https://www.nature.scot.

Websites - Specific Sources

Chapter 1: (Page 9)
Reference to the Gaelic Fonn -
https://www.ceilede.co.uk/company/the-fonn.

Chapter 1: (Page 14)
David McPhee, writing in Energy Voice article, and also printed in Press and Journal newspaper, 13th May, 2021:
"In the hillside around the 22-mile loch, 363 operational onshore wind turbines have been built - with a further 20 under construction and 29 developments awaiting approval.
Another 198 wind developments are currently in pre-application or scoping with 109 awaiting applications or a final decision on whether they can apply to build."
David McPhee quoting Lyndsey Ward in the same article:
{Lyndsey Ward: "I would ask people to look at this map and understand these are primarily wealthy companies from

overseas harvesting our heritage with thousands of tonnes of concrete poured into our hillsides."}
https://www.energyvoice.com/renewables-energy-transition/wind/uk-wind/322405/calls-to-stop-installation-of-more-wind-turbines-at-loch-ness/.

Chapter 1: (Page 15)
Val Sweeney, "Glenurquhart protest group raises fears over impact of wind farms in Loch Ness and Glen Affric areas on Highland tourism", Inverness Courier, 15th Feb., 2021,
https://www.inverness-courier.co.uk/news/protest-group-fears-impact-of-wind-farm-plans-on-highland-tourism-227925/.

Chapter 7: (Pages 72-73)
Reference to name of River Nairn - Roddy Maclean quoting William Watson,
https://www.nature.scot/doc/place-names-inverness-and-surrounding-area (p. 177).

Chapter 7: (Pages 75-76)
Reference to wells -
https://www.nature.scot/doc/place-names-inverness-and-surrounding-area (p. 43).

Chapter 14: (Page 135)
Reference to Port of Nigg - base for Offshore Wind Tower Factory, Global Energy Group Newsletter, 3rd December 2021,
https://gegroup.com/latest/nigg-offshore-wind-announcement#:~:text=Nigg%20Offshore%20Wind%20(NOW)%20will,in%20the%20UK%20and%20abroad.

Chapter 19: (Page 176)
Reference to Shenachie -
Seoras Macpherson, Seanachaidh of Glendale, Skye
https://tracscotland.org/storytellers/seoras-macpherson/.

https://www.luath.co.uk/george-macpherson.

Chapter 19: (Page 175)
Reference to The National Centre of Excellence in Traditional Music -
https://www.musicplockton.org/

Chapter 23: (Page 218)
References to a community wind farm, and a sewerage system using a 'whole systems' approach to biological technology' -

Findhorn Wind Park:
https://findhornwind.co.uk/.

Findhorn Ecovillage:
https://www.ecovillagefindhorn.com/index.php/water.

Chapter 26: (Page 243)
Reference to large wind farm on Isle of Lewis -
Martyn McLaughlin writing in The Scotsman newspaper, 31st January, 2021,
https://www.scotsman.com/news/environment/massive-wind-farm-lewis-gets-backing-local-planners-3117873.

I have quoted from this article:
"If completed, the revised wind farm would have installed capacity of 184MW, capable of supplying electricity to nearly 230,000 homes ... across Scotland a year, and it is estimated it could directly support up to 208 FTE jobs during its 25 year operational phase.
... the council itself has admitted that given the openness of the surrounding landscape, the wind farm would be visible across Lewis and swathes of northern Harris, with 'widespread significant adverse effects,' particularly on the 'intimate scale and richly diverse character' around Stornoway."

Chapter 26: (Page 244)
Reference to Beinn Ghrideag, a small community wind farm on the Isle of Lewis -
http://www.pointandsandwick.co.uk/about-us/our-wind-farm/.

Chapter 30: (Page 268)
Reference to Loch Duntelchaig -
https://www.nature.scot/doc/place-names-inverness-and-surrounding-area (p. 176).

Website - Garden Project

Mandala Garden
https://mandalagarden.uk/web?n=Main.HomePage.

Please also see Notes Pages where you can add your own favourite groups and personal inspirational ideas.

Image Credits

Front cover graphics:
Mandala Pattern Design Illustration
© GDJ pixabay via Canva.com

Back cover graphics:
Gradient Gold Oval frame © sparklestroke via Canva.com
Green Wreath Leaves © sketchify via Canva.com
Gold Glitter Background
© Pezibear from pixabay via Canva.com

Book text graphics:
Title page: Mandala Pattern Design Illustration
© GDJ pixabay via Canva.com
All leaves and blossoms designs © sketchify via Canva.com
Green Eucalyptus Leaves (main motif) for Chapter headings,
Chapter Parts pages: Pink and Brown Gum Nut Blossom,
Green Eucalyptus Leafs and Yellow Blossom,
Pink Closed Blossom Flower,
Pink Flowering Blossom Branch, Yellow Gum Nut Branch.

Chapter 1
Two-Toned Green Leaf © sketchify via Canva.com

Chapter 1
Flat Textured Risograph Vibrant Autumn Multicolor Rowanleaf
© Trendify via Canva.com

Chapter 3
Handdrawn organic Autumn Hawthorn Leaf
© sketchify via Canva.com

Map by *Laura Newbury*
Map Text in Shadows into Light Two via Canva.com
Metatron's Cube watermark design by *Laura Newbury*
Flower of Life watermark design by *Laura Newbury*

Photographs

V Father climbing on Sàil Gharbh, Quinag, Assynt, Scottish Highlands, 1953. *Credit: Family Collection.*

V Father and companion, ice climbing in north-west Scotland, 1950s. *Credit: Family Collection.*

V Mother and a donkey, Culloden Moor, 1958. *Credit: Family Collection.*

VI Mother, Nairnside, 1958. *Credit: Family Collection.*

VI Mother at the washing line at Nairnside, late 1950s. *Credit: Family Collection.*

VI Father on Loch Meiklie, Glenurquhart, Inverness in his traditional Canadian canoe, late 1950s. *Credit: Family Collection.*

XII A pastel painting of the Birchwood at Balloch, 1978. *Credit: Laura Newbury.*

2 The A9 at Drumochter Pass. *Credit: Laura Newbury.*

3 Praying hands stones at Corrimony. *Credit: Laura Newbury.*

4 Calanais central stones, Isle of Lewis. *Credit: Laura Newbury.*

10 At Loch Morlich with beloved Grandpa Arthur, early 1960s. *Credit: Family Collection.*

42 Curtain of ice on the lower pool. *Credit: Laura Newbury.*

78 The Clava Viaduct in moonlight. *Credit: Simon MacLennan.*

83 The author, age 3½ playing on the garden swing, Nairnside. *Credit: Family Collection.*

89 The author on the Moor, with views towards the Moray Firth and Ben Wyvis. *Credit: Simon MacLennan.*

90   View of Ben Wyvis from Craggie. *Credit: Laura Newbury.*
93   Cairngorms from a road near Granton-on-Spey.
     Credit: Laura Newbury.
94   A circle of ice on the lower pool. *Credit: Laura Newbury.*
96   Immortelle! Is it you in the ice? *Credit: Laura Newbury.*
102 Monolith at Gask, near Inverness.
     Credit: Laura Newbury.
126 The author painting in a field near Craggie, 1983.
     Credit: Simon MacLennan.
146 Notice board at Strathdearn. *Credit: Laura Newbury.*
149 Wind farm at the source of the River Nairn at Càrn Ghriogair, Monadhliath Mountains.
     Credit: Laura Newbury.
173 Looking from the Stones towards the motte at Cantraydoune. Credit: *Laura Newbury.*
174 Stones at Cantraydoune. *Credit: Simon MacLennan.*
179 Gate and forestry plantation, with Moray Firth beyond.
     Credit: Laura Newbury.
182 Painting made on the Moor of view (see photo 179) before forestry plantation. Laura Newbury, 1983.
     Credit: Laura Newbury.
187 The author (in pushchair) with sister and family dog, Nairnside, early 1960s. *Credit: Family Collection.*
199 Oh Immortelle, your pool is so beautiful!
     Credit: Laura Newbury.
210 Painting made on Clava Moor. Laura Newbury, 1983.
     Credit: Laura Newbury.
216 19th century farms and barns near Craggie.
     Credit: Laura Newbury.
220 Immortelle's pool. *Credit: Laura Newbury.*
230 The upper pool and waterfall. *Credit: Laura Newbury.*
256 Horse plough, early 20th century. Unknown location, possibly Strathnairn.
     Credit: Collection of Simon MacLennan.

257 A scene of daily life in the country. Unknown location, possibly Strathnairn.
Credit: Collection of Simon MacLennan.
267 Loch Duntelchaig. *Credit: Laura Newbury.*
268 Loch Duntelchaig. *Credit: Laura Newbury.*
280 From Ben MacDui Looking towards Cairn Toul, Sgòr an Lochain Uaine and distant Ben Nevis.
Credit: Laura Newbury.
298 The author's notebook. *Credit: Laura Newbury.*
343 About the Author. *Credit: Simon MacLennan.*

Cover Photos

Front cover: Immortelle! Is it you in the ice?
Credit: Laura Newbury.
Back cover: The author on Clava Moor looking towards the Moray Firth, Scotland. *Credit: Simon MacLennan.*
Inset: Clava Cairns, Strathnairn, Scotland.
Credit: Laura Newbury.

Appendices

Appendix A
A Message about the Trees, 2011

This is a channelling that I received from the Angels in November 2011 on behalf of a client who has given permission to share this.

You are very much connected with the devas, the beautiful shining ones, guardians of the trees, waters, rocks and the earth. These are our dearly beloved sisters and brothers. We angels are not of their kin, but they are beloved of us, and have belonged to Earth since eternity. They are living vibrations of love and life and without their continual devotion to love and Light, your planet would not even exist. They are the heart throb of your planet. They need you now.

For you are aware that the turbulence of the winds and fires and seas in the form of tornadoes, drought and flood are not merely aberrations of the natural rhythm (of Nature) but are caused by the abuse and greed of humans, through taking and plundering, without giving back. Now the Earth can no longer support any system that is based on fear, that comes from fear, that comes from false belief. Only love is real. Only love creates life. Only love will survive.

You are not the only beings on Earth; there are other souls there too. Even the trees are sentient and the pure waters are filled with life. You are all connected.

We angels are here to help humankind. We are the guardians of humans. The devas are the guardians of the Earth and all that lives thereon.

We angels are in support of the devas, and we are also guardians of the vibration of your planet, the movement of wind, stars and seas.

Ariel speaks:

The devas are calling now. They need our help and they need humans' co-operation. Their world is diminished and retracting. They have shrunk away from their beloved dwelling places and exist in their full majesty and power only in the wild places that have not been touched by humans.

Scotland is a heartland for the devas, yet the very last places wherein they dwell are being devalued and debased by development in the name of 'progress'.

Anyone who has a heart can see this. No! Anyone who has a heart can feel this. Anyone who will cut through the heartland of the devas in the cause of 'progress', 'sustainable energy' or for material profit is serving a false god. That person is cutting off their nose to spite their face, as your saying goes.

Your beautiful trees are the lungs of a living Earth given for your joy and pleasure, and for your shelter, to purify the air and support the creatures in their millions. Even in the carving of the wood of the tree, there is beauty in its shape and form and feel. In its death, the tree leaves imprint of its life. In the rings of its cut trunk it records its life and the seasons and weathers as a barometer. In its death, it gives warmth in the fire of your hearth and uplifting scent of bark. The tree rejoices and sings in the breeze and throws down its carpets of glorious leaves and flowers, season after season in great rejoicing of life, in true spirit of giving. Without the trees, we your angels weep, for you have destroyed the very lungs of the Earth; the breathing in of joy and pure air, which is life force in the physical dimension.

Without the trees, the devas have fled and have become poisoned and deformed and lost their way. Some are made enemies of humans. Some of them are now so debased and depleted that they wish that all may die.

There are others that are so highly evolved that they are wishing to join their prayers with human prayers to bring the Earth's healing. As the Earth heaves in turbulence it seeks to heal itself and as the fires rage and the droughts purge, a new world is to rise from the ruins. Salvation is possible. A time of great Peace is coming. A time of great joy is coming. We need you.

There are now so many of you sending Light to the world though your prayers, that you are creating a fire that cannot be put out. It is through your hearts that the world is saved, person by person. It is through your gratitude for the Earth and appreciation of the Earth and for your lives, that the power of healing proliferates and grows, and the transformation takes place. Through the power of your hearts you are building a new world. That power is the only true power. It is the power that turns your world on its axis and gives life to every beautiful living thing. That power is Love. Shine your lights!

We ask that you pray for the devas of the Earth.

We intercede with the devas and ask for prayer for the trees.
We thank you for your help.

Our radiance is upon you all.

Appendix B

These are extracts from a channelled message that I received from the Angels on 16th March 2011 and quoted here with kind permission from Colin Fraser-Malcolm.

The great traumas that are happening in your world now are on a massive scale and affecting the Earth. The Earth is healing, and as it does so, it is throwing up the poisons from its system and purifying itself by way of volcanoes, earthquakes, and torrential rain and gales; all of these are shifts in the Earth's structure to bring back balance. The imbalance has been caused by humans.

The devas, as we say are powerful, but cannot heal their territories without humans' help, because it is through the relentless greed, plunder, and disrespect of the environment, that the devas' powers are weakened.

When humans begin to respect the Earth again, then the devas can combine forces with humans to make the changes.

…….. You can understand that fire and flood alone can be healed and are transmutations that herald new growth and new life, but where there is pollution of chemicals or energies that would affect the Earth's ability to repair, such as poisons or negative energies such as nuclear or electricity of high voltage, then the damage is far greater. In this case, it is necessary to heal the cause rather than the symptom. We mean that replanting trees for instance may not work as the devas will not return to abide there.

It is necessary to treat the cause by contacting the devas (through your angels) and asking them to join you in prayers of healing and sending of Light.

.... The climate that has brought bountiful years to Scotland has changed since prehistoric times. It is changing again as the Earth heals itself. You are seeing these changes. It is a time of tumult but this tumult is a sign of healing. We need you to trust and stay in the Light and not to follow anyone else's programme. Everything you do must come from the heart and all that you do - you do from your heart.

Appendix C

In Chapter 25, the Role of Humans
as Caretakers of Planet Earth was referred to
by Laura's angel guides
in the following excerpt on page 240.

Many World Faiths offer such teachings. Human responsibility in caring for the environment is named in Buddhist, Hindu, Sikh, Baha'i, Muslim, Jewish, Christian, and Chinese Daoist teachings. The list of resources below is partial and not to be considered complete, but may direct the reader to further material on this topic.

Chapter 25: page 240

Did we ever promise that we would look after Earth?

Yes, humans were given Earth to look after.
They disobeyed.

Who did we humans make a promise to?

    Gaia.

Who is Gaia?

    Mother Earth.

Thank you, angels.

Selection of websites - with information on religious teachings about our relationship to the environment:

BBC Bitesize guides for students e.g., Christian teachings:
https://www.bbc.co.uk/bitesize/guides/zr3c7ty/revision/3

Islamic teachings on stewardship of the environment:
http://www.khaleafa.com/khaleafacom/caretakers-of-the-earth-an-islamic-perspective

The International Environment Forum - a Bahá'í inspired organisation for the environment and sustainability:
https://iefworld.org/cmpquotes.htm

Sacred Mountains of China:
https://sacredland.org/nine-sacred-mountains-china/

Quaker programmes:
https://www.quaker.org.uk/our-work/our-stories/inspiring-children-with-a-love-of-the-natural-environment-1

Indigenous peoples' relationship to our planet, Earth as Caretakers:
https://www.culturalsurvival.org/publications/cultural-survival-quarterly/our-existence-dependent-us-being-land-caretakers

Acknowledgements

I gratefully acknowledge all who have helped to bring this book into reality.

I wish to thank my friends who have accompanied me on this path, some physically walking with me or appearing in my life during the writing process. I thank everyone who has expressed interest in the book's progress over the years, patiently waiting to read it. Your trust in me as a channel for the messages of the Nature guardians has kept me going when the road was bumpy. I am grateful and feel honoured to share with you our common desire to be human guardians for our beautiful Earth. You all know who you are!

I gratefully acknowledge my father's influence. He has always championed the indigenous societies, who lived in harmony with Nature, and he introduced me to Scotland's mountains and wilderness.

I thank my three Angel guides. Particularly, I thank Immortelle as the star of the show for bringing Earth's voices into the physical dimension with the help of my angel Ariel.

I'd like to acknowledge my human helpers behind the scenes for all the technical aspects of preparing this book for publication. It takes more than one pair of hands to make a book and I am indebted to several people who did not wish to be named. I thank my personal assistants and proof-readers for their unstinting dedication and devotion to this project. Finally, I'd like to thank John King of Tatterdemalion Blue for his patience and care in creating this book.

I wish you all many Angels' blessings!

May all beings everywhere be happy and free.

About the Author

Laura was born in Inverness in the north of Scotland, where from her early teenage years she accompanied her father on walks in some of the wildest and remotest of Scotland's Highland landscapes. The Cairngorm mountains is a unique region of Arctic tundra in the UK with several mountains over 4000 feet. Experiencing this environment from a young age fostered Laura's long-lasting reverence for and appreciation of Nature's beautiful and sacred places.

Inspired by her love of trees, mountains and wilderness, she became an artist and educator after completing her MA (Hons) degree in Fine Art and postgraduate degree in Art Teaching from Edinburgh University.

As a practising artist and educator, Laura has taught children and adults in both schools and private settings. Following the publication of her book, *An Angels' Guide to Working with the Power of Light* in 2011, Laura began teaching workshops throughout the UK based on material from the book. She also travelled to Finland and the USA.

Since 2020 Laura has created flourishing online groups such as *Angel Sisters Round the Kitchen Table*, which bring together small groups of friends to create their own curriculum in a short series of sessions. Other classes have included creating Vision Boards and Mandalas. The main focus of her work is *channelling* of Angel messages, which she also offers as personal Angel guidance for her clients.

Laura has also teamed up with Scottish musician Mairi Campbell to create weekly *Prayers for Nature* online gatherings which combine meditations, singing, music, poetry, and guest contributions from among the participants. Everyone has something to contribute towards the theme of caring for our natural world. Each series lasts for a period of 7 weekly sessions, and is based on donation.

To find out more visit: *www.lauranewbury.co.uk*

Notes Page

As this book was begun whilst I sat with a notepad at a waterfall, listening and writing down the messages I received, I'm offering these pages for you to write about your own connection with the nature spirits of your land. What is your role to play as a caretaker of the Earth?

Create your own Resource List (of books, websites, podcasts, music, storytelling, art, etc.) that inspire and support your own contributions as an Earth guardian.

Notes...

Notes...

Notes...

Notes...

Notes...

Notes...

Ingram Content Group UK Ltd.
Milton Keynes UK
UKHW020615160323
418667UK00013B/1169